The Parthenon Code
Mankind's History in Marble

From the east pediment of the Parthenon, Atlas pushes
away the heavens, and with them, the God of the heavens.
Computer reconstruction
by Holmes Bryant.

The Parthenon Code
Mankind's History in Marble

Robert Bowie Johnson, Jr.

SOLVING LIGHT BOOKS

He is revealing the deep and the concealed things;
knowing what is in the darkness since with Him
a stream of light solves them.

Daniel 2:22

©2004 Robert Bowie Johnson, Jr.

Solving Light Books

727 Mount Alban Drive

Annapolis, Maryland 21401

Computer Renders by Holmes Bryant

©2004 Holmes Bryant

and Robert Johnson

ISBN 0-9705438-3-2

Library of Congress Control Number: 2003098932

TheParthenonCode.com

SolvingLight.com

Cover Illustrations:

Atlas and the Garden of the Hesperides on the east pediment of the Parthenon (front) and the Three Fates from the east pediment (back) by Holmes Bryant. Cover design by Holmes Bryant.

All Scripture passages, unless otherwise noted, are from the Concordant Translation, Concordant Publishing Concern, Santa Clarita, CA 91387 (Concordant.org).

Material from the Perseus Library, noted in the photo credits, is copyrighted by the Corporation for Public Broadcasting and the President and Fellows of Harvard College.

First Printing.

Acknowledgements

The author is very grateful for the immense contributions to our knowledge of the ancient Greek world from the following scholars: Bernard Ashmole, Sir John Beazley, Sir John Boardman, T. H. Carpenter, David Castriota, Peter Connolly, B. F. Cook, Gregory Crane (Editor-in-Chief of the Perseus Project) and all of his associates, Hazel Dodge, Richard G. Geldard, Robert Graves, Peter Green, Evelyn B. Harrison, Jane Ellen Harrison, Kristian K. Jeppesen and the many other scholars who participated in the Parthenon Kongress in 1982, Carl Kerényi, Mary R. Lefkowitz, Jenifer Neils, J. Michael Padgett, Olga Palagia, Carlos Parada, John Pinsent, J. J. Pollit, Ellen D. Reeder and all of the other scholars who contributed to her marvelous book, *Pandora: Women in Classical Greece*, Noel Robertson, H. A. Shapiro, Erika Simon, Panayotis Tournikiotis, Edward Tripp, Nicholas Yalouris, Froma I. Zeitlin, and the many others, here unnamed.

Thanks to The Perseus Library, and all those who have written detailed descriptions of vase-paintings and sculpture for it including Deirdre Beyer-Honça, Nick Cahill, Suzanne Heim, Kathleen Krattenmaker, Anne Leinster, and Beth McIntosh.

Thanks to John Rothamel, Frank Bonarrigo, Michael Thompson, and Mark Wadsworth for their valuable insights, and thanks to Ric and Patsy Davis, John Gauthier, Ron Pramschufer, Ian T. Taylor, and Jamie Zahn-Cohagen for their encouragement. Thanks to Veronica Velines for her timely legal assistance.

Thanks to Dr. Pierre Jerlström, editorial coordinator of *TJ: The In-Depth Journal of Creation*, a publication of Answers in Genesis. Chapter 2 of this book appeared in Volume 17(3) of that international journal in slightly different form under the title, "*Athena and Eve*."

For their detailed critiques of the manuscript, thanks to Stella Stershic, Frank Bonarrigo, Nancy Beth Johnson, and Richard Elms.

Thanks also to Lisa Marone, Peter Perhonis, Richard Burt, Don MacMurray, Peggy Griggs, Jay Joseph, and Kelly Machande.

Special thanks to Dean H. Hough and James R. Coram, co-editors of *Unsearchable Riches*, a publication of the Concordant Publishing Concern, for their inspired and enlightening writings.

For Nancy Lee

Contents

Contents, Continued

Preface

[Greek civilization at last almost welcomed] those conquering Romans through whom dying Greece would bequeath to Europe her sciences, her philosophies, her letters, and her arts as the living cultural basis of our modern world.

Will Durant, *The Life of Greece*

Athens was the shining star of the ancient world, dominating almost every field of human endeavor.

Peter Connolly, *The Ancient City*

Athens is the original home of Western civilization.

John M. Camp, *The Athenian Agora*

Learned men have written great books about the building that rose before us; mighty battles of logic or opinion have been fought over almost every detail; each of its marble blocks has been measured with a painstaking accuracy that would be ridiculous were it any other building than the Parthenon: but "all the Old World's culture culminated in Greece, all Greece in Athens, all Athens in its Akropolis, all the Akropolis in the Parthenon."

Eugene P. Andrews in 1896, from *The Parthenon*

One always has the sense in approaching the Akropolis of Athens of being in the company of all mankind. It is one of the universal places, where the collective mind and soul meet and gather to a point of perception. Even the most dull of heart have been transformed by this space.

R. G. Geldard, *The Traveler's Key to Ancient Greece*

[T]he Akropolis is certainly the focal point of any visit, and every archaeo-logical tour inevitably starts from the Parthenon, the temple that symbolizes Greek architecture and, in its structure and ornamentation, represents the very essence of the spirit of Greek civilization.

Furio Durando, *Ancient Greece*

And I, in the trials of war where fighters burn for fame, will never endure the overthrow of Athens—all will praise her, victor city, pride of man.

Aeschylus, *Eumenides*

Our city is an education to Greece . . . Future ages will wonder at us, as the present age wonders at us now.

Perikles

But the more one contemplates the Greeks, who have played this enormous part in the forming of our own lives, the more one wants to find out how it all began.

Michael Grant, *The Rise of the Greeks*

We are now ever more cognizant that Classical Greece was not only a foun-dation of Western civilization, but also a bridge to prehistoric times.

Ellen D. Reeder, *Pandora*

Yes, and who of my generation does not remember that the democracy so adorned the city [Athens] with temples and public buildings that even today visitors from other lands consider that she is worthy to rule not only over Hellas but over all the world.

Isokrates, *Areopagiticus*

Introduction

Where Does Greek Myth Come From?

My neighbor and friend, Mike Thompson, and I recently attended a lecture about the Parthenon at a museum in Baltimore. Although the speaker had received many prestigious awards for her work, her theme did not resonate with us. The ancient Greeks created the living basis of our culture, and yet from her obscure interpretations of certain sculptural depictions, you would have thought that the Greeks' most glorious monument had been created by architects and artists from a different planet. During the question period, I tried to think of something to ask that would respect the lecturer's extensive erudition, and yet shed some light on the true meaning of the Parthenon sculptures and their relevance to our lives today. As I searched my brain for the question that wasn't there, a middle-school girl, sitting with members of her class, stood up behind us and asked, "Where does Greek myth come from?"

The lecturer stood stymied. After one of those knowing academic chuckles and a short silence, she explained that Greek myth is "dynamic" and "ever-changing," and that there was "much metaphor involved." She dodged the question because she didn't know the answer to it. I doubt that she had ever been asked that question before.

Education is not necessarily enlightenment. Education, in fact, sometimes casts a dark pall over the truth. We can be thankful that Greek art was not meant for some super-educated class: it was meant for all thinking Greeks. And that, in turn, means that we can understand it as well.

Greek myth and Greek art are inseparable. Greek art depicts the myth: Greek myth explains the art. And Greek myth, it turns out, is the story of mankind told from the Greeks' religious perspective. It follows logically that within surviving Greek art, Greek myth's visual counterpart, *we have in our possession today a pictorial record of the history of the human race.* And even more exciting, *we have the keys to decoding the ancient sculpted and painted images.* With these things in mind, let's set about answering that young student's very perceptive and very basic question: *Where does Greek myth come from?*

PART I

Background

Greek artists tell us the truth about their culture's origin, depicting characters, gestures, and symbols we can all understand. In their vase-paintings and sculptures, they tell the same story as the early chapters of the Book of Genesis, but they tell the story from a very different standpoint.

sts' Code

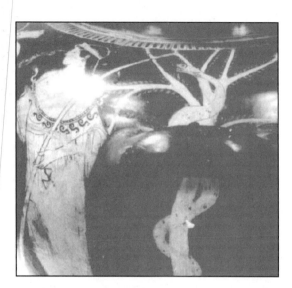

municated in a universal language that we can un-
he early events described in the Book of Genesis
hat understanding. The meaning of Greek "myth"
r to us, and we will at long last grasp what the an-
g us about themselves on the magnificent sculptures

Figure 1. The Parthenon atop the Akropolis of Athens, from the Northwest.

As we look to the basis of our essentially Greek civilization, we find the Parthenon at its focal point. This imposing Classical structure, built during the imperial apogee of our culture's youth, boasted more sculptural decoration than any other temple in Greek antiquity. And yet, for more than 2,000 years, the true meaning of these depictions has remained hidden beneath distracting myths and explanations which strain our credulity: the lame god Hephaistos cracks open the head of Zeus with his axe and out pops Athena (east pediment), Poseidon and Athena compete in a contest for control of Attika (west pediment), the gods fight the Giants (east metopes), Greeks fight Amazons (west metopes), Lapiths battle Kentaurs (south metopes), Greeks destroy Troy (north metopes), a great procession presents Athena with an embroidered cloak (the frieze). We don't understand what these things mean. How incongruous that this should be so! It is as if a vaunted oak with branches extending across the earth and up into the heavens should look down at the acorn and say, "I don't recognize you; I don't understand what you are."

Let me put it a different way. Charles Freeman, in his book *The Greek Achievement*, has written, "The Greeks provided the chromosomes of Western civilization." We know that the Parthenon stood at the very center of Classical Greek civilization, the basis of our own. We should comprehend, intuitively even, what the Parthenon is. And yet one of the great scholars of the ancient Greek world, Sir John Boardman, has written, "[T]he Parthenon and its sculptures are the most fully known, if least well understood, of all the monuments of classical antiquity that have survived." Where is the lost understanding?

The lost understanding is with us, and it is surprisingly easy to recover. It is staring us in the face on the sculptures that survive from the Parthenon and other temples, and on thousands of vase-paintings with simple messages about Greek history and religion which we erroneously categorize as "myths."

4

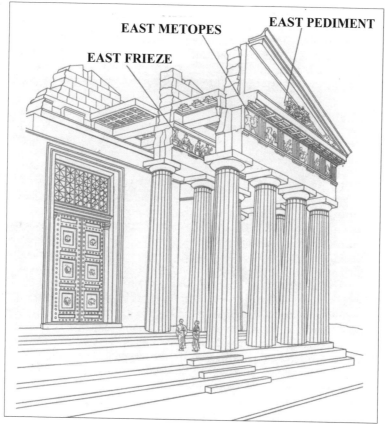

Figure 2: Cutaway drawing of the Parthenon from the East.

What is the Parthenon Code?

The Parthenon Code is a simple method of expression devised by ancient Greek artists to communicate religious ideas and historical information to their fellow countrymen. The artists' painted and sculpted declarations were very simple and far less abstract than writing. We can compare them to other types of visual language such as stained-glass windows in the Medieval period, and even comic strip panels and story-boards for television in our own day.

I call it the Parthenon Code because it was on Athena's temple that this artistic communication reached its highest, and in many ways, its most straightforward and simple form. The seven sculptural themes on the outside of the temple and Athena's gold and ivory idol-image on the inside portrayed interconnected truths about Greek origins. These historical and religious truths all appeared in similar ways on vase-paintings or on other temple sculptures, or on both. Greek artists went to great pains to tell us who they were and where they came from. It's time we took them seriously.

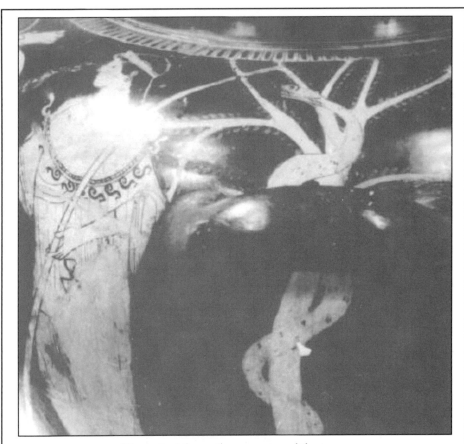

Figure 3: Athena, the serpent, and the tree.

Athena's familiar and endearing intimacy with the serpent is undeniable, and it points straight to Eden. Her being is indissolubly coupled with the serpent: she is the goddess of the serpent's wisdom. Above, in this rare and revealing partially damaged vase-painting from ca. 450 BC, Athena, identified by her serpent-trimmed *aegis*, stands proudly by the tree. The serpent appears to be giving her instructions; the serpent has her ear. She is the woman who has received and welcomed the enlightenment of the serpent.

What do the artists tell us by fringing her aegis with serpents? The aegis signifies authority, and the serpents *outline* and *encompass* the source of her authority. This simple message comes through in any language.

The spear is Athena's identifying weapon; she is almost always pictured grasping it. On the vase, she holds what appears to be her spear, but notice: her spear is actually a branch of the serpent's tree. What is the artist trying to tell us? Athena's weapon, a symbol of her strength, originates directly from the serpent's tree.

Massive amounts of religious and historical information survive from the ancient Greek world. The ancient artists had all of that available to them and more. They learned their history from the previous generations' artists; and, distilling the information they received from them and from the ancient poets, they presented what they knew in the simplest possible images. As we shall see, sometimes they competed with each other to develop the clearest or most creative way to convey an historical fact or religious idea.

Ancient Greek artists remind me of the people who published the Classics Comics in the 1940s and 1950s. They'd take a book like *Uncle Tom's Cabin* or *Ivanhoe*, and present the story in color pictures. Many young students availed themselves of those comic books to write what would have otherwise been very tedious book reports. Ancient vase-artists painted scenes which are very akin to a modern-day comic strip panel. Those who penned the Classics Comics had to know the original story. Greek artists who themselves dealt with a most basic Classical theme—humanity's beginnings—had to know the original story as well. On the temple sculptures and on the vase-paintings, they are not trying to trick us; and they are not presenting us with unintelligible, obscure symbolism: they are telling us their version of the original story—their history—in the simplest visual terms possible.

Let's get right to the basic truth of ancient Greek religious history which its art and myth chronicle, and which finds its fullest expression in the sculptures of the Parthenon. That begins with understanding the identity of Athena, the goddess for whom the Greeks built their most magnificent temple. To truly grasp who she is and what Greek artists are trying to tell us with their simple code, we need a frame of reference outside of Greek myth/art. That all-important frame of reference is the Book of Genesis; specifically, the early events regarding mankind's origins described in it. When we measure Greek myth/art against those events, we find that the Greek poets and artists are telling the same story from an opposite viewpoint—one that says that the serpent did not delude Adam and Eve in the ancient garden, but rather, enlightened them. Athena represents Eve, Athena *is* Eve, the woman described in the Book of Genesis. But Athena is not the original Eve—Hera is. This important difference is explained in detail in the next chapter and in Chapter 15. Athena is the new Eve of the Greek age, the one honored and worshipped for bringing the serpent's enlightenment *back to mankind* after the Flood. The next chapter, a detailed summary of ancient Greek religion and its meaning, will help you see just how surprisingly obvious this is.

Chapter 2
Ancient Greek Religion—A Summary*

Ancient Greek religion, what we call mythology, tells the same story as the Book of Genesis, except from the point of view that the serpent is the enlightener of mankind rather than our deceiver. Zeus and Hera, a husband/wife and brother/sister pair, are pictures of Adam and Eve. Athena represents Eve also—the *re-born* serpent's Eve in the new Greek age. She and the Parthenon and the entire ancient Greek religious system celebrate the rejuvenation and re-establishment of the way of Kain (Cain) after the Flood. Though on one hand Greek idol-worship contradicts the teaching of the Word of God, on the other, if properly understood, it reinforces the truth of the Scriptures.

---

*This chapter is a summary of my book *Athena and Kain: The True Meaning of Greek Myth.*

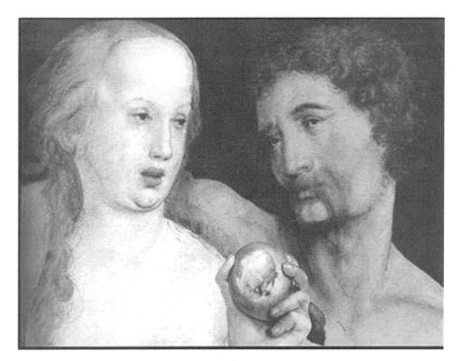

Figure 4: Hans Holbeins' *Adam and Eve.*

Athena's magnificent temple, the Parthenon, is the national monument of Greece. From 447 to 432 BC, during the Classical Age, the ancient Athenians built for Athena one of the most superb architectural works of antiquity. Featuring more sculpture than any other Greek temple, the Parthenon dominated their Akropolis—the high place of the city. Inside stood her forty-foot-tall gold and ivory idol-image. Later in this summary of the meaning of Greek myth, we are going to take a close look at Athena's famous Parthenon statue as it has been reconstructed in the Parthenon in Nashville, Tennessee, from ancient replicas and descriptions of it. We are not going to be able to understand very much about Athena's idol-image, however, unless we see where she fits into the history of humanity as the Greeks saw it. We need some background. Fortunately, the Greeks provided it in their myths and art.

The First Couple

There is no Creator-God in the Greek religious system. The ancient Greek religious system is about getting away from the God of Genesis, and exalting man as the measure of all things. You may think to yourself that the Greeks are exalting gods, not man; but haven't you ever wondered why the Greek gods looked exactly like humans? The answer is the obvious one: for the most part, the

Figure 5: Hera and Zeus from the east frieze of the Parthenon, ca. 438 BC.

gods represented the Greeks' (and our) human ancestors. Greek religion was thus a sophisticated form of ancestor worship. You have no doubt heard of the supposedly great philosopher, Sokrates. In Plato's *Euthydemus*, he referred to Zeus, Athena, and Apollo as his "gods" and as his "lords and ancestors." Greek stories about their origins are varied and sometimes contradictory until their poets and artists settle upon Zeus and Hera as the couple from whom the other Olympian gods and mortal men are descended. This brother/sister and husband/wife pair, the king and queen of the gods, are a match for the Adam and Eve of Genesis. Figure 4, on the opposite page, is Hans Holbein's *Adam and Eve*. This couple is the beginning of the family of man, and the origin of the family of the Greek gods, Zeus and Hera. Figure 5 shows us Zeus and his wife Hera, sculpted on the east frieze of the Parthenon, ca. 438 BC. With no Creator-God in the Greek religious system, the first couple advances to the forefront.

Hera, the Queen of the Gods, is the Primal Eve

According to the Book of Genesis, Eve is the mother of all living humans, and the wife of Adam. Since God is the Father of both Adam and Eve, some consider them to be brother and sister as well. After they had both eaten the fruit, Adam named his wife Eve (which in Hebrew means "Living") and Genesis 3:20

explains why: "... for she becomes mother of all the living." In a hymn of invocation, the 6th-century BC lyric poet, Alcaeus, refers to Hera as *panton genethla*, or "mother of all." As the first mother, the Greeks worshipped Hera as goddess of childbirth; as humanity's first wife, the Greeks worshipped her as the goddess of marriage.

We are told in Chapter 2 of Genesis that Eve was created full-grown out of Adam. Before she was known as Hera, the wife of Zeus had the name *Dione*. The name relates to the creation of Eve out of Adam, for Dione is the feminine form of *Dios* or Zeus. This suggests that the two were, like Adam and Eve, the first male and female humans.

The attribute most often associated with Hera in ancient art was the scepter. She is often depicted as enthroned and holding it in her right hand. She is, and always will be, the queen of Olympus. As the sister/wife of Zeus, Hera is a deification of the original Eve, the motherless mother of all humanity. She holds the scepter of rule by birth.

Zeus, the King of the Gods, is Adam

From the Judeo-Christian standpoint, the taking of the fruit by Eve and Adam at the serpent's behest was shameful, a transgression of Yahweh's commandment. From the Greek standpoint, however, the taking of the fruit was a triumphant and liberating act which brought to mankind the serpent's enlightenment. To the Greeks, the serpent freed mankind from bondage to an oppressive God, and was therefore a savior and illuminator of our race. The Greeks worshipped Zeus as both savior and illuminator; they called him Zeus *Phanaios*, which means one who appears as light and brings light. The light that he brought to the ancient Greeks was the serpent's light that he received when he ate the fruit from the serpent's tree.

In his *Zeus and Hera*, mythologist Carl Kerényi suggests that the name Zeus or Dios, at its deepest level, means "the actual decisive, dynamic moment of becoming light." Thus, the very meaning of the names of the first couple, Dios and Dione, points to that time when they ate the fruit of the Tree of the Knowledge of Good and Evil, and first embraced the enlightenment of the serpent. The natural force, lightning, depicts who Zeus is and what he brings to mankind perfectly. It should not surprise us, then, that the attribute most closely associated with Zeus in ancient art was the lightning bolt. On most of the vases on which he is depicted, Zeus holds the lightning bolt in his right hand. From the Greek viewpoint, there is no more "actual decisive, dynamic moment of becoming light" in human history than the time Adam and Eve received the serpent's enlightenment, and no

Figure 6: On a vase from ca. 410 BC, Zeus holds the lightning bolt and scepter of rule.

more appropriate symbol for it than the lightning bolt of Zeus.

On a Greek vase from ca. 410 BC, a naked Zeus holds the scepter of rule in his left hand and the lightning bolt in his right (Fig. 6). He is the naked and unashamed king of Olympus. The fruit of the tree—the serpent's enlightenment—has been passed to him. It is the true source of his power.

Zeus and Hera Are the First Couple Described in Genesis

In his *Works and Days*, the ancient poet Hesiod wrote of "how the gods and mortal men sprang from one source." The first couple, Zeus and Hera, were that source. Hera is the single mother of all humanity, and Zeus is, according to Hesiod, "the father of men and gods." The term "father Zeus" is a description of the king of the gods which appears over one hundred times in the ancient writings of Homer. As the source of their history, Zeus and Hera became the gods of their history.

According to Genesis, Adam lived 930 years. The length of Eve's life is not mentioned but there is no reason to think that it wasn't about as long as Adam's. That by itself would confer a godlike status on them. And who came before them? No one. It is only natural that the Greeks worshipped Adam and Eve as Zeus and Hera. Those without a belief in the Creator have only nature, themselves, and their progenitors to exalt.

The Greek tradition insists that Zeus and Hera were the first couple; the Judeo-Christian tradition insists Adam and Eve were the first couple. Two opposite spiritual standpoints share the same factual basis. If the above is true, then the Greeks ought to have directly connected Zeus and Hera to a paradise, a serpent, and a fruit tree. They did, indeed, make such a direct connection.

Figure 7: Vase-depiction of the serpent and the apple tree in the Garden of the Hesperides.

The Garden of the Hesperides—Eden's Greek Counterpart

The Greeks remembered the original paradise. They called it the Garden of the Hesperides, and they associated Zeus and Hera with its enticing ease, and with a serpent-entwined apple tree. The Hesperides, the spirit-beings associated with this tree, its apples, and its serpent, get their name from *Hespere* in Greek, which means evening, and that signifies the West where the sun sets. This matches the Genesis account which describes civilization developing to the east of Eden. A return to Eden would mean traveling west. The Greeks put the Garden of the Hesperides, with its serpent-entwined apple tree, in the Far West.

Some mythologists have mistaken the Hesperides for guardians of the tree, but they certainly are not. Their body language, their easy actions, and their very names serve the purpose of establishing what kind of a garden this is: a wonderful, carefree place. In Figure 7, we see the Garden of the Hesperides depicted on a water pot from ca. 410 BC. The serpent entwines the apple tree with its golden fruit. The names of the figures are written on the vase. Two of the Hesperides, Chrysothemis (Golden Order) and Asterope (Star Face) stand to the immediate left of the tree. Chrysothemis moves toward the tree to pluck an apple. Asterope leans pleasantly against her with both arms. To the left of them, Hygeia (Health) sits on a hillock and holds a long scepter, a symbol of rule, as she looks back towards the tree. To the right of the apple tree, Lipara (Shining Skin) holds apples in the fold of her garment, and raises her veil off her shoulder.

The names of the Hesperides describe what the garden is like. It's a land of soft starlight, gold for the taking, perfect health, and wondrous beauty. Apollodorus, writing in the 2nd-century BC, gives four different names for the Hesperides: Aegle (Dazzling Light), Erythia (Red Land), Hesperia (Evening Star), and Arethusa (Water Fountain). The sound of a water fountain is one of the most peaceful sounds. What an enchanting and delightful place! The Hebrew word for Eden means "to be soft or pleasant," figuratively "to delight oneself." The Garden of the Hesperides is, with little doubt, the Garden of Genesis.

If Adam and Eve, in the Greek religious system, have become Zeus and Hera, there should be literary evidence for their presence in this garden, and there is. Apollodorus wrote that the apples of the Hesperides "were presented by Gaia [Earth] to Zeus after his marriage with Hera." This matches the Genesis account: Eve became Adam's wife right after she was taken out of Adam (Genesis 2:21–25), and the next recorded event is the taking of the fruit by the first couple. Connecting Zeus and Hera with the Hesperides automatically connects them with the serpent and the fruit tree with which they are always represented.

The chorus in Euripides' play *Hippolytus* speaks of "the apple-bearing shore of the Hesperides" where immortal fountains flow "by the place where Zeus lay, and holy Earth with her gifts of blessedness makes the gods' prosperity wax great." Thus Euripides put Zeus in the garden, and his language affirms that this is where Zeus came from.

You have probably heard at one time or another about Eve eating the apple. The Hebrew word for fruit in Chapter 3 of Genesis is a general term. The idea that Adam and Eve took a bite of an apple comes to us as part of the Greek tradition.

The Greek poets placed a figure named Atlas in the ancient Garden of the Hesperides. Hesiod wrote in his *Theogony*:

And Atlas through hard constraint upholds the wide heaven with unwearying head and arms, standing at the borders of the earth before the clear-voiced Hesperides; for this lot wise Zeus assigned him.

His presence in the Garden of the Hesperides clarified the Greeks' religious viewpoint, for it was his job to put the authority of heaven at a distance from them. In Figure 8, we see part of a plate scene depicting Atlas pushing away the heavens. We can see where the artist has drawn stars. As Atlas pushes away the heavens, he also pushes away the God of the heavens—the very object of his efforts. Victory for the Greek system means that the Creator is kept at bay, pushed out of the picture, and His influence nullified, so that men become free to believe

Figure 8: Atlas pushes away the
heavens, and with them,
the God of the heavens.

and do what they will. The way of Greek religion, which is nothing less than the way of Kain (Cain) referred to in the Scriptures, is a life lived without God's interference with mankind's desires. The Creator must be pushed away and ignored if Zeus-religion is to succeed.

Yahweh cursed and condemned the serpent in Genesis 3:14: "On your torso shall you go, and soil shall you eat all the days of your lives." As God is pushed out of humanity's realm, the curse on the serpent becomes void. The serpent rises up, as on the plate depiction, to take his place as the illuminator and enlightener of the human race.

The Two Antagonistic Sons of the First Family

Now if Zeus and Hera are pictures of Adam and Eve, we would expect them to have two antagonistic male children just as the first man and woman did. Zeus and Hera had two male children: Hephaistos, the elder, and Ares; and they were as averse to each other as Kain and Seth.

Adam and Eve had three sons: Kain, Abel, and Seth. But Kain killed Abel, evidently before the latter had offspring. Since Seth replaced Abel, we look at Adam and Eve as having two sons, each of whom, in turn, had offspring. In the Scriptures, the line of Seth is the line of Christ. The Book of Matthew traces the lineage of Christ through David to Abraham; and the Book of Luke further traces the lineage of Abraham to Adam through his son Seth. This is often referred to as the line of belief in the Creator-God or the line of faith. On the other hand, the Scriptures define the line of Kain as one of unbelief in the Creator-God. According to I John 3:12, "Kain was of the wicked one," a straightforward reference to what the Scriptures refer to as "the ancient serpent called Adversary and Satan, who is deceiving the whole inhabited earth" (Revelation 12:9).

The Greeks deified Kain as Hephaistos, god of the forge. They deified his younger brother, Seth, as Ares, the troublesome god of conflict and war. In the Judeo-Christian tradition, Kain is the evil one whose way is to be shunned. In the Greek religious system, Ares, the Seth of Genesis, is the traitor and the one who causes ruin and woe.

16

Hephaistos/Kain

By his Roman name, Vulcan, we associate Hephaistos, the deified Kain, immediately with the forge and the foundry. According to Genesis 4:22, the members of Kain's family were the first to become forgers "of every tool of copper and iron." These surely included the hammer, the axe, and the tongs—the tools most often associated with Hephaistos in Greek art.

Hephaistos' banishment from, and return to, Olympus (a place where the Creator is excluded from the pantheon) is a "myth" which constituted an essential element of Greek religion; it appeared painted, sculpted and bronzed throughout the Archaic and Classical periods. In the Greek religious system, the banishment of Hephaistos corresponds, in Genesis, to Kain's being commanded to wander the earth by Yahweh: "A rover and a wanderer shall you become in the earth" (Genesis 4:12). According to Greek sources, it was Hera or Zeus, or both, who banished their eldest son. Since the Greeks rejected the Creator-God, it makes sense that they would attribute the banishment of Hephaistos to his parents instead.

According to Genesis, Kain wandered for a time, but then settled in one place in complete disobedience to Yahweh's instructions for him to remain a rover:

And knowing is Kain his wife and she is pregnant and bearing Enoch. And coming is it that he is building a city, and calling is he the name of the city as the name of his son, Enoch (Genesis 4:17).

The return of Hephaistos to Olympus in Greek religion corresponds to Kain's ignoring Yahweh's command to wander, and his building a city instead. Out of that city, the defiant line of Kain prospered as he and his offspring embraced the wisdom of the serpent.

As a reward for his return, Hephaistos received the beautiful and sensuous Aphrodite as his wife. Just as Kain's wife was most likely his sister, so Aphrodite was the sister of Hephaistos. Zeus is the father of both Aphrodite and Hephaistos, and Aphrodite's mother, Dione, is the same woman/goddess as Hera, but from a different and more ancient oral tradition.

In Plato's dialogue, *Cratylus*, Sokrates describes Hephaistos as "the princely lord of light." According to Robert Graves, his name is a contraction of *hemeraphaestos*, which means "he who shines by day." On a vase scene from the Archaic period (Fig. 9), the young Hephaistos stands on his father's lap in the presence of his mother, Hera. He holds two torches and is hailed as "light of

Figure 9: Vase-depiction from ca. 500 BC of Zeus (Adam), Hera (Eve), and their eldest son, Hephaistos (Kain), "the princely lord of light."

Zeus." Hephaistos shines because he is Eve's eldest son, Kain, who rejects the Creator and embraces the serpent's enlightenment, the very basis of Zeus-religion.

Ares/Seth

Zeus was fond of his son Hephaistos, who performed an indispensable and appreciated function as armorer of the gods. On the other hand, Zeus considered his youngest son, Ares, to be worthless, calling him "hateful" and "pestilent" and a "renegade." The ancient poet, Homer, referred to Ares as "the bane of mortals." The only reason Ares has a place in the Greek pantheon is that he is the son of Zeus; that is, he is one of the two actual sons of the first couple, Adam and Eve, of whom Zeus and Hera are deifications. Zeus hates Ares, but accepts responsibility for siring him: "for thou art mine offspring, and it was to me that thy mother bare thee," and then rails at this son of his, telling him that if he were born of any other god, he would have been "lower than the sons of heaven" long ago. Some scholars say Greek religion is anthropomorphic; that is, gods take human form. That's not quite right. What happens is that real human ancestors retain their original identities and take on godlike qualities. Ares, as a deification of Seth, is trapped, in a sense, by the historical framework. His father, Zeus, had to hate him, and Greek heroes were expected to kill his children.

While the scriptural viewpoint defines Ares/Seth as the Yahweh-believing, or spiritual son, Greek religion defines him as hated by, and antagonistic to, the ruling gods who are part of the serpent's system. Likewise, while Zeus-religion looks on Hephaistos/Kain as the true and devoted son, the scriptural viewpoint defines him as part of the wicked one's system. Jews and Christians dislike and shun the line of Kain, but they can't get rid of him or his line without altering their spiritual standpoint and history itself. Kain is part of the Scriptures, and he is there to stay. Zeus-religion has the same kind of situation. It hates the line of Ares, but it cannot eliminate the line from its history, for, as we shall see, the basic achievement of Zeus-religion, its grand celebration, is the triumph of the way of Kain over the way of Seth. Ares is part of Greek sacred literature and art, and he is there to stay.

The Flood wipes out the way of Kain

According to Genesis, the Flood temporarily wiped out the way of Kain. Noah, in the line of Seth, "a just man" (Genesis 6:9), survived with his wife, three sons, and their wives in the ark. All but these eight people disappeared into the earth. The Greeks pictured this cataclysmic event as half-men/half-horses known as Kentaurs (Centaurs) pounding a man named Kaineus into the ground with a rock (See Fig. 10). The artist of the François Vase (Fig. 11) wrote the name "Kaineus" next to the man being pounded into the earth by the Kentaurs. Kaineus means "pertaining to Kain," or more directly, "the line of Kain."

Who were the Kentaurs? The original Greek word for Kentaur, *Kentauros*, means hundred (where we get century and cent) and most likely relates to the fact that Noah, the chief of the line of Seth, warned of the Flood for one hundred years. In most vase-paintings of them, the Kentaurs carried symmetrical branches, a sign that they belonged to a certain branch of humanity. The Greeks, who embraced the way of Kain, did not acknowledge the Creator God, and so they couldn't blame Him for the Flood. They blamed the survivors of it, that strange branch of humanity they didn't really understand—the line of Seth that came through the flood waters on the ark.

Figure 10: Kentaurs pound Kaineus into the ground with a boulder. West frieze of the
Temple of Hephaistos (the deified Kain), Athens, ca. 440 BC.

Figure 11: The vase-artist of the François Vase writes the names of the Kentaurs, and the
name of the man being pounded into the earth—Kaineus—the line of Kain.

Figure 12: On this shield band panel, Herakles, the Nimrod of Genesis, accosts Nereus, the Greek Noah, who has a flame and a snake coming out of his head. Herakles is demanding to know where he can find the enlightenment of the serpent.

The Resurgence of the Way of Kain after the Flood

For a number of years after the Flood, God's awesome and decisive intervention in human affairs remained fresh in the minds of Noah's descendants, and the way of Kain remained dormant. Then, gradually, a yearning for the serpent's wisdom began to take hold. On a shield band panel from about 550 BC, a Greek artist depicted this all-too-human desire perfectly (Fig. 12).

The characters are the great hero, Herakles, the Nimrod of Genesis transported to Greek soil, and Nereus, the Greek Noah. Nereus means the "Wet One." His bottom half is a fish, signifying that he came through the Flood. The inscription on this panel refers to him as *Halios Geron*—"The Salt Sea Old Man." Herakles demands to know something that only the Salt Sea Old Man can tell him. A flame and a serpent come out of Nereus' head. Herakles wants to know where to find the enlightenment of the serpent. According to Apollodorus:

Herakles seized [Nereus] while he slept, and though the god turned himself into all kinds of shapes, the hero bound him and did not release him till he had learned from him where were the apples of the Hesperides.

Life in service to the God of Noah seemed boring. Humanity wanted another big bite of the apple from the serpent's tree in the Garden of the Hesperides. Ancient Greek religion commemorates the return and triumph of the way of Kain after the Flood, and it is celebrated in many interrelated ways in myth and art:

- Hermes, the Cush of Babylon, embraces the serpent's system and becomes deified as the chief prophet of Zeus-religion.
- Poseidon, a "brother" of Zeus marries a daughter of Nereus/Noah and replaces him as god of the sea.
- The gods inspire Greek heroes to wound Ares/Seth and kill his offspring.
- A special child, the seed of Hephaistos/Kain, is reborn from the earth in the city of Athens.
- In one of his famous twelve labors, Herakles, the Nimrod of Genesis, kills the three-bodied Geryon who represents the spiritual authority of the three sons of Noah.
- As his final labor, Herakles returns to the serpent's tree in the Garden of the Hesperides and obtains the sacred apples for Athena.
- In the great culminating and decisive battle, the gods in concert (as a religious system) overwhelm and defeat the Giants who represent the Yahweh-believing sons of Noah.

Athena—the Serpent's Eve Reborn after the Flood

In one way or another, Athena is involved with or connected to all of these events. She is the ultimate symbol of the great victory of Zeus-religion over the religious system of Nereus/Noah. She is the serpent's Eve, reborn and exalted after the Flood. According to the Greek myth, she was born full-grown out of Zeus, an unmistakable picture of Eve being born full-grown out of Adam. And she was born in the presence of Hera, the primal Eve, meaning that she (Athena) is the new representation of Eve in the Greek age. As a sign of this change, Herakles made his way back to the serpent's tree in the garden, obtained the golden apples which once belonged to Hera, and presented them to his patron goddess, Athena. Hera and Athena each had possession of the sacred fruit from

Figure 13: Metope from the temple of Hephaistos in Athens and a drawing of it. Herakles presents the apples he has obtained from the serpent's tree to Athena. This affirms that she now represents the serpent's Eve and the serpent's wisdom in the new Greek age.

the serpent's tree in the garden at one time, sure evidence that they are both pictures of Eve.

The extant metope at the northeast corner of the temple of Hephaistos in Athens (Fig. 13) still depicts Herakles presenting Athena with the three apples from the Garden of the Hesperides. The drawing fills in the figures. The Greeks knew from the stories they heard and from other art they had seen that these golden apples came from a serpent-entwined tree in a place called the Garden of the Hesperides, and that Hera was the original recipient and owner of them. On the sculpture itself, Herakles may as well be saying, "Here Athena, these golden apples from the serpent's tree which once belonged to Hera, now belong to you. By guiding me in all my labors after the Flood, you have proven that you are the one who enlightens and empowers mankind with the knowledge of good and evil, and offers the promise and hope of immortality."

Now that we understand what Greek religion was about, we are in a position to understand the religious statement the Athenians made to their world and to posterity when they erected Athena's ivory and gold-plated idol-image in the Parthenon (Fig. 14).

The Judeo-Christian tradition traces the current state of humanity back to a woman, a serpent and a tree. Athena's idol-image shows us the woman and the serpent, but where is the tree? The very core of the statue is wood—a tree. In both the Greek and Judeo-Christian traditions, a tree is at the core of what happened between a woman and a serpent in paradise.

Note that the serpent rises up next to Athena as a friend. In Genesis, Yahweh had condemned the serpent to crawl on its belly as a deceiver of humanity, yet all who entered the Parthenon to worship or admire the great statue were forced to look up to both Athena and the serpent. That is because the Greek religious system, the very opposite of the Judeo-Christian, was based on the notion that the serpent had enlightened humanity in paradise.

Athena holds Nike in her right hand, the hand of power. Nike symbolizes victory—Eve's "victory" for humanity when she ate the fruit offered by the serpent. Athena is the only goddess in Greek art who is ever pictured holding Nike.

Athena's very name speaks of Eve. In Genesis 3:4, the serpent promised Eve that when she ate the fruit of the tree she would not die. In the most ancient Greek writing (Linear B), the name of the goddess first appears as *Athana*. The word *thanatos* in ancient Greek means death. A-thanatos signifies deathlessness. A-thana is the shortened form of Athanatos meaning the deathless one, or more specifically, the embodiment of the serpent's promise to Eve that she would never die, but would be as the gods, knowing good and evil. Through Athana (tos), later called Athena, the serpent has made good his promise to Eve.

On the front of her *aegis*, or goatskin, which covered the top of her chest, Athena wore the head of the Gorgon Medusa—the head of serpents. The aegis is a symbol of authority. The symbolism is straightforward: the source of Athena's authority is the head of serpents.

Atop Athena's helmet, between winged griffins, crouched an inscrutable sphinx. As we know from the story of Oedipus, Hera originally controlled this riddle-uttering winged monster with the head of a woman and the body of a lion. But it is now after the Flood. Athena's possession of the sphinx shows that her authority supersedes that of Hera in the new Greek age. The wings of the sphinx symbolize power in the heavens; the body of the lion, power on Earth; and the woman's head represents the mysterious Eve, mother of all living. As we have seen, Hera, the primal Eve, carried the scepter of rule by birth. Athena, the new Eve of the Greek age, carries a deadly spear, a sign that she led the great spiritual battle to defeat the Yahweh-believing sons of Noah and re-establish the way of Kain after the Flood.

There is even a more obvious demonstration of Athena's identity as the re-born serpent's Eve. Meeting the ancient Greeks at eye level as they entered the Parthenon was the statue base of the great idol-image of Athena. In the center of it, surrounded by the gods giving her gifts, stood a sculpted Pandora—the woman who, according to Greek myth, was responsible for letting evil out into the world. Athena's gold and ivory grandeur above Pandora was literally based on this obvious picture of Eve.

Eve was the most important woman in human history, and Athena is Eve. No wonder the Athenians named their city after her, and elevated her to a position of such undisputed supremacy.

Figure 14: Athena Parthenos, full-size reproduction in the Nashville
Parthenon by Alan LeQuire <www.Parthenon.org>.

Athena's Idol-Image—A Key Element of the Parthenon Code

Let's examine Athena's Parthenon idol-image as an example of the Greek artists' simple form of symbolic communication to the average Greek.

As a Greek entered the Parthenon and viewed Athena's great idol-image, the first thing he or she would have noted is that it is a woman, a woman six or seven times taller than normal wearing clothes made of gold with skin of ivory. The message: **This is the woman we worship as our goddess.**

The visitor then notices the huge serpent rising at her side. The message: **This is the woman who befriended the serpent**, and/or, **This is the woman befriended by the serpent.**

Then the visitor sees Nike, the goddess of victory, in Athena's right hand. The message: **This is the woman whose befriending of the ancient serpent led to her (and now our) victory.**

Then perhaps the visitor would think of the depiction of Athena having been born full-grown out of Zeus in the center of the east pediment under which she had just entered the temple. The message: **This is the woman born full-grown out of a man.**

Then the visitor looks at the statue base and sees Pandora depicted receiving gifts from the gods. The message: **This is the woman whose gold and ivory grandeur is based (literally as well as figuratively) on the time evil was let out into the world.**

Then perhaps the visitor's eye would be drawn to the Gorgon Medusa, the head of serpents, on Athena's aegis, or goat skin, a symbol of authority. The message: **This is the woman who gets her authority from the head of serpents.**

Then the visitor notes that Athena's goat skin is fringed with serpents. The message: **This is the goddess whose authority is outlined, or bounded, by serpents**.

The overall message of Phidias, the sculptor of the idol-image, could not be any plainer: Athena is the Eve we recognize from Genesis worshipped as the one who brought the serpent's enlightenment to mankind. When we factor in the post-Flood time frame of Athena's ascendancy, of which the artists were well-aware, we see that **Athena is the woman we recognize from Genesis, Eve, whom the Greeks exalted as the goddess who *brought back* to mankind the serpent's enlightenment *after the Flood*.** The Greek religious system and the Judeo-Christian religious system are exact opposites, both of whose origins go back to the same place—the Garden of Eden (in the Greek system, the Garden of the Hesperides). The Judeo-Christian tradition says that the serpent deluded Eve; the Greek religious tradition says the serpent enlightened Eve, and through her, all of mankind. The Judeo-Christian tradition says God is the measure of all things; the Greek religious system says man is the measure of all things. Both stem from the same source. This is the key to understanding Greek myth and art.

Figure 15: On this storage jar from ca. 525 BC, Athena's aegis is positioned over her right shoulder so that the Gorgon head—the head of serpents—is seen in full frontal-face.

The Curse of the Gorgon Medusa

Once you see it, Athena's true identity becomes self-evident. She may as well have worn a sign around her neck saying, "Hello, I'm the serpent-worshipping Eve of Genesis." Why haven't the great scholars of Greek myth been able to see her from this perspective? I attribute their misperceptions to the curse of the Gorgon Medusa on Athena's aegis (Fig. 15), the focal point of her idol-image. If you remember the myth, the look of the Gorgon Medusa had the power to turn men to stone. The hero, Perseus, who cut off the Gorgon's head and presented it to Athena, used his polished shield as a mirror to view her indirectly, negating the power of her gaze. Most of the revered teachers of mythology and anthropology (J.J. Bachofen, Jane Ellen Harrison, Robert Graves, Joseph Campbell et al.) were at worst atheists, and at best contemptuous of the Book of Genesis. As they looked to Athena herself for their understanding, the stare of the Gorgon on her aegis turned their minds figuratively to stone—a kind of mental paralysis set in. In this intellectual stupor, they were unable to recognize Athena as the serpent's Eve. As mockers of the validity of Scripture, they would never have considered looking away from Athena and toward Genesis in order to understand the identity of the goddess. This is the atheists' dilemma: if they don't look to Genesis, they will never understand Greek myth; if they take Genesis seriously, they cease to be atheists.

The curse of the Gorgon Medusa loses its power when we look away from Athena and toward the Scriptures for our understanding. When we view Athena's image indirectly, as it is clearly and simply reflected in the Book of Genesis, we get a true picture of her identity, and understand her role in Greek religion as a depiction of Eve—the serpent's Eve.

Conclusion

Without reference to the early events described in the Book of Genesis, it is not possible to make any real sense of Greek mythology. Without Genesis as a benchmark, Athena's significance and identity must remain a troubling enigma, and the entire formidable religious framework of ancient Greek society will continue to mean virtually nothing to us.

That is not to say that understanding Greek myth is a matter of blind faith in the Book of Genesis: quite the contrary. This entire book is a systematic presentation of abundant evidence that the events of Eden were part of the Greeks' collective cultural memory, and that their special interpretation of those events made up the very *raison d'etre* of their religious system. Greek myth/art is human history. The Book of Genesis is human history. *While the viewpoints of each are opposite, the recounted events and characters match each other in convincing detail.*

The Greeks knew a lot about Noah and his sons and daughters. While it is true that the Greeks built the Parthenon to glorify the serpent-worshipping Eve of Genesis, it is also true that they built it to celebrate their "victory" over Noah and his God. It's time to look more deeply into that idea.

Figure 15.1: The Parthenon atop the Akropolis of Athens during the Classical period.

PART II

Noah and His Children in Greek Vase-art, in Greek History, and on the Parthenon

Adventurous believers in the truth of Genesis have searched the Mountains of Ararat in modern-day Turkey for the remains of Noah's ark, most recently using satellite cameras to aid in their quest. Their idea is that by finding what remains of Noah's ark, they prove that Noah existed, that the Book of Genesis is true, and that the God of Genesis is the one, true God.

Little did they realize that proof of Noah's existence has stood atop a much smaller mountain—the Akropolis of Athens—in plain sight for nearly 2500 years. The sculpture of Athena's great temple, the Parthenon, celebrates the triumph of the Greek religious system over Noah and his Yahweh-believing children. All seven of the sculptural themes of the Parthenon (on the two pediments, on the four sets of metopes, and on the frieze) relate to Noah in some significant way. We may not have found the ark yet in Turkey, but in ancient Greece we have found Noah as painted on vase after vase, as sculpted on the Altar of Zeus at Pergamum, and as the specifically acknowledged but unseen background figure on the Parthenon.

Chapter 3

Nereus—The Greek Noah

The Greeks knew exactly who Noah was. They called him Nereus, the "Wet One." Greek artists chronicled the rise of their religion from his lifetime, and often depicted Nereus/Noah on vases with the bottom half of a fish and/or holding a fish, signifying that this fish-man had brought humanity through the Flood.

Figures 16, 17, and 18: Nereus, the Old Man of the Sea depicted by three different vase-artists.

Nereus, the Greek Noah

Above, we see three different depictions of Nereus from ancient Greek vases, ca. 500 - 450 BC. On all three he looks very old, he is seated as if on a throne, and he holds a scepter, a symbol of rule. The simple artistic communication is this: Here is the old man who ruled, or this is the ruling old man, or perhaps, this is the man who ruled by virtue of his age and stature.

In *The Meridian Handbook of Classical Mythology*, here is how Edward Tripp describes Nereus:

An ancient sea-god. Nereus, a son of Pontus (Sea) and Ge (Earth), may have had considerable importance before Poseidon became the ruling sea god. He is referred to by both Homer and Hesiod as the Old Man. Hesiod explains that this is because he is kind and just. He was the father, by the Oceanid Doris, of the fifty sea-nymphs—the Nereïds. Like other sea-deities, he had prophetic powers. Herakles, led to his home by the Nymphs, captured him sleeping. Herakles bound him and re-fused to release him until he revealed the location of the Garden of the Hesperides.

According to Robert Graves, Nereus means "Wet One." He is Noah, the fish-man, the one who came through the Flood; that's why the Greeks associated him with Sea and Earth. The ancient poets called Nereus the "Old Man of the Sea." According to Genesis, Noah lived 600 years before the Flood, and 350 years after it. As we saw in Chapter 2, one ancient artist referred to Nereus as the "Salt Sea Old Man." After the Flood, Nereus/Noah lived long enough to sire fifty daughters whom the Greeks called Nereïds.

The Book of Genesis does not name Noah's wife, but the Greeks said that the wife of Nereus was the Okeanid (Oceanid) Doris. What made her an Okeanid was the fact that she rode the ocean in the ark with Nereus/Noah and their family for a year.

Figures 19, 20, 21, and 22: Sometimes Greek artists depicted Nereus as an old man with the bottom half of a fish holding one or more fish (top left); sometimes as an old man with the bottom half of a fish holding his scepter (top right); sometimes as a full-bodied old man holding a fish (bottom left); and sometimes simply as an old man (bottom right).

And of course Nereus/Noah was known for having prophetic powers: for a hundred years he had predicted the Flood that eventually wiped out the line of Kain.* Hesiod wrote in his *Theogony*, "And Sea begat Nereus, the eldest of his children, who is true and lies not: and men call him the Old Man because he is trusty and gentle and does not forget the laws of righteousness, but thinks just and kindly thoughts." In Genesis 6:9 we read: "Noah is a just man."

The memory of Nereus, to the Greeks, was indeed of "considerable importance" (as Tripp writes) for Hesiod took the time to name all fifty of his daughters whom, he wrote, "sprang from blameless Nereus, skilled in excellent crafts." Greek artists and poets treated the Old Man of the Sea as a personage of permanent significance, giving him the respect his patriarchal standing was due. The vase-artists competed with each other to express in different creative ways the historical truth that the Greek religious system took over from Nereus/Noah.

As we have seen in Chapter 2, Nereus/Noah was the living link to the days before the Flood, and so Herakles, the Nimrod of Genesis, had to go to him to find out the location of the serpent's ancient garden—the Garden of the Hesperides. Getting back to the serpent's tree for another bite of the fruit was the twelfth and final labor of Herakles. That's precisely what ancient Greek religion was about—replacing the authority of Nereus/Noah with that of the ancient serpent from the garden paradise.

---

*According to Genesis, the Flood occurred 100 years after Yahweh told Noah to build the ark. And II Peter 2:5 indicates he was a herald or proclaimer during that period.

Figure 23: A seated Nereus and two of his daughters, the Nereïds.

On the vase-depiction above from ca. 490 BC, Nereus appears as a seated spiritual figure enjoying the devotion and affection of his daughters, the Nereïds. On other vases as well, he appears as a man of paternal tenderness whom his daughters seek to embrace. On the depiction of him to our right from ca. 450 BC, the artist has given Nereus a scepter, suggesting regal authority.

Figure 24: Nereus with scepter.

Nereus at the Birth of Athena

The storage jar opposite (Fig. 25) from ca. 525 BC depicts the birth of Athena. Zeus sits holding lightning bolts in his right hand as a sign of the moment of lighting up in paradise. Athena has emerged full-grown from Zeus with spear and shield and stands on his lap facing the two goddesses of childbirth. These are children of Hera, the chief goddess of childbirth. I haven't been able to identify the figures behind Zeus, but the old man to our right facing Athena and Zeus is Nereus, the Greek Noah.

The lion under Zeus' chair is a symbol of kingship or rule, and that is what the painting is about. The artist has made Nereus a witness to the rebirth of the serpent's Eve which, of course, means an end to his rule, an end to the dominance of his own line of Seth, and the resurgence of the way of Kain. Athena may be the nemesis of Nereus, but she is not going to hurt him physically—Greek gods and heroes never do—she and her Zeus-religion are going to take

Figure 25: Nereus, far right, is forced by the artist to witness the birth of Athena—the rebirth of the serpent's Eve after the Flood—signaling an end to the rule of the Old Man of the Sea who brought surviving humanity through the Flood.

over from him spiritually. That's the message repeated over and over in ancient Greek art and myth.

We don't want to overlook a very simple point the artist is making in this scene. The birth of Athena, the rebirth of the serpent's Eve, signals the establishment of Zeus-religion, and by putting Nereus/Noah in the scene, the artist is telling us that this happened, or began to happen, during his lifetime.

As on the vase above, Greek artists made a habit of placing Nereus in scenes as a passive witness to key events in the development of the antithetical Greek religious system. One artist put him as a witness to Herakles killing a Kentaur, a member of the line of Seth (Fig. 72, page 80). Another artist made Nereus a witness to the abduction of his daughter, Thetis, by the Zeus-worshipper, Peleus (Fig. 130, page 130), while another artist made Nereus and his wife, Doris, witnesses to that couples' wedding which was attended by all the Greek gods (Fig. 129, page 130). Yet another artist showed Nereus looking on helplessly as Herakles wrestles away his power and gives it to Poseidon, the brother of Zeus (Fig. 32, page 43). On the Altar of Zeus at Pergamum, the sculptors put Nereus and Doris in the corner of the main frieze to witness the utter rout by the gods of the Giants, who represented their Yahweh-believing sons (Fig. 97, page 98). All of those scenes share the same basic message: the man-centered, religious outlook of the Greeks replaces the God-centered spiritual outlook of Noah.

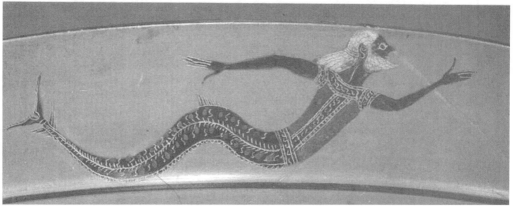

Figure 26: A Greek artist tells us where the people of Crete came from.

Nereus/Noah, Zeus, and Europa

Greek myth/art and the Book of Genesis tell basically the same story because that's what really happened in our past. Greek artists knew where they came from, and they often expressed it with great simplicity. In a recent issue devoted to ancient Crete, the editors of an archaeological journal made a point to emphasize that European civilization began there. In about 540 BC, as we can see on the above vase (Fig. 26), a Greek artist expressed that truth very simply.

Michael Padgett writes in *The Centaur's Smile* that this cup "may have been the earliest representation of Europa and the bull in Attic art yet known to us." He summarizes the story thus:

Europa, daughter of Phoinix, king of Tyre, was picking flowers in a meadow with her friends when she caught Zeus' eye. He transformed himself into a saffron-breathing bull, attracted her attention, and carried her off across the sea to Crete, where she bore him Minos, Radamanthys, and, in some versions, Sarpedon.

On the vase, the artist depicts the voyage from Tyre on the eastern Mediterranean coast to Crete. On one side, Europa rides through the sea on the back of Zeus the bull, and on the other side we learn the timeframe; for there, Nereus, the Old Man of the Sea, is pictured. According to Genesis, in the latter part of Noah's life, Yahweh dispersed humanity after their attempt to unite in Babylon by confounding their one language into many. Genesis describes those who then sailed about the Mediterranean as "coastlanders" (Genesis 10:5). The Greeks ignore Noah's God and instead give Zeus credit for bringing humanity to Crete from the Mideast, thereby establishing on that island the earliest foundations of Greek civilization.

For the most part, Greek art/myth is a record of where the Greeks came from and what kind of religious/spiritual orientation they developed. Again, let's trust the artists: they knew enough to pinpoint the location where their civilization first developed, and they knew enough to date its establishment from the time of Nereus/Noah. Let's now take a look at how these artists pitted Herakles against Nereus in various vase-scenes to depict the developing dominance of their man-centered religious outlook.

Chapter 4

Herakles Seizes the Authority of Nereus/Noah

Herakles is the first great "master in the earth" from Genesis, Nimrod, transplanted to Greek soil. The Hebrew word for Nimrod means "Rebel." Greek artists depicted Herakles as carrying out a successful rebellion directed against Nereus, the Greek Noah. At that time, Noah's was the only system to rebel against.

Victorious rebels become heroes and replace one system with a different one. The meaning of the great hero's name in Greek explains his new system as concisely as possible: Herakles means "the glory of Hera." Hera's glory was her place in the Greek pantheon as the queen of all mankind. Herakles' rebellion replaced the authority of Noah with the authority of the gods of Zeus-religion.

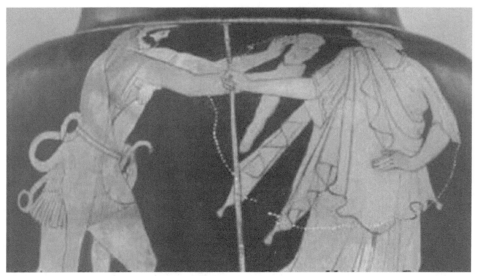

Figure 27: Herakles forces Nereus back, showing him the physical power of his club.

Herakles Comes to Grips with Noah's Authority

Most of the extant vases featuring Nereus/Noah show him being disempowered in some way. In almost all cases, his authority is being taken away, and yet he never resists. As we'll see in Chapter 9, sometimes he receives the news of his disempowerment indirectly from his daughters. Sometimes the artists picture Herakles taking the authority of Nereus/Noah directly from him. On the red-figure storage jar for wine, above, Herakles chases after Nereus, pointing to his club, a symbol of his strength. Nereus is backing up, reacting to the aggressive body language of Herakles. The artist's message is simple: Herakles is telling Nereus/Noah that he is in charge now. Note that the serpent coils itself into Herakles' belt. This tells us that the serpent is intricately related to this takeover. The weaponless Nereus/Noah does not fight back; he always remains passive, stoic even, in the face of this great religious transformation.

Figure 28: Nereus depicted with his trident.

In Figure 29, opposite, a different vase-artist depicts the same idea a different way. The nude Herakles, brandishing his club in his right hand, comes astride Nereus and grasps his neck with his left hand. He is bringing the momentum of Nereus to a halt, and by extension, he is bringing the rule of

Figure 29: Herakles brings the rule of Nereus/Noah to an abrupt halt.

Nereus/Noah to an end, replacing it with Zeus-religion. Behind Nereus, Poseidon, a "brother" of Zeus, steps up and replaces the "Wet One" as god of the sea. Herakles may as well be saying, "Hold it, Nereus, your reign is over. Poseidon is in charge now."

On Figure 28, an artist painted Nereus carrying the trident to let us know that to begin with, it was his symbol of power. In Figure 29, above, the Greek god Poseidon has now taken it for himself. We'll see in subsequent chapters that the theme of Greek gods and heroes taking what belongs to Nereus/Noah continues: Zeus will take his scepter, Athena will take his cloak, and Poseidon and the Zeus-worshipper, Peleus, will take his daughters.

There is another way the artists used Herakles to express the idea that Nereus/Noah lost his power to the Greek religious system. In order to show Nereus losing his authority, artists created a figure who came to be known as Triton (Fig. 30). Triton represents Nereus himself at the height of his powers. Basically, the artists created two different images for Nereus, one which represented his authority, and the other which represented the helpless and usurped old man himself. Using these two related images, the artists could picture the authority of Nereus/Noah being wrestled away without showing any harm coming to the Old Man of the Sea.

Figure 30: Triton, a depiction of Nereus at the height of his powers.

Figure 31: Herakles wrestles away Triton, who represents the authority of Nereus/Noah.

Herakles Wrestles Away Triton—Noah's Authority

Above, we see a depiction from ca. 520 BC of Herakles coming to grips with Noah's authority represented by the fish-tailed Triton. If the artists had wanted to show Herakles killing a monster, they would have made it very obvious as they did on many other vases where killing was part of the action. But on these vases and many others, the artists make Herakles' grip on Triton the focal point of the encounter. The artists invented Triton as a symbol with which Herakles was able to grapple. He is wrestling away Triton—Noah's authority and power—seizing it for the developing Greek religious system. After the Flood, humanity ceased fearing the God of Nereus/Noah, and instead began to fear the great hero, Herakles, and worship the gods of Zeus-religion.

On the vase above, one of the daughters of Nereus sees what is happening and gestures to her father as if to say, "What's happening, Dad? Aren't you going to do something about this?" The answer is no. Nereus will do nothing. According to Genesis, Yahweh actually spoke to Noah, then guided him for a hundred years in the building of the ark, and then took him and his family through the Flood. Noah had a profound understanding of what was happening, and he knew that the One "Who is operating all in accord with the counsel of His will" (Ephesians 1:11) had a purpose in it. The Greek artists faithfully recorded the historical facts that Nereus/Noah was never harmed and that he never physically resisted the takeover of Zeus-religion.

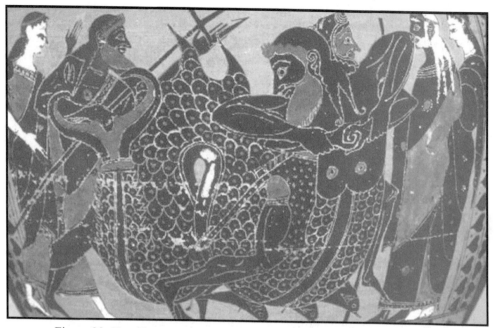

Figure 32: Herakles wrestles away Noah's authority, giving it to Poseidon.

The vase-depiction of Herakles and Triton, above, tells the story in more detail. Herakles harms or kills many of his opponents, but never Nereus or Triton (the younger Nereus). Here, he wrestles with Triton, grabbing him from behind. Notice the interlocking hands of Herakles. He is coming to grips with Noah's legacy. On the vase, he is wrestling it away from the Old Man of the Sea who stands to the right leaning on his staff with a daughter (or perhaps his wife, Doris) disconsolate at the turn of events he will do nothing to prevent. On the left, behind Triton's tail, stand Poseidon (with trident) and his wife, the Nereïd Amphitrite, both of whom bend toward the action with their arms upraised, in gestures that indicate their involvement with its outcome.

What a magnificent painting! Herakles is wrestling away Nereus' authority and his association with the power of the sea and giving both to Poseidon, a brother of Zeus. Poseidon becomes god of the sea and its power. Nereus still has a place in Greek history, but as a believer in Yahweh, no place on Olympus.

Greek artists tell us that Herakles (the Nimrod of Genesis) as a powerful young man, came to grips with the authority of the old Nereus, and wrestled it away from him. According to Genesis, at the end of Noah's life, Nimrod became "a master in the earth." *Strong's Concordance* defines the Hebrew word for master as "powerful; by implication, warrior, tyrant:—champion, chief, mighty one, strong man, valiant man." Those same words precisely describe the Greek Herakles. Here again, the Greek and the Judeo-Christian historical traditions match.

On this Attic black-figure cup from ca. 520 BC (Figs. 33, 34, and 35), the artist takes the seizure of power from Nereus/Noah a step further. On one side of the cup, he shows Herakles wrestling with Triton. We now understand what the Greeks understood from such an image: this depicts the power of the Greek religious system coming to grips with the authority of Noah and wrestling it away from him. But what happens once that authority is wrestled away? The artist tells us on the other side of the cup.

There we find Herakles chatting with Dionysos, the god of wine and revelry. Nereus/Noah was a spiritual man. Dionysos represents the soulish man, the man who lives according to his senses. In the center of the inside of the cup, the artist has painted the head of the Gorgon Medusa—the head of serpents. Around the Gorgon head, six Greeks relax at a drinking party (symposium). Humanity is free from the God of Noah, free to follow its soulish and sensual urges.

On the cup, Dionysos holds a kantharos in his hand. Greek artists used this drinking cup as their basic symbol of transformation. The artist's painting is celebrating humanity's change in orientation from the spiritual to the soulish—from a God-centered system of belief to a human-centered system. Who are the most important figures in a human-centered system? The great humans of history such as Kain (Hephaistos), Cush (Hermes), Nimrod (Herakles), and especially the first man and the first woman whom the Greeks deified as Zeus and Hera.

Figure 33: The Gorgon Medusa and symposiasts on the interior of the cup.

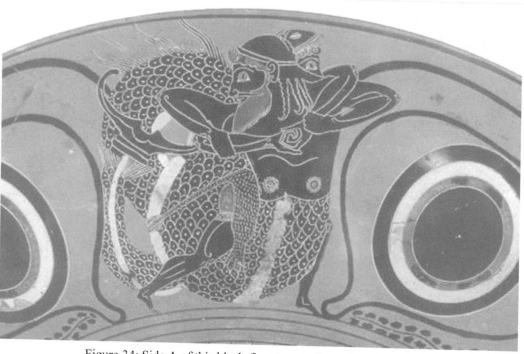

Figure 34: Side A of this black-figure cup tells us that Herakles has wrestled away the authority of Nereus/Noah.

Figure 35: Side B of the same vase. Herakles talks with Dionysos, the god of wine and revelry who pursues soulish pleasures related to the senses. The spiritual reign of Noah is replaced by the soulish reign of Zeus-religion.

Figure 36: Amphitrite (daughter of Nereus), Nike, and Amphitrite's husband, Poseidon.

On the vase-depiction above from ca. 480 BC, Nike stands in the center between two folding stools, where Amphitrite and Poseidon sit facing each other. Nike, with her wings spread, turns her head toward Amphitrite. She holds a wine jug in her right hand and a small red flower in her left hand (the red blends into the black in the illustration). Amphitrite also holds such a flower in her left hand; and in her right hand, she holds a drinking bowl out of which she is pouring into the ground the wine Nike has given her. Poseidon also pours out the wine from the bowl in his right hand. His left hand holds his trident.

The flowers in the hands of Amphitrite and Nike represent the beginning of the flowering of the Greek religious system. As a daughter of Nereus, Amphitrite used to belong to him. As the wife of Poseidon, she now belongs to the new god of the sea, and has become part of the Greek religious system. This is the victory they are celebrating. By pouring out wine into the earth, they are ritually sealing their victory over Nereus, and affirming their place in the Greek pantheon.

The average Greek looking at this scene would have known that it was Herakles who made this celebration possible, that he was the one who had pushed Nereus/Noah out of the picture. As we look at the Parthenon sculptures in the following chapters, we will see that they relate directly to many of these vase-scenes the Greeks encountered as part of their daily lives.

Chapter 5

The Flood Depicted on the Parthenon

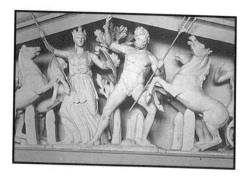

The west pediment of the Parthenon depicted the Flood and its aftermath. Poseidon left behind a pool of saltwater as the ocean receded from the Akropolis. Then Athena presented the people of Athens with an olive tree, the symbol of the new age after the Flood.

Poseidon usurped the power of Nereus, the Greek Noah, by taking his daughter Amphitrite. The pediment does not feature Noah, but alludes to him through the presence of his daughter and son-in-law.

The West Pediment

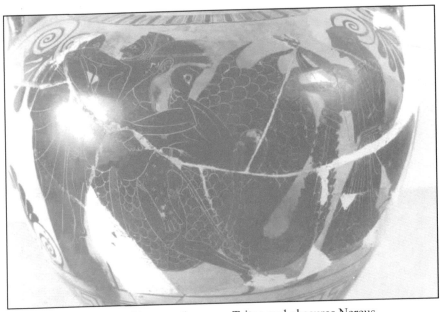

Figure 37: Herakles wrestles away Triton and obscures Nereus.

Before we get to the Flood depicted in the center of the west pediment, we need to grasp its underlying theme. Two vase-artists give us the background we need using very simple images. On the above vase (Fig. 37), the scene is familiar to us. Herakles wrestles away the authority of Nereus/Noah as Nereus and one of his daughters look on. In Chapter 4, we've seen that Herakles gives this authority (represented by Triton) to Poseidon who has taken one of Nereus' daughters, Amphitrite, for himself. On the vase, the artist makes a point to obscure part of the face of Nereus. Nereus is being elbowed out of the way, shoved out of the picture. Herakles and Poseidon barge into the family of Nereus and take over. The belief system of Nereus contradicts the reemerging way of Kain: the Old Man of the Sea and his God must be pushed out of the way.

The two sides of the Attic red-figure storage jar pictured opposite (Figs. 38 and 39) affirm that Nereus has been replaced. On one side, a daughter of Nereus runs to him. From the sense of urgency in her body language and her extended, pleading arm, we see that she is insisting that he take action in regard to something that is occurring. What the daughter of Nereus/Noah is worried about is pictured on the other side. There, Nike, the winged goddess of victory, pours a drink offering to the newly-enthroned Poseidon, the "brother" of Zeus. A new religious system has taken over, and the daughter of Nereus/Noah wants to know what he is going to do about this usurpation.

Nereus receives the news stoically. He is not going to do anything about it. This is history, and historically, Nereus/Noah did nothing about the takeover of

Figure 38: A daughter of Nereus wants to know what he is going to do
about what has happened on the other side of the vase.

Figure 39: On this side of the vase, Nike celebrates Poseidon's takeover.

Zeus-religion. The center of the west pediment celebrates this takeover without
picturing the Old Man of the Sea. We'll see Poseidon and Amphitrite in the center of the west pediment, but not Nereus. From the Greek standpoint, it's over for
him. His authority has been usurped and he must remain obscured. While history
demands his acknowledgement, Zeus-religion demands he be supplanted.

Figure 40: Reconstruction of the west pediment of the Parthenon.

Noah's Flood—Retold the Greek Way

The celebration of the triumph of Zeus-religion begins on the west pediment with the purposeful exclusion of Nereus/Noah. The central sculptures tell essentially the same Flood story as the Book of Genesis except that Nereus/Noah has been shoved aside and replaced with Poseidon. To "read" the Greek version of that story, we're going to have to cut through some very befogging "myths" and think about what they really mean. To get to the truth, we're going to trust the ancient sculptors, and give them credit for knowing who they were and where they came from.

According to the conventional view, the center of the west pediment of the Parthenon depicts the so-called contest between Athena and Poseidon for control of the Akropolis, the city itself, and all of Attika, the surrounding region. In some versions of the myth, the contest was held to determine whose name the city would bear. Athena and Poseidon each were to give a gift, and the greater gift would win the city. The exact identity of the judges of this "contest" is muddled. They are variously said to have been the other Olympian gods, Zeus alone, one of many kings of Attika, or the populace as a whole.

Poseidon went first. He raised his trident and struck the earth atop the Akropolis. It trembled and split apart in that place. Then, right there—four miles inland—a salt spring miraculously appeared where no water had been before. This demonstration of Poseidon's great power impressed the judges, whoever they were.

Now it was Athena's turn. She caused an olive tree to sprout up nearby. Without hesitation, the judges favored Athena's gift and named the city after her.

Athena's gift makes sense if we relate it to the Book of Genesis. There, the dove returns to Noah with a torn-off olive leaf in its beak, and the olive tree becomes a sign of the new age after the Flood. Athena takes the olive tree as her own symbol, establishing herself as humanity's source of direction and enlightenment. Poseidon's side of the story, however, is unconvincing. His gift of a salt

Figure 41: Athena and Poseidon in the center of the
west pediment of the Parthenon.

spring on the Akropolis is a worthless offering to the people of Athens. It must mean something else, and it does: it is a straightforward representation of the Flood and its aftermath.

In the book, *Worshipping Athena: Panathenaia and Parthenon*, edited by Jenifer Neils, contributor Noel Robertson relates that no well of any kind exists on the top of the Akropolis, and concludes that "this strange well with sea-water did not go down very far; perhaps it was more of a basin." This crucial bit of research helps substantiate the idea that, rather than depicting a preposterous contest between deities, the west pediment of the Parthenon portrayed part of humanity's history—the Flood and its aftermath. During the Flood, Poseidon, the god of the sea, covered the Akropolis. What Poseidon left behind as his waters receded was a basin, or pool, of salt water—not a spring. Thank you, Professor Robertson.

What is framed in myth as a contest between Athena and Poseidon is in reality a vivid depiction of a familiar, earth-shaking historical event. Poseidon is the god of the sea, or more accurately, the god of the *power* of the sea. During the Flood, Poseidon's salt water covered the Akropolis. As the waters subsided, he left a salt water pool as a reminder of his power. Following Poseidon's (the sea's) departure from the Akropolis, the goddess Athena usurped the symbol of the olive tree and began her rule of the new Greek age. It's as simple as that.

Figure 42: Jacques Carrey's drawing of part of the west pediment in 1674.

Let's look at the central figures in more detail. Fortunately, we have the drawings of Jacques Carrey from 1674 to help us. I'd like to have Poseidon where he belongs, on the same page with Iris and Amphitrite, but that's not the way Mr. Carrey drew the scenes.

We'll examine those three figures first. In the reconstructed model of the west pediment on the previous page, Poseidon holds his trident in his left hand. But both extant vase-depictions of the central scene show Poseidon holding his trident in his right hand, apparently pulling it up and away (see pages 56 and 57). I appreciate the work of those who put the west pediment model together, but in this case, I'm going to trust the ancient vase-painters. Poseidon, the power of the sea, is depicted as having struck the ground with his trident, causing the earth to quake and split. When he did that, water gushed forth. This matches the account of the Deluge in Genesis. Water came first from below, then from above:

On this day rent are all the springs of the vast submerged chaos, and the crevices of the heavens are opened, and coming is the downpour on the earth forty days and forty nights (Genesis 7: 11-12).

Poseidon has rent "all the springs of the vast submerged chaos" releasing the great Flood upon the earth. The poets Pindar and Homer both call him "the Earthshaker." But he is stepping back from his action of striking the earth with

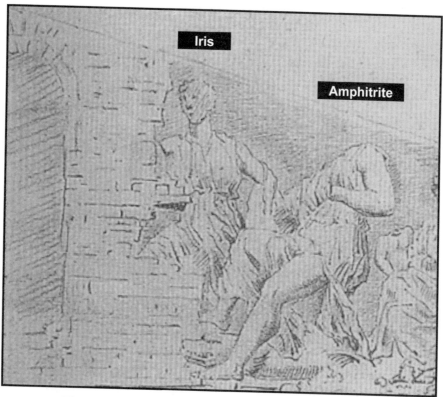

Figure 43: Jacques Carrey's drawing of Iris and Amphitrite.

his trident, indicating that the Flood is over. Amphitrite, Poseidon's chariot-driver and wife, tells us what happened next. In Greek myth, Amphitrite, a daughter of Nereus, is associated with dolphins because she was reluctant to marry Poseidon until a messenger named Delphin persuaded her to do so. Delphin is a word related in meaning to Delphi, the site of Apollo's oracle, thus suggesting their marriage was ordained by the gods. Dolphins appear as the sea grows calm. Amphitrite here represents the calm sea, the non-threatening sea. This also agrees with the Genesis account:

And the Elohim [God] is causing a wind to pass over the earth, and subsiding are the waters. And being held in check are the springs of the submerged chaos and the crevices of the heavens, and being shut up is the downpour from the heavens, and returning are the waters off the earth, going and returning.

Note that the wind caused the waters to subside. The same thing happens to-day, at least where I live. After it rains, the wind comes and takes the dampness away with it. Amphitrite's garb depicts the wind. This is the observation of B. F. Cook, the former Keeper of Greek and Roman Antiquities in the British Museum. He bases it on Amphitrite in the above drawing. Mr. Cook writes:

Figure 44: Amphitrite from the 1674 drawing of Jacques Carrey.

The goddess [Amphitrite] wears a peplos girt with a belt high below the breasts and open at the side so that, as the drawing shows, the lower part was swept back by the wind, leaving the left leg bare.

Thus it is very possible that her figure represents not only the calming sea, but the wind which dried it up as well. The ripples in the dress of Iris, whose figure survives as a headless, armless torso with legs to the knees (Fig. 45, opposite) also depict the action of the wind.

As we have seen, Amphitrite is one of the Nereïds, the fifty daughters of Nereus, the Greek Noah. This is a direct connection to the Flood-events described in Genesis. Nereus can't be depicted here because he is part of the line of Seth, and what the Greeks are affirming on the west pediment is that the serpent's system, the way of Kain, has taken over after the Flood. Undue attention to Nereus distracts from that. That's why Poseidon, the brother of Zeus, has become the god who represents the awesome power of the sea.

Behind Amphitrite and the chariot stands Iris. Iris means "Rainbow" in Greek. According to Olga Palagia, author of *The Pediments of the Parthenon*, two large symmetrical cuttings at her back, made with large diameter drills, indicate the attachment of marble wings, suggesting that she is delivering a message to earth from the celestial realms. The rainbow's message is that the seas will remain calm. This also accords with the Genesis account. The rainbow's association with the Deluge is widely known. In Chapter 9 of Genesis, Yahweh explains that He will not inundate the world again, and as a sign of this covenant with humanity, He leaves the rainbow:

"My [rain]bow I bestow in a cloud, and it comes to be for a sign of the covenant between Me and the earth. And it comes, when I cloud over the earth with a cloud, then appears My [rain]bow in the cloud, and I am reminded of My covenant, which is between Me and you and every living soul in all flesh, and there is not to come a future deluge of water to wreck all flesh."

While Amphitrite portrays the calming sea and the wind which causes it to recede and make the land reappear, Iris brings the rainbow's message that such a Flood will not occur again. These depictions of Poseidon, Amphitrite, and Iris on the right of the pediment express the essential elements of the Genesis account of the Flood. The difference is that Yahweh is behind the Genesis event and Zeus is behind the rendition of it on Athena's temple, the Parthenon. And of course, Nereus/Noah and his wife have been replaced by Poseidon and Amphitrite.

With the depictions of Athena, Nike, and Hermes to our left of the center of the pediment, the Greeks give us

Figure 45: Iris, or "Rainbow," from the west pediment of the Parthenon, now in the British Museum, London.

a concise overview of what happened after the waters of the Deluge receded. Athena, a chosen instrument of the serpent's system, takes over. Her birth after the Flood (the rebirth of the serpent's Eve) is the theme of the east pediment. Back on the west pediment, Nike guides her chariot establishing the goddess' victorious preeminence in this age. If this great Greek goddess is to rule the minds and hearts of humanity, she needs the help of a believer and a prophet. She needs Hermes. According to Greek myth, Hermes assisted the Three Fates in the cultivation of the olive tree. That means Hermes was the first, after the Flood, to receive the serpent's enlightenment from Athena, nurture it, and develop it into a religious system. Nike's presence speaks of Athena's and Hermes' joint victory.

Chapters 2, 8, and 20 discuss Hermes' identity and role in Zeus-religion, so I'll just remind the reader that he is a deification of Cush, who founded Babylon and led the effort to unite humanity—without Yahweh—in the building of the infamous tower there.

Figure 46: Late Classical vase-painting of the center of the west pediment of
the Parthenon. Hermes approaches from the left. On the
right, Iris, the Rainbow, floats above Poseidon.

To my knowledge, there are only two extant vase-depictions of the center of
the west pediment of the Parthenon: the one above (Fig. 46), and the partially
damaged one (Fig. 47), opposite, both from the Late Classical period. Each artist
has put what appears to be an olive tree in the center. On one, a serpent coils upward on the tree. On the other, the lightning bolt of Zeus comes down on the top
of the tree.

On the vase above, Hermes appears to our left of Athena, just as on the Parthenon; and Iris appears flying in the sky next to Poseidon. A fish swims between
Poseidon's legs indicating the receding flood waters. On the depiction opposite,
the woman next to Poseidon looks to be Amphitrite, wife of Poseidon and the
daughter of Nereus/Noah. A sea creature swims at their feet, probably Triton, the
symbol of the sea's power and the authority of Nereus that Herakles has wrestled
away from him.

The lightning bolt of Zeus and the serpent, as symbols, relate to the same
event. The lightning bolt signifies the enlightenment of the serpent from Eden.
Now that the Flood is over, the serpent returns to enlighten humanity and to rule
the Greek age, symbolized by the olive tree, through Athena. The lightning bolt
has the advantage of representing the serpent's enlightenment *and* calling attention to a sudden, significant change on earth directed by Zeus.

Figure 47: On this water pot from ca. 400 BC, the artist has painted his rendition of the center of the west pediment of the Parthenon. Poseidon's body language matches Carrey's drawing and the surviving sculpture.

Chapter 6

Before the Flood, the Kentaurs Take the Line of Kain's Women

Before the Flood, the line of Seth intermarried with the line of Kain, and over time merged into it, leaving Noah's family as the only one with an untainted connection to Seth. Those events are related in Chapter 6 of the Book of Genesis.

The Greeks remembered these same events as the stealing of the line of Kain's women by the Kentaurs, and they depicted this embarrassment on the south metopes of the Parthenon.

Furthermore, they remembered the trauma of the Flood itself as the line of Kain being beaten into the earth by these same Kentaurs.

The South Metopes

Figures 48 and 49: In south metope # 30, a Kentaur kills a Lapith.
On metope # 29, a Kentaur carries off a Lapith woman.

The Kentaurs Defeat the Lapiths and Take Their Women

The generations after Noah wanted to know what happened before the Flood, and why it occurred. Noah, his three sons, and their wives passed on this knowledge to succeeding generations. In recounting the story, the members of Noah's family would have explained to their offspring basically what is written in Chapter 6 of Genesis; namely, that the line of Seth took women from the line of Kain for their wives, that these women clung to their idolatrous ways until, with the exception of Noah's family, the line of Seth became indistinguishable from the line of Kain. All humanity, except for the family of Noah, thus came to embrace the way of Kain, a way which excluded reverence for the Creator. Thus, the Deluge and Noah's ark coming through it.

After the Flood, those who sought to exalt mankind (as opposed to the God of Noah), began to look back fondly upon the civilization and people who had been destroyed by the Flood. To them, the wrong people got wiped out. The Zeus-worshipping Greeks put a different "spin" on the story when they retold it. They made the line of Seth look brutal and uncivilized; and the line of Kain, noble and victimized. Let's look into some of the details which the Parthenon sculptors and other Greek artists were kind enough to leave with us.

The theme of twenty-three of the thirty-two south metopes on the Parthenon is the Lapiths fighting the Kentaurs (Fig. 53, pages 64-65). In most of the scenes that depict one-on-one combat, as in Figure 48, the Lapiths are getting the worst

Fig. 50: On this oil jar from ca. 465 BC, Herakles grasps the hand of Perithous in Hades. He can't bring him back because he is from the pre-Flood age. Their eye contact and hand grip show agreement. Herakles vows to avenge the taking of the Lapith women by the Kentaurs.

of it. Not only that, the Kentaurs are carrying off the Lapith women as on the metope depicted in Fig. 49. What is going on here?

First, it's important to emphasize that these are not Greeks but Lapiths, a word that, according to Robert Graves, means "Flint-chippers." This suggests great antiquity. Some ancients write that the Lapiths were from Northern Greece, but there is no record of any Lapith settlements. The Lapiths existed before the Flood, and Greek myth bears this out.

This taking of the Lapith women occurred at the wedding of a man named Perithous. The Kentaurs showed up and supposedly got drunk (they don't look drunk in any of the sculptures), and carried off Perithous' wife, Hippodameia, and other women. Some chroniclers get mixed up as to when this happened. We know it happened before the Flood because the Greek hero, Herakles, went to Hades to retrieve Perithous and the hero Theseus (Fig. 50). Herakles was able to bring Theseus out of Hades because that Greek hero lived in Herakles' own era. He could not bring back Perithous, because he had lived before the Flood.

The Kentaurs represent the line of Seth; the Lapiths, the line of Kain. Let me suggest two possibilities for the origin of the name Kentaur, both of which may

Figure 51: Three Kentaurs on a vase, each carrying that "strange" branch.

be true. The root meaning of the Greek word *Kentauros* is hundred. The Romans took it over as *kenturion* (centurion), the leader of a hundred soldiers, and it comes down to us as a cent, and a century. Not only did Noah build an ark, he heralded for a hundred years that the Flood was coming: "[For God] spares not the ancient world, but guards Noah, an eighth, a herald of righteousness, bringing a deluge on the world of the irreverent" (II Peter 2:5).

Noah was 500-years-old when he learned of the coming Flood and 600-years-old when it happened (Genesis 5:32, 9:28-29). As a herald or proclaimer of righteousness (belief in Yahweh), Noah warned for a century that the world would be inundated. The unbelievers derided him, and most likely said words to this effect: "That moron has been proclaiming that nonsense for a hundred years." As Noah was part of the line of Seth, it is natural that the Greeks would associate his relatives with this hundred-year-long proclamation.

Then, in the Chaldean language from Babylon where the image of the Kentaur originated, the word *çûwç* means horse, and the Kentaurs were depicted as half-men/half-horses. A word that is pronounced almost identically in Chaldean, *çûwph*, means "terminate, or have an end, perish." The horse-part of the Kentaur may have been a homophonic word-picture which connected to the reason that the line of Kain perished during the Flood. As we shall see later in this chapter,

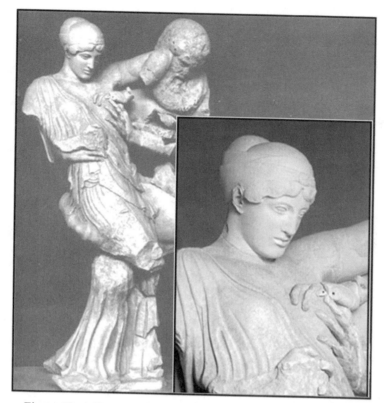

Figure 52: A Kentaur abducts Hippodamea, the "Horse-tamer."
From the east pediment of the temple of Zeus at Olympia.

Genesis suggests very strongly that it was this taking of the women that led to the Flood. We'll also see that the Greeks specifically blamed the Kentaurs for bringing an end to the line of Kain during the Flood.

On the storage jar, opposite, from ca. 530 BC (Fig. 51), three Kentaurs walk to our left, each carrying a symmetrical branch over their left shoulders. From the perspective of the line of Kain, this branch identifies them as part of that "strange branch" of humanity, the line of Seth.

Kentaurs dominated 5th-century BC Greek public sculpture. The west pediment of the temple of Zeus at Olympia featured the Kentaurs seizing the Lapith women at the wedding of Perithous, the king of the Lapiths. The Greek myth that Ares/Seth had an affair with Aphrodite, wife of Hephaistos/Kain, expresses the depth of the desire of the Seth-men for the beautiful Kain-women.

In Figure 52 above, from that pediment of the temple of Zeus, a Kentaur grasps Hippodameia, the wife of Perithous, to carry her off. Hippodameia does not fight him. Her impassiveness indicates that she is going to be carried off no matter what she does. This is the sculptor's way of telling us that this is not about women fighting the Kentaurs, but women being carried off by them.

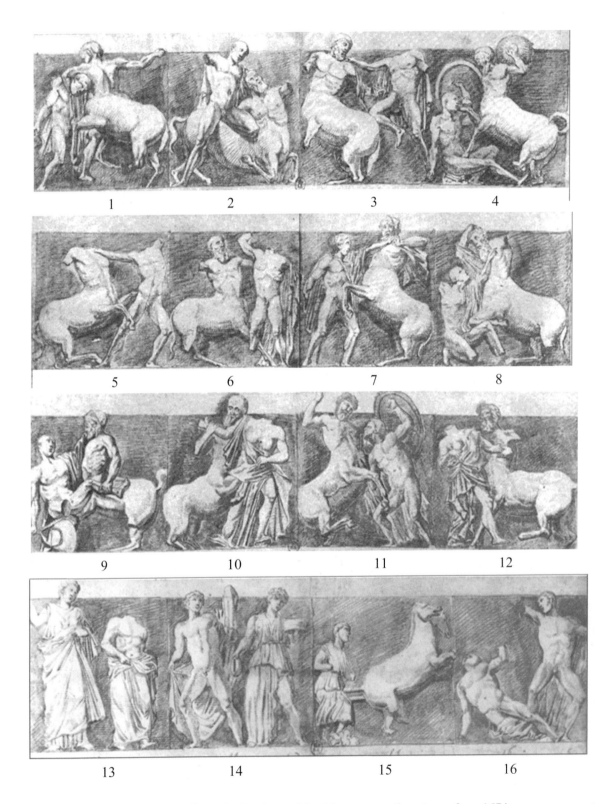

Figure 53: Jacques Carrey's drawings of the thirty-two south metopes from 1674.

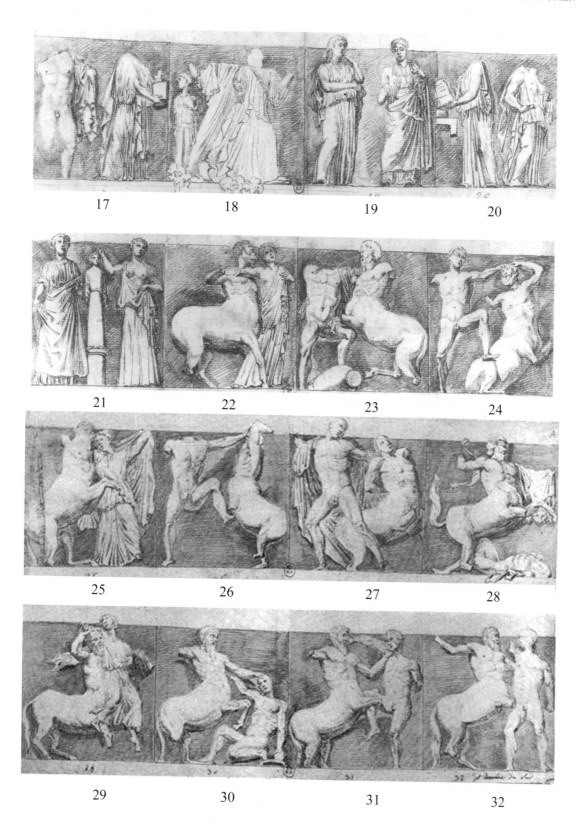

17   18   19   20

21   22   23   24

25   26   27   28

29   30   31   32

Seth, Kain, and Subjection

The difference between the line of Kain and the line of Seth concerns the question of subjection. El in Hebrew means Subjector. Kain and his line reveled in their insubjection to the Supreme Subjector, El, also called Yahweh. The name of Kain's great-grandson, Mehujael (*Mchui-El*), expresses his line's great antipathy to the Supreme: it means "Wipe-out Subjector."

Seth was subject to God, and he was expected to subject the rest of humanity in his domain, especially his direct offspring, to God. The subject of Chapter 5 of Genesis is the annals of Adam—the record of the whole line of first-borns through Seth down to Noah. Each of these men, when his father died, was to function as the subjector of humanity while he lived, and then at death pass the rule on to his son. But something happened to the line of Seth before the Flood. Only Noah's family escaped the Deluge. Why? Wasn't the line of Seth in subjection to the Subjector? Genesis 6:9 reads:

These are the genealogical annals of Noah: Noah is a just man. Flawless became he in his generations. With the Elohim walks Noah.

Noah was flawless in his generations, but the rest of the line of Seth, by taking women from the line of Kain, had become flawed in their generations. While the line of Kain refused to be subject to God, the line of Seth failed in not subjecting *others*.

Seth, and after him, each successive first-born son, lived about two hundred years after the death of his predecessor, when he took over the place of Adam as the head of humanity. Yet, at the end of the line, only Noah, with his family, was free from the prevailing insubjection. If the reason for the prevailing insubjection to God was that the men in the line of Seth had taken women from the line of Kain for their wives, where does it say so in Genesis? It says so in Genesis 6:1-8, but before I cite that, we need to look at the meaning of the words Elohim (capitalized) and elohim (not capitalized), which appear in that passage.

We already know that the term El for God in Hebrew means Subjector and refers to the Supreme Subjector Who is Yahweh, or God the Father, the omnipresent Spirit. Elohim (capitalized in English) refers to God as He is working through others, especially Christ. When in the Hebrew texts, Elohim, a plural word, is used to refer to the Supreme Spirit, it always takes a singular verb. That is because, according to Scripture, God always operates through Christ and sometimes in turn through lesser beings, as One Spirit. The word **Elohim** refers to the One True God, **El**, as He is subjecting His creations through other beings.

The word elohim (not capitalized in English) refers to human subjectors, or ruling magistrates. For example, the words of Moses brought many into subjection to the God of Israel, and in that sense he is one of the elohim, one of those who played a part in subjecting others to God.

Before the Flood, God established Adam and his first-born successors through Seth as elohim, or subjectors of humanity. Genesis 5:1 states that the Supreme Subjector created Adam in His likeness; that is, as a subjector. Genesis 5:3 states that Adam, in turn, begot Seth "in his likeness, according to his image." This shows that Adam was the subjector, or ruling magistrate, of humanity while he lived, and that he passed this on to Seth. Seth inherited Adam's authority because Abel had no offspring before he was murdered by Kain, and Kain did not honor God or wish to bring any into subjection to Him. Thus Seth inherited the rights as Adam's first-born elohim, or subjector, by double default.

Now we are in a position to understand Genesis 6:1-8:

And coming is it that humanity starts to be multitudinous on the surface of the ground, and daughters are born to them. And seeing are sons of the Elohim* [human subjectors in the line of Seth] the daughters of the human, that they are good, and taking are they for themselves wives of all whom they choose.

And saying is Yahweh Elohim "Not abide shall My spirit in the human for the eon, in that moreover, he is flesh. And come shall his days to be a hundred and twenty years."

Now the distinguished** come to be in the earth in those days, and, moreover, afterward, coming are those who are sons of the Elohim* [human subjectors in the line of Seth] to the daughters of the human, and they bear for them. They are masters,** who are from the eon, mortals with the name.

And seeing is Yahweh Elohim that much is the evil of humanity in the earth, and every form of the devices of its heart is but evil all its days.

. . . Yet Noah finds grace in the eyes of Yahweh Elohim.

Men in the line of Seth took "for themselves wives of all whom they choose" (Genesis 6:2). Subsequent verses in the above passage reiterate this intermarriage

---

*This phrase "sons of the Elohim" is translated as "sons of God" in the King James Version. Taken to mean spirit beings, this has resulted in much illogical and unscriptural speculation. For more information, see "Studies in Genesis" in the September 2002 issue of Unsearchable Riches (www.Concordant.org).

**As far back at the *Septuagint*, the pre-Christian Greek translation of Hebrew Scriptures ca. 270 BC, two words meaning "distinguished" and "masters," in the cited passage were both mistranslated "giants." This has led to all kinds of fallacious interpretations and fables.

Figure 54: South metopes # 21 and # 22 drawn by Jacques Carrey in 1674.

of the lines, saying it happened after the days in which the distinguished came to be in the earth. It seems evident that the "distinguished" were Lamech's father, Methuselah, and Lamech's grandfather, Enoch. Why were they distinguished? Genesis 5:22 says "And walking is Enoch with the Elohim, after his begetting Methuselah, two hundred years." Walking with the Supreme is something that would set any man apart from his associates. Methuselah is distinguished because he was alive during the time his father walked with Elohim and because he lived for nine hundred and sixty-nine years, the longest of any human in Scripture.

The final breakdown of the ruling order of subjectors in the line of Seth occurred sometime during the lifetime of Noah's father, Lamech. Of the eight generations from Seth to himself, Lamech is the only one whose words are recorded in Scripture, so we know that they are very significant. He says of his son, Noah, "This one will console us because of our doings, and because of the grief of our hands, because of the ground Yahweh Elohim makes a curse" (Genesis 5:29). It remains for Genesis 6:1-4 to explain what "our doings" refer to. What went wrong in Lamech's time was this: Lamech's brothers and sons (other than Noah), and his uncles, took their wives from the line of Kain.

The taking of the Lapith women is the way the Greeks remembered this traumatic reality from before the Flood. Greek sculptors took great pains to associate the Lapith women with their goddess, undoubtedly an Eve/Hera figure. As we look at the Parthenon's south metopes numbers 21 and 22, above, as drawn by

Figure 55: Kain women cling to their goddess as the Kentaurs (Seth-men) abduct them.

Jacques Carrey in 1674, we see a Kentaur carrying off a woman from the line of Kain, as other women in the line of Kain cling to their goddess. Above, from the temple of Apollo at Bassae, we see the same theme depicted with more intensity. In the face of the onslaught of the Kentaurs, the women in the line of Kain exhibit fierce determination to keep their religion intact.

The Kentaurs (Seth-men) overpowered, abused, and carried off the Kain-women, yet these women refused to change their beliefs! That is what the clinging women represent, and that is how the line of Seth became corrupted. Of course, the Greeks didn't see it that way.

We've seen that according to the Greeks, the key Kain-woman taken by the Seth-men was Hippodameia, the wife of Perithous, king of the Lapiths. Hippodameia means "Horse-tamer." The half-men/half-horses may have taken the women of the line of Kain by force, but those same devoted Kain-women eventually tamed their captors from the line of Seth!

In a nutshell, to use Paul's words in II Corinthians 6:14, the line of Seth became "diversely yoked with unbelievers." And according to the apostle, that is the same as trying to establish a partnership between "righteousness and lawlessness," and the same as trying to create a communion between "light and darkness." "Or what part [has] a believer with an unbeliever?" According to the scriptural viewpoint, God's judgment on the ancient world is inevitable.

Figure 56: Kentaurs pound Kaineus into the earth on the west frieze
of the temple of Hephaistos in Athens.

The Greeks Blamed the Kentaurs for Wiping Out
the Line of Kain during the Flood

The above sculpture is part of the west frieze on the temple of Hephaistos in Athens. Built from 460 to 450 BC, the temple of Hephaistos stood on a little hill across from the agora, the hub of ancient Athens. It was the Athenians' most easily accessible major temple.

What's happening in the above scene? Two Kentaurs grasp a large rock. Working in concert, they pound a man into the ground. We don't know how many artists worked on this sculpture, but we can estimate that it would have taken one sculptor between a year-and-a-half to three years to complete it. That was a very serious undertaking; the figures are quite plain to us even after about 2,440 years. That is because they were meant to last and mean something to us.

This sculpture was part of a public building in ancient Athens. As the heirs of ancient Greek culture, it belongs to us now. In order to understand it, we need to establish some missing connections.

The theme of a man, whose name we will find to be *Kaineus*, being beaten into the ground is not original with this sculpture. Many ancient vases depicted this event including the famous François Vase from the 6th century BC, opposite.

Figure 57: On this partially damaged part of the François Vase from ca. 550 BC, three
Kentaurs pound Kaineus (the line of Kain) into the ground.

On it, three named Kentaurs pound the man into the ground, and to our right of
him, the vase-painter has written that man's name—KAINEUS. The word for the
eldest son of Adam and Eve as it appears in the Greek Scriptures is KAIN. And
we've seen that the eldest and favorite son of Zeus and Hera is Hephaistos, a deification of the Kain of Genesis.

The Flood temporarily wiped out the line of Kain. The Greeks pictured this
cataclysmic event as Kentaurs pounding a man named Kaineus into the ground
with a rock.

Kaineus does not represent just one man. In Greek, *eus* at the end of a noun
very often means "stemming from or pertaining to" that particular noun. For example in Greek, *Hippo* is a horse; *Hippeus* means pertaining to a horse, or horse-
like. So with Kain-eus, we have pertaining to Kain, stemming from Kain, or the
offspring of Kain. Kaineus is the human representation of the entire line of Kain.
The sculpture and the many vase-paintings tell us that which pertains to Kain;
that is, the line of Kain, gets pounded into the earth by a strange branch of humanity. Note that the Kentaur to our left, above, carries a branch which he may
be using as a weapon as well. We have already seen that this "strange branch" of
humanity is the line of Seth.

Figure 58: The shield device of Kaineus identifies him with the serpent.

Above, we see a drawing by Sir John Beazley of a vase from ca. 550 BC depicting two Kentaurs beating Kaineus into the ground. The shield of Kaineus features the ancient serpent, to whose religious system Kain is devoted. One Kentaur holds a branch which represented, to the Greeks, that other "strange branch" of humanity—the line of Seth. In the above scene, the artist has drawn the branch as a weapon. Perhaps he is trying to tell us that it's that "branch" (the line of Seth) that drives Kaineus into the earth.

Is there a special reason why Kain must be pounded in the head, as opposed to being stabbed in the heart or neck, for instance? That's a very good question with a very revealing answer. In Genesis, the line of Kain is considered to be the serpent's seed. They were the humans who embraced the way of Kain, welcomed the serpent's enlightenment, and rejected the rule and worship of Yahweh. Adam's and Eve's offspring before the Flood knew of Yahweh's curse on the line of Kain. It appears in Genesis 3:15:

"And enmity am I setting between you and the woman and between your seed and her seed. He shall hurt your head and you shall hurt his heel."

The Greeks looked back at the pounding of Kaineus into the ground by rock-blows to the head as the fulfillment of this curse. If that were the end of the story, there wouldn't be any Greek religion embracing the way of Kain. But that wasn't the end of the story. The line of Kain came back into being after the Flood. Thus, the hurting of Kain's head put an end to the curse without putting an end to the line of Kain.

Two Perceptions of the Same Horrendous Event

Figure 59: Michelangelo's painting of the Flood.

"And I, behold Me bringing a deluge of water over the earth to wreck all flesh, which has in it the spirit of the living, from under the heavens. All that is in the earth shall expire" (Genesis 6:17).

[For God] spares not the ancient world, but guards Noah, an eighth, a herald of righteousness, bringing a deluge on the world of the irreverent (II Peter 2:5).

Above, we see Michelangelo's painting of the destruction of all humanity save Noah and his family. Below, we see the ancient Greek interpretation of that same horrifying, traumatic event depicted on a vase from ca. 550 BC.

Figure 60: Kentaurs drive Kaineus (the line of Kain) into the earth.

The Reemergence of the Way of Kain after the Flood

The Greeks referred to Kaineus, the line of Kain, as invulnerable, and since they wholeheartedly re-embraced the way of Kain after the Flood, thus it seemed to them to be true. But how, specifically, did they account for Kain's line coming back into being after the Flood? The way the Athenians told the story, Athena took the sperm, or seed, of Hephaistos (the deified Kain), put it on a piece of wool and placed it into the ground. And out of that same ground into which Kaineus had been pounded, the line of Hephaistos, or Kain, reemerged in the form of a very special child, Erichthonios, "the Earth-born One."

The vase-depictions opposite tell the story of Kain's disappearance into the earth during the Flood, and his reappearance from the earth after the Flood. On the top vase, Kentaurs pound Kaineus into the ground. On the bottom vase, Gaia (Earth) brings forth the Earth-born One, the seed of Hephaistos who stands to our left of the child. The artist has painted Erichthonios white to emphasize his purity and importance. Athena reaches out and receives him. Nike, her head cocked lovingly to the side, holds Athena's shield and spear, indicating that the defeat of the Yahweh-believing sons of Noah is complete. Hephaistos wears an olive wreath; and the owl has an olive wreath for the child, as the olive tree is the symbol of the post-Flood age.

Aphrodite sits as if she were queen. As the wife of Hephaistos, she is entitled to revel in this great event. Hermes looks on the scene from above and gestures as if he were conducting an orchestra. As the deified Cush of Babylon, he is the one who orchestrated the reestablishment of the way of Kain after the Flood. Behind Aphrodite stands Zeus (we can only make out the very front of him) with his scepter suggesting that the child will partake of the god's rule. In his other hand, out of the picture, Zeus has his lightning bolt, representing his power and the moment of lighting up in paradise.

The Greeks understood the intrinsic relationship between these two vase-depictions. The major effect of the Flood was that the line of Seth (the Kentaurs) beat the line of Kain, or Kaineus, into the ground. But as the Greek legend says, Kaineus is invulnerable. With Athena's protection and the seed of Hephaistos nourished by the earth, the line of Kain comes back into being after the Flood in the form of the child, Erichthonios. Gaia presents the invulnerable, Earth-born One to Athena in the presence of Zeus, and the line of Kain is reestablished.

With Kaineus having been bruised severely on the head and yet coming back into existence after the Flood, the curse of Genesis was finally overcome, as was the patriarchal rule of Noah. In the Greek world, Noah's God, the God who had issued the curse, disappeared into the background, obscured by deified humans.

Figure 61: On this vase from ca. 475 BC, the artist tells us that Kaineus (the line of Kain) disappeared into the earth at the hands of the Kentaurs.

Figure 62: A red-figure vase depicting the birth of Erichthonios. The essence of ancient Greek religion is very simple. After the Flood, Athena, the reborn serpent's Eve, nurtures the reborn line of Kain.

Figure 63: The long south side of the Parthenon.

The Mysterious South-Central Metopes

Unlike the metopes from the east, west, and north, many of those from the south have survived in good shape. That is because the south side is the back side of the temple, very close to a steep cliff of the Akropolis where vandals and de-facers didn't venture. The south-central metopes were blown to bits in the explosion of 1687 when the Turks, besieged by the Venetians, used the Parthenon as a gunpowder magazine. Fortunately, Jacques Carrey had drawn all thirty-two metopes in 1674. Had the other sets of metopes not been battered beyond recognition by that time, he undoubtedly would have drawn them as well.

Both pediments, the metopes below them, and the north metopes which faced the center of the Akropolis were in plain view to those who frequented the area. The south metopes, on the long back side of the temple, were "behind the scenes," so to speak. And this is where the sculptors went into some depth about the origins of the their religious history. Metopes 1 through 12 and 21 through 32 pertain directly to Kentaurs seizing the Lapith women before the Flood. Centered between these twelve scenes on each side, metopes 13 through 20 depicted something "central" to Greek religion, perhaps taking us back to the original events upon which their system was based.

Let me give you my interpretation of metopes 13 through 16, opposite. Metope 13: two men talk. One is taller and presumably older than the other. Kain and Abel. Metope 14: Kain becomes upset over a sacrifice his wife is planning to offer. The dispute with Abel had affected Kain's domestic life. Metope 15: We read in Genesis: "And saying is Kain to Abel, his brother, 'Go will we to the field.'" Kain's intentions startle Abel and his horses in the field. Metope 16: Genesis again: "And coming is it, at their coming to be in field, rising is Kain against Abel, his brother, and killing him."

Figure 64: South metope 13.

Figure 65: South metope 14.

Figure 66: South metope 15.

Figure 67: South metope 16.

The other four south-central metopes, numbers seventeen through twenty, remain very mysterious.

In metope 17, a woman with an object in her hands, turns away from a man. Perhaps the man is Kain, and the turning of the woman's back to him signifies Kain's banishment for killing his brother, Abel. Is the woman Eve? Does she turn away because Kain is asserting that he is naked and unashamed?

In metope 18, the gender of the figures is not clear. The figure to our left gestures with the right arm. The figure to our right gestures with the left arm. A child has entered the scene in the background. Is this Seth? In Genesis 4:25, Eve says that she has named the child Seth (meaning Set) "For set for me has the Elohim another seed instead of Abel, for Kain kills him." What are the cloud-like images Carrey has drawn at the feet of the figures?

In metope 19, we see a woman and a man. The woman's arm positions indicate that she is thinking something over, or trying to figure out something. The man appears to be pondering the situation with her.

In metope 20, both figures appear to be female. The one to our left examines a scroll near what may have been a table with another scroll. The figure to our right walks away from the other, grasping what looks like a small scroll in her right hand. Are the Greeks telling us that all of this is written in a scroll somewhere? Did the Greeks know about the Scroll of Genesis? Or is it another scroll, a lost Greek scroll which told the same story as the Parthenon sculptures? And what was written on the part of the scroll that we can see?

Without Kain, there would be no Greek religion. The whole outlook of Zeus-religion is based upon the reestablishment of the way of Kain after the Flood. It makes sense that these eight "hidden" yet "central" metopes would pertain directly to him.

These eight scenes don't relate to any of the standard stories from Greek mythology. All scholarly attempts to offer cogent explanations for them have proven very unsatisfactory. Perikles, the driving political force behind the building of the Parthenon, would have known what these sculptures meant. So would have Phidias, the chief artist and general supervisor of the work. The architects, Iktinos and Kallikrates, would have been able to tell us what's going on in these scenes as well. In his *The Parthenon and Its Impact on Modern Times*, Panayotis Tournikiotis has pointed out that according to Vitruvius, Iktinos and a man named Karpion composed treatises on Athena's temple but none of these have survived, and neither have any of the other ancient Greek texts on architecture mentioned by Vitruvius. It's very sad that no accounts by contemporary writers of the planning and construction of the Parthenon have made it to our day. Will someone please organize a search-party for the treatises of Iktinos?

Figure 68: South metope 17.

Figure 69: South metope 18.

Figure 70: South metope 19.

Figure 71: South metope 20.

Figure 72: A vase-artist forces Nereus to witness Herakles pummeling a Kentaur.

Kain's Revenge after the Flood

Remember that the south metopes are background. They tell what happened before the Flood. Greek religion cannot be separated from that background because it defines itself in relation to it. There is continuity and logic in the Greek religious system. Greek artists depicted what they knew happened before the Flood; they depicted Nereus/Noah, the man from the line of Seth who came through the Flood; and they depicted as a celebration the triumph of their religious system—the way of Kain over the way of Seth—after the Flood.

Before the Flood, Kentaurs (Seth-men) abducted Kain-women. After the Flood, as we shall see in Chapter 9, Zeus-worshippers such as Peleus, abduct Noah's daughters. When Kentaurs try to abduct Kain-women after the Flood, Herakles kills them (See Fig. 73, opposite).

During the Flood, the Kentaurs beat Kaineus (the line of Kain) into the earth with huge rocks. After the Flood, the great hero, Herakles, who provides the muscle to reestablish the way of Kain, takes revenge against the Kentaurs. In Figure 72, above, Nereus/Noah is forced to watch as Herakles pummels a Kentaur. As Zeus-religion develops after the Flood, the Kentaurs' rocks get smaller and the club of Herakles, more powerful. The artist has made Nereus stand as a mute and powerless witness to the great spiritual change to come.

As we shall see in the following chapter, the Greek gods in concert overwhelm the Yahweh-believing sons of Noah after the Flood. In Figure 74, the god Dionysos conquers one of Noah's sons whom the Greeks referred to as Giants.

Figure 73: On a storage jar from ca. 550 BC, Herakles kills the Kentaur Nessos who is thus unsuccessful in his effort to carry off the hero's wife, Deïaneira.

The vase shape itself relates to the scene for it is a drinking cup, a kantharos which means "dung-beetle" in Greek. This is an ancient symbol of transformation going back to Egypt. The vase scene is a summary of the great spiritual/religious transformation that Greek artists depict over and over again in different ways: the god's friendship with the serpent enables him to overcome a Yahweh-believing son of Noah. Let's now take a look at the story of the gods defeating the Giants in some detail.

Figure 74: On this kantharos from ca. 460 BC, Dionysos and the serpent subdue a Giant, one of the Yahweh-believing sons of Noah.

Chapter 7
The Conquest of Noah's Yahweh-believing Sons

The defeat of the Giants is the culminating event, the great celebration, of ancient Greek religion. The rebellion of Hermes in Babylon, the rebirth of the serpent's Eve, the replacement of Nereus with Poseidon as god of the power of the sea, the rebirth of the line of Kain in Athens, and the labors and conquests of Herakles, all pertain to it or lead up to it.

This is the fundamental assertion made by the ancient poets, vase-artists, and sculptors: the Greek gods have defeated the Giants; the Greek religious system has overcome the Yahweh-believing sons of Noah.

The East Metopes

Figure 75: The east façade of the Parthenon. The pediment depicted the birth of Athena—
the rebirth of the serpent's Eve after the Flood. The fourteen metopes below it depicted
the gods (Zeus-religion) defeating the Giants (the Yahweh-believing sons of Noah).

The Gods Crush the Giants

The fourteen metopes below the east pediment of the Parthenon depicted the gods defeating the Giants. They are in a sadly battered state, and identifying the figures in the individual metopes is highly speculative. We know from other sculptures, vase-paintings, and literature that all the Olympian gods took part in this decisive victory, with Zeus and Athena in the forefront, and the mortal hero Herakles playing the key, even indispensable role. As all the gods were triumphant in concert, the defeat of the Giants represents the victory of the Greek religious system over another religious system.

According to Pindar's *Nemean Ode*, the prophet Teiresias predicted that Herakles would receive Hebe (Youth) as his bride after his death as a reward for his heroism in the battle of the gods against the Giants—formidable foes of the gods who could not be defeated without Herakles' help. When that battle came about, the shining hair of many Giants was "stained with dirt beneath the rushing arrows of that hero." Thus after Athena brought Herakles to Olympus in her chariot, he married Hebe, becoming immortal in accord with the prophecy.

But what did this mean? What was its historical basis? We have to look to Genesis to find out. There, we discover that after the Flood, Nimrod became the first great hunter and king. And we have seen that Herakles is Nimrod transplanted to Greek soil.

Figure 76: Zeus with his lightning bolt, Herakles with his bow, and
Athena with her spear, attack and vanquish the Giants.

Right after the Flood, faith in Yahweh was very strong, obviously. Within a few generations and a couple of hundred years, that faith began to wane. This period is described thus in Acts 14:16: "God . . . in bygone generations, leaves all the nations to go their ways . . ." In the Greek story of the gods defeating the Giants, the Giants are the Yahweh-believing sons of Noah, and the gods represent the Greek religious system. The fact that the gods could not win without the help of a man points directly to the historical figure, Nimrod, who began the organization of humanity into armies, cities, and nations, embracing the religious ideas of his father, Cush—the ring-leader at the Tower of Babel. We read in I Chronicles 1:10 that "Cush was the father of Nimrod, who grew to be a mighty warrior on earth." Herakles' given name in Greek was Alcaeüs, meaning "Mighty One." On the above vase (Fig. 76), Herakles, between Zeus and Athena, leads the charge against the Giants.

Some scholars still describe this momentous action as "the *battle* between the gods and Giants." It was an armed encounter, certainly, but as you will see throughout this chapter, the artists portray it as the resounding and decisive *victory* of the Greek gods over the Giants—Zeus-religion over the Yahweh-believing sons of Noah.

Figure 77: Zeus and Athena kill Giants.

Above we see Zeus and Athena routing the Giants on a cup from ca. 410 BC. Zeus holds a lightning bolt in his raised right hand and his scepter in his left hand, as he prepares to kill the Giant, Porphyrion. Porphyrion flees to the right but turns to look back at Zeus as he prepares to throw a stone, a futile gesture. The artist is most likely engaging in irony, evoking the memory of the huge rock used to beat Kaineus into the ground. It is now a laughably smaller rock and worthless against the relentless onslaught of the gods.

Next to Zeus, Athena is about to spear the Giant, Enkelados. This Giant has fallen onto one knee. Athena has caught him by surprise: his shield is on the wrong side and his sword is still sheathed. Athena extends her left arm over him, and with it, her serpent-fringed aegis, or goat skin. Enkelados has turned his head toward Athena as she advances toward him, spear raised. He sees his own demise coming.

As we see by looking carefully at Zeus and his opponent, the artist has provided four important symbols of the victory's significance. First, Zeus wears an olive leaf wreath, a symbol of the new age after the Flood; second, Zeus holds the lightning bolt, a symbol of the serpent's enlightenment; third, he holds the scepter of rule; and fourth, the serpent itself appears on the Giant's shield. The symbols tell the story: the defeat of the Giants is about the rule of the serpent's enlightenment after the Flood. Or we could put it another way: this is the beginning of the transfigured serpent's enlightened rule.

Figure 78: Athena thrusts her spear into a kneeling Giant as Hermes watches.

Above, from ca. 525 BC, a Giant kneels before Athena and Hermes. Athena thrusts her spear into the Giant's torso. The artist seems to be telling us that it's the end of the old guard. The rebirth of the serpent's Eve has finally put an end to the belief system of the Yahweh-believing sons of Noah.

In Figure 79, an Attic red-figure vase from ca. 510 BC, Dionysos kills a Giant. The soulish man overcomes the spiritual man. The leopard on the arm of Dionysos lets us know of Nimrod's (Herakles') crucial presence in the victory. One interpretation of the meaning of "Nimrod" is that it comes from *Nimr*, a leopard, and *rada* or *rad*, to subdue. The subduer of the leopard, Nimrod, brought back the religious system of the ancient serpent (shown on the vase with a beard), and thus the Greek gods overcame the religion of the Giants.

Scenes such as the ones on these pages appeared sculpted on

Figure 79: Dionysos and the ancient serpent put an end to a Giant.

the fourteen metopes under the east pediment of the Parthenon. The artists sculpted and painted true pictures of the history of humanity: the way of Kain has overcome the way of Seth. Zeus-religion has overcome the Yahweh-believing sons of Noah.

Figure 80: Athena kills a Giant, from the east pediment of the old temple of Athena.

Above, we see part of the east pediment from the old temple of Athena on the Akropolis, ca. 520 BC, now in the Akropolis Museum. Athena kills a Giant.

Below, on a water pot from ca. 480 BC, Athena and Zeus kill Giants. Zeus strikes with his lightning bolt, a sign of his power and the serpent's enlightenment. The Giant succumbs to the might of Zeus, and, holding a huge rock above his own head, falls. The rock is probably an allusion to the rock the Kentaurs used to pound Kaineus into the ground before the Flood, but it is of no avail now. The Giant will wind up crushing himself with his own rock.

In many of these scenes, Athena is pictured as on this page, extending her aegis, a symbol of her authority. She is extending the authority of Zeus-religion over the Yahweh-believing sons of Noah.

Figure 81: Athena and Zeus kill Giants.

Figure 82: Poseidon about to crush his opponent with a rock.

The message on the partially damaged storage jar, above, from ca. 525 BC seems to be one of paybacks. Poseidon is about to pummel one of the Giants into the earth with a huge rock, in the same way that the Kentaurs pummeled Kaineus into the ground before the Flood (inset). On many vases, Poseidon is pictured fighting Giants using the trident he usurped from Nereus, so the rock must have special significance, and I think we know what it is.

Below, and on the page opposite, we see a total of six images from an Attic red-figure oil jug from ca. 480 BC, now in the Cleveland Museum of Art. Curator Arielle P. Kozloff writes of it:

Here Douris [the Greek artist to whom the painting is attributed] portrays the death of the giant Enkelados at the hands of Athena in the legendary war between the gods and the giants. The artist has given us the most dramatic, most evanescent moment of this episode, and on this vase has rendered it timeless. Athena, intent on her prey, strides purposefully forward ready to give the coup de grace with her spear. This final blow is not necessary and this the goddess knows, for victory gleams in her eye . . . She has already wounded Enkelados; blood is pouring from his left thigh and rib cage. Douris has caught the giant just at the last excruciating moment before death as he reels backward, releasing his grip on his short sword, his eyes glazing over and turning skyward. Athena's emblem, the Gorgon head, appears to cheer her on with its open mouth just as the centaur [Kentaur] device on Enkelados' shield futilely enjoins the giant to keep up the battle. He shouts encouragement to Enkelados and lifts a barely visible branch as a replacement to the giant's fallen arms.

Let me add a few observations to Ms. Kozloff's insightful description. The Gorgon head represents the source of Athena's authority, "the head of serpents," and it is proclaiming victory as well as cheering on Athena. The branch held by the Kentaur is not a weapon but a symbol of that "strange branch" of humanity, the line of Seth, here soundly defeated by the line of Kain. It appears to me that the Kentaur is giving up. The gods defeating the Giants is not a "battle." The artists make it clear to us that this is an horrendous defeat for the Giants, and a glorious and total victory for the gods of Zeus-religion.

Figure 83: Blood streams from Enkelados' rib cage as his eyes glaze over.

Figure 84: Athena.

Figure 85: Enkelados.

Figure 86: Kentaur on the shield of Enkelados.

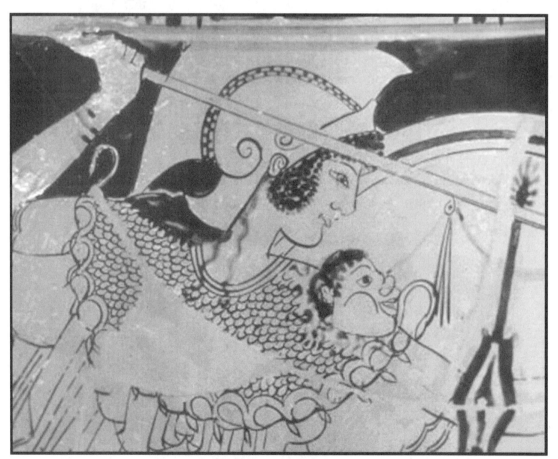

Figure 87: The Gorgon Medusa on Athena's aegis.

Figure 88: Hypnos puts the Giant Alkyoneus to sleep as Herakles approaches.

The language of Greek artists is universal. Above, from ca. 510 BC, Hypnos, the god of sleep, has put the Giant, Alkyoneus, to sleep as Herakles approaches. Herakles acted so aggressively and so decisively that the Giants hardly new what happened. Many of the Yahweh-believing sons of Noah didn't pay attention to the momentous spiritual changes; they remained oblivious, asleep. On the drinking cup below from ca. 525 BC, Herakles and Hermes offer gestures of congratulations to each other. They have caught the Giants unawares. They have put the serpent's system of worship and sacrifice in the place of Noah's.

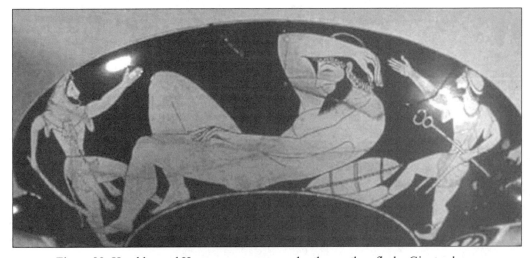

Figure 89: Herakles and Hermes gesture to each other as they find a Giant asleep.

Figure 90: The Altar of Zeus at Pergamum as reconstructed in Berlin

Figure 91: A close-up of some sculptures on the west side of the Altar of Zeus at Pergamum.

The Altar of Zeus at Pergamum

The Greek gods defeating the Giants was portrayed most vividly in the 120-meter-long frieze surrounding the great Altar of Zeus at Pergamum. Much of it survives and the entire altar with most of the sculpture has been reconstructed in the Pergamon* Museum in Berlin. The kings of Pergamum looked across the Aegean Sea to Athens for their inspiration in religion and art. For Pergamum as well as Athens, Athena was protectress of the city. The outer friezes depicted the gods, led by Zeus, Athena, and Herakles, vanquishing the Giants.

King Eumenes II ordered the great altar built as a tribute to both Zeus and Athena in 183 BC, and it was most likely completed in 178 BC.

---

*The city is variously referred to as Pergamum, Pergamon, and Pergamos.

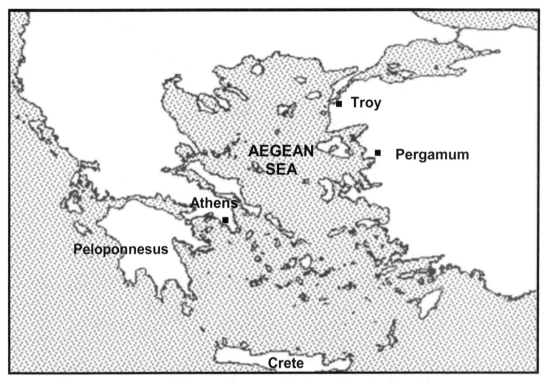

Figure 92: Athens and Pergamum in the ancient Greek world.

The victory of the gods over the Giants virtually wiped out belief in Noah's God throughout the ancient Greek world. Zeus-religion relegated the Supreme God of the Scriptures to the status of a non-entity, and elevated the serpent and humanity to the supreme heights. Overlooking their city, high atop a hill, pictured opposite, the Pergamenes built the Altar of Zeus, flagrantly boasting of the triumph of the serpent's system.

Since Jesus is the One Who said, "[W]hat is high among men is an abomination in the sight of God," it should not surprise us to find that He identified the Altar of Zeus with the rule of the Adversary or Satan. In Revelation 2:13, He speaks to His Jewish followers in Pergamum thus: "I am aware where you are dwelling—where the throne of Satan is." From a scriptural standpoint, the Altar of Zeus is the throne of Satan, the seat of the Adversary of God and His Christ.

When you understand what Zeus-religion really is—the way of Kain triumphant, mankind exalted, and God discarded—many aspects of the spiritual history of humanity fit together like the pieces of a black-and-white jigsaw puzzle.

The great Altar of Zeus remained intact until the tenth century. Then, the Byzantines used many parts of the altar, including the frieze plates, to construct a defensive wall on the fortress-hill in their war against Islam, and the ancient treasures gradually disappeared into the dirt.

Figure 93: The site of the ancient Altar of Zeus overlooking the city of Pergamum.

In the early 1870's, a German engineer named Carl Humann who had been hired to build a highway in Asia Minor, was drawn to Pergamum where he discovered and unearthed some of the frieze plates. In 1878, a planned excavation of the fortress-hill terrain began under Humann's direction. Over the years, the Germans conducted negotiations with the Turkish government, making possible the acquisition of the Pergamum findings for the Berlin Museum. There, in 1880, some sculptures were shown for the first time. It was not until 1930, however, that the western side of the Altar of Zeus, the throne of Satan, was erected in a room in the newly built Pergamon Museum. Shortly after that, Adolph Hitler seized power. He was a man determined to eradicate Yahweh's chosen people, the Jews. These were a people who directed their worship exclusively to the God of Nereus/Noah. The rest of the story you know.

I look at the development of Zeus-religion as part of God's operations, for as Paul wrote in Romans 11:36, "out of [God] and through Him and for Him is all." Why didn't the Greeks have a clear perception of God? Paul wrote in II Corinthians 4:4 that "the god of this eon blinds the apprehensions of the unbelieving." If Greece and other nations understood God and His purpose, and remained steadfast in their worship of Him, Israel would not be His chosen people, and more to the point: without a deluded and lost humanity, there is no reason for the cross of Christ which conciliates God's enemies to Himself (Romans 5:10).

Figures 94 and 95: Aphrodite steps on the head of a fallen Giant.

The ancients approached the Altar of Zeus from the east. Their first view was of Zeus and Athena—victors in the front rank of the battle which surged toward all sides. The image of Herakles does not survive but an inscription puts him to the left of Zeus. According to the ancient lyric poet, Pindar, and others, the Giants could not be defeated without the help of the great hero whom we know to be the Nimrod of Genesis transplanted to Greek soil.

Taking part in this great victory are all the chief Greek gods: Zeus, Athena, Nike, Hera, Herakles, Artemis, Apollo, Dionysos, Hephaistos, Ares, Poseidon, Aphrodite, and Hermes. The Altar of Zeus includes all of these, and it is so epically grandiose that it makes room for lesser deities such as the Three Fates, Amphitrite, Leto, Helios, Eos, Themis, Hekate, Nyx, and Selene to play a part in the utter routing of the Giants.

Above, from the north part of the frieze, Aphrodite, a deification of the wife of Kain, stomps on the head of an unfortunate Giant. Genesis 3:14 implies that the head of the serpent will eventually be crushed. The Greeks saw their gods as crushing the heads of the line of Seth.

Figure 96: Athena and the serpent kill a Giant.

Above, from the east frieze, Athena and the serpent bring down the winged Giant Enkelados. Athena drives his head downward as the serpent, entwined about his body with fangs locked into his breast, pulls him to the earth. The wings are an indication of Enkelados' great spiritual power. A victory over beings with such a connection serves to emphasize the fearful and ultimate power of Athena, the serpent, and Zeus-religion.

Figure 97: Nereus and Doris forced to witness the triumph of the serpent's system.

Here is a man on the frieze that you should be able to identify because you have seen him depicted on vases already. His face is solemn and sad, and he is the only man on the entire frieze who is not actively engaged in the battle. From one of the corners, the sculptors have made him an observer of this horrendous defeat of the line of Seth.

This is Nereus, the Greek Noah. We've seen this same kind of theme on a vase where Nereus stoically observes the birth of Athena (the rebirth of the serpent's Eve), and on a vase where he stands by as Poseidon takes his daughter, Amphitrite, and Herakles wrestles away his power. Greek myth and art chronicle the great spiritual change which took place after the Flood. Greek artists often used Nereus/Noah as a constant against whom they were able to portray this great change. This device was artistically effective and historically accurate.

Next to Nereus stands his wife, Doris. I thought at first that she was actively engaged in subduing one of the Giants; that is, one of her own Yahweh-believing

Figure 98: Amphitrite, daughter of Nereus and Doris, fights as the
serpent's ally against her brothers, the Giants.

sons. Then I thought about the fact that the son's legs were turning into serpents.
It is more likely that she is hopelessly trying to save a son who is figuratively
turning to the serpent's system.

If Nereus and Doris were to look around the corner, their dismay would only
increase; because there stands their daughter, Amphitrite, pictured above, fighting on the side of the Greek gods, her exertions in that regard allied with the ancient serpent's. She has married Poseidon, the brother of Zeus, betraying her parents by joining the serpent's cause.

From the point of view of Scripture, Noah and his wife are forced to witness
an "abomination of desolation." Faith in Yahweh ends, and humanity elevates
and worships Zeus, the serpent's Adam, and Athena, the reborn serpent's Eve,
after the Flood.

Chapter 8
Noah's Cloak on the Parthenon

The Greeks memorialized their annual celebration of the birth of Athena on the 160-meter-long Parthenon frieze. It depicted a grand parade leading up to the presentation to the assembled gods of a very special cloak. The cloak had once belonged to Nereus/Noah, the great patriarch of the new age after the Flood and the acknowledged ancestor of all. Now that Greek humanity had dispensed with the God of Noah and re-embraced the way of Kain, the cloak belonged to Athena and the other Greek gods. On the cloak, the Greeks embroidered scenes of the gods defeating the Giants—the Yahweh-believing sons of Noah—as a sign of their ownership of the cloak and the triumph of their religious system and man-centered culture.

The Frieze

Figure 99: Cutaway Drawing of the Parthenon from the East.

The Parthenon Frieze

The Parthenon had eight outer columns in the front (east), eight in the back (west), and seventeen columns running along the north and south sides, counting the corner columns twice. Inside the outer columns, a porch ran all the way around the temple building itself. Near the very top of the outside of the temple building, above the inner columns, the artists sculpted a continuous low-relief Ionic frieze that ran all the way around the building. It measured about 160 meters long and approximately one meter high. It depicted a grand parade of Greeks moving from the southwest corner and up the long north and south sides of the temple to its culmination in a ritual event sculpted in the center of the east frieze. The ritual involved the presentation of an embroidered woolen cloak (called a *peplos*) to twelve seated gods, and Iris and Eros who were standing.

Jenifer Neils' research and writing on the frieze are crucial to our ability to understand what the artists were trying to tell us when they carved it. Along with

Figure 100: Part of the west frieze *in situ* seen through the outer columns.

many other scholars, she identifies the parade of people and animals toward the enactment of a ritual event as the depiction of an actual, annual celebration in ancient Athens called the Panathenaic Festival. The following quotes are from her excellent book, *The Parthenon Frieze*:

The most famous religious procession . . . [was] the Panathenaia, the annual festival honoring the city's patron deity. Celebrated since at least 566 BC, it was conducted with special pomp every four years, in emulation of the games in honor of Zeus at Olympia.

In the case of the Panathenaia we know that, in addition to animal sacrifice, a special gift, an elaborately woven robe known as the peplos, was prepared every four years for the goddess and carried in the procession to her temple.

With its some 378 dramatis personae, accompanied by 245 animals, [the frieze] is a tour de force of planning and carving.

In spite of the fact that the carving is spread over 114 rectangular blocks, the design presents to the viewer a seamless whole gliding effortlessly and inexorably toward the east.

Ms. Neils also writes, "It is obvious from its position in the center of the east frieze that this ceremony involving five figures [the cloak ceremony] was the high point of the narrative." A narrative is a story. What story are the Greek art-

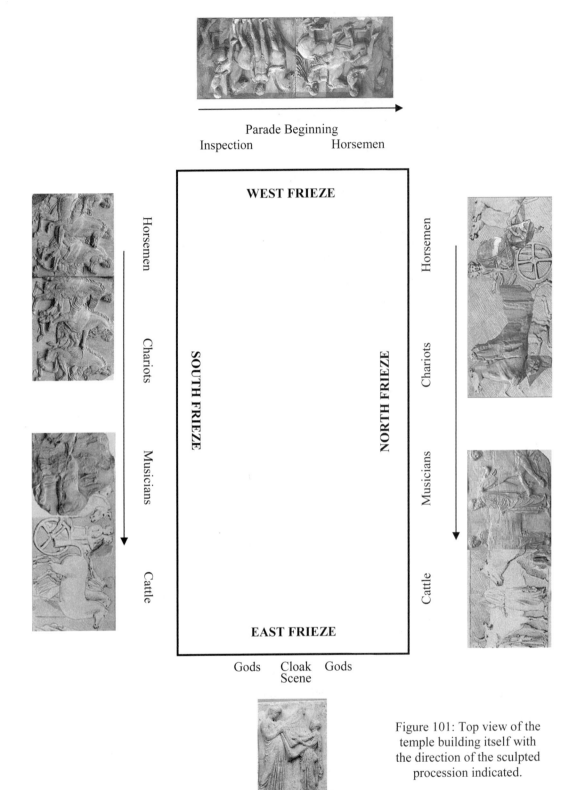

Parade Beginning
Inspection   Horsemen

WEST FRIEZE

Horsemen

Chariots

SOUTH FRIEZE

Musicians

Cattle

NORTH FRIEZE

Horsemen

Chariots

Musicians

Cattle

EAST FRIEZE

Gods   Cloak   Gods
        Scene

Figure 101: Top view of the
temple building itself with
the direction of the sculpted
procession indicated.

Figure 102: In this combination of surviving sculpture and Jacques Carrey's drawing from 1674, men lead sacrificial animals up the north side of the frieze toward the East.

Figure 103: Horsemen advance along the south side of the frieze toward the East.

ists telling us here? The whole city turned out to watch the presentation of this cloak. Not only did they repeat this ceremony every four years for more than a thousand years, but they memorialized it and the procession leading up to it on the most glorious Greek temple in the ancient world. This was their greatest and most important festival, a grand parade, an unforgettable party, a religious system celebrating itself. What is the story behind the cloak? Where did it come from, and why did it mean so much to the Greeks?

When the commissioner of the National Football League in America presents a trophy to the owner of a football team with much fanfare, we know exactly what it means. His team has won the Super Bowl. When the Greeks presented a meticulously embroidered cloak to the gods for their approval on the Akropolis of Athens, they also knew exactly what they were doing and why.

Jenifer Neils writes that this frieze depicting the Panathenaia—the festival for all Athenians—which culminated in the presentation to the gods of a sacred cloak, "is unique and thus the most intriguing feature of the entire temple." Unique it is, indeed. What makes it even more intriguing, and especially revealing for us as to the meaning of ancient Greek religion, is the fact that this cloak, centrally depicted on the east frieze of this magnificently sculpted band, once belonged to Noah.

Noah's Cloak

Just as Herakles' determination to get back to the serpent's tree in the Garden of the Hesperides and Athena's friendship with the serpent don't make much sense to us without reference to the early events described in Genesis, so neither will the Greek cloak ceremony make sense without reference to Genesis. The interpretive understanding we need appears in the ninth chapter of Genesis. Genesis 9:18-21 reads:

Figure 104: The cloak as it appeared on the east frieze of the Parthenon, held by a priest and his assistant.

And the sons of Noah who fare forth from the ark are Shem and Ham and Japheth (And Ham, he is the father of Canaan). These three are sons of Noah, and from these the entire earth is scattered over.

And starting is Noah as a man who serves the ground, and planting is he a vineyard. And drinking is he of the wine and is drunk, and is exposing himself in the midst of his tent.

This is a very strange passage. It is understandable that, after a year in the close quarters of the ark with only his family, Noah wanted to grow some grapes, make some wine, and have a drink. But why report his drunkenness and his nakedness in the scrolls? Furthermore, his "drunkenness" was not the rowdy kind: he drank in his own abode, and he undoubtedly was drinking "wine that makes the heart of a mortal rejoice" (Psalms 104:15). The root of the Hebrew word for "is drunk" in the sense used in the passage, according to *The New Strong's Exhaustive Concordance of the Bible*, means "to become tipsy; in a qualified sense, to satiate with a stimulating drink or (figuratively) influence:— (be filled with) drink (abundantly), (be, make) drunk (en), be merry." Noah drank wine until he fell asleep. Big deal.

His nakedness was not a problem either. He had every right to fall asleep naked within the privacy of his own tent. This episode is not really about his drunkenness or his nakedness. It is about his garment, about being viewed by another human without his garment. The succeeding verses make this clear:

And seeing is Ham (father of Canaan) the nakedness of his father, and, faring forth, he is telling his two brothers outside. And taking are Shem and Japheth a garment, and are placing it on the shoulders of the two, and they are going backward, and covering the nakedness of their father. And their faces were backward, and the nakedness of their father they did not see (Genesis 9:22-23).

Clothing represents the position and authority of the person. We use the phrase "under the mantle of so-and-so's authority." Kings and queens wear their royal garb, and we respect their office or station in life. The Hebrew word for garment in the passage conveys "the idea of a *cover* assuming the shape of the object beneath." Noah's garment stood for Noah's authority, a very awesome authority at that time. Noah had brought himself and seven others through the Flood as its only survivors. After the Flood, he became the living father of all mankind. No wonder his cloak meant so much.

What happened in the Genesis passage is that the young son, Ham, seeing his father separated from the mantle of his authority, got the idea that it was time for his elderly father to give up his authority to him and his brothers. Ham's brothers, Shem and Japheth, did not agree. They were especially careful to walk backwards as they replaced their father's garment so as not to see him then, or be able to visualize him in the future, as separated from it.

When Noah awoke, he realized what had happened, and placed a curse on one of Ham's children, Canaan. The curse must have applied to Ham in some way, because he, after all, was the one who wanted to take Noah's authority in the form of the cloak in the first place. Ham had other children, and they too must have been influenced by their father's usurping desire. Ham's eldest son was Cush and he eagerly embraced the idea of taking Noah's authority. Cush was instrumental in the building of the Tower of Babel, and became deified in the Greek religious system as Hermes, the chief prophet of Zeus-religion (see Chapter 20). The most famous son of Cush, in turn, was Nimrod. Genesis 10:8-10 says this about Nimrod:

And Cush generates Nimrod. He starts to become a master in the earth. He becomes a master hunter before Yahweh Elohim. Therefore is it being said, "As Nimrod, the master hunter before Yahweh." And coming is the beginning of his kingdom to be Babel and Erech and Accad and Calneh, in the land of Shinar.

In the Greek religious system, this "master hunter" and first king of humanity was know as Herakles. Herakles was, in fact, Nimrod, transported to Greek soil. In the last chapter, we saw that Greek artists depicted Herakles on many different vases wrestling away the power of Nereus/Noah or simply pushing him out of the

Figure 105: Herakles seizes Nereus/Noah who is wearing the star-studded cloak.

way. On the vase-depiction in Figure 105 above, Nereus/Noah is wearing his cloak. On it, the artist has drawn stars signifying authority from the heavens. Herakles' authority comes from his own strength. With that strength, he is seizing Nereus/Noah, garment and all, pushing him out of the way, and replacing the prophet who receives his authority from the God of the heavenly realms, with himself and his own earth-bound authority. Herakles embraced the religious orientation he learned from his father, Hermes/Cush.

What happened to the star-studded cloak of Nereus? We find out when we take a look at the vase, opposite, which depicts the birth of Erichthonios in Athens after the Flood. We've seen in Chapter 6 that this child is the seed of Hephaistos, the deified Kain. On the vase, the child emerges from Gaia (Earth) and reaches out with his arms toward Athena, while his father, Hephaistos, looks on as any proud father would. Gaia, wearing two serpent bracelets, lifts up the "Earth-born One" by his buttocks and left side. The goddess has shifted her serpent-fringed aegis to her back so as not to frighten the child. Note that Athena's cloak is studded with stars. The garb could not be any more perfect for the occasion. The arms that deliver Erichthonios are adorned with the serpent. This child

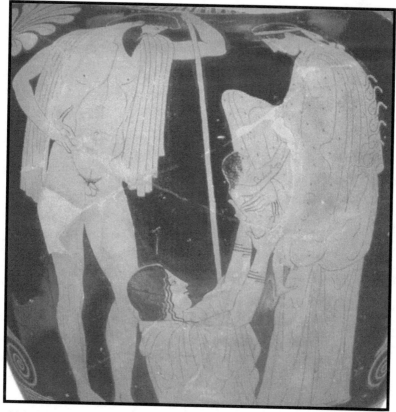

Figure 106: On this vase from ca. 410 BC, Gaia (Earth) presents the child Erichthonios (the Earth-born One) to his step-mother, Athena. The child's father, Hephaistos (the deified Kain), looks on. The line of Kain has reemerged in Athens after the Flood.

will seek and welcome the serpent's enlightenment. The child symbolizes Greek humanity honoring the deified Kain and looking to the reborn serpent's Eve in worship. From the Greek perspective, the cloak of Nereus/Noah, the cloak that symbolizes ruling authority in the post-Flood age, now belongs to Athena and the Greek religious system.

But what did the Greeks embroider on the cloak which they presented to the gods for their approval during the Panathenaic ritual? Certainly something that the gods would be very pleased to see. And what could make them happier than viewing scenes of themselves conquering the Giants? Their whole religious system was about overcoming these Yahweh-believing sons of Noah. Embroidering the cloak with such scenes put Greek religion's indelible mark upon it. The embroidery had the same kind of effect as the brands on cattle—Noah's cloak *belongs* to Athena and the other gods of Zeus-religion. Athena's sculpted cloak was visible on the east frieze. The fourteen individually sculpted scenes on the east metopes of the Greek gods defeating the Giants were a constant reminder of the scenes the cloak depicted, and of the ultimate success of Zeus-religion.

Noah's Cloak and Chiron—The Transitional Kentaur

Herakles/Nimrod, the powerful first king of humanity, became very prominent in Greek art. He appears on thousands of extant vases. His father, Hermes/Cush, as the chief prophet of Zeus-religion, appears on almost as many vases. Hermes' father, Ham, appeared far less than his son and grandson in Greek art. The reason is that although he initiated the idea of taking from Nereus/Noah the cloak, or mantle of authority, he was far less influential on the actual development of Zeus-religion after the Flood. The Greeks called Ham Chiron. In Hebrew Ham is Châm pronounced *khawm*. In Greek, Chiron is χειρον, most likely a homophone for Châm. The literal meaning of Chiron is hand, and he was the first after the Flood to give a hand to the fledgling development of what ultimately matured into Zeus-religion.

Chiron/Ham did not develop what ultimately came to be Zeus-religion; his son Hermes/Cush did. But the authority which originated in Noah after the Flood came *through* Chiron/Ham to Hermes/Cush, and so Greek artists depicted Chiron as wearing the cloak of Noah.

Greek artists painted Chiron on vases as a friendly Kentaur. The Kentaurs, representing the line of Seth, were mortal enemies of Greek religion, and so depicting Ham as a Kentaur seems very strange at first, but we will soon see that the artists were very logical and true to the historical situation when they depicted him thus.

Chiron was known as the great teacher of the Greeks. In his Nemean Ode, Pindar referred to him as "Deep-thinking Chiron," and stated that he reared the Greek hero, Jason (of Jason and the Argonauts), taught to Asklepios "the gentle-handed laws of remedies" who then became a god of healing, arranged for the Zeus-worshipper, Peleus, whom he taught, to marry Thetis, "the lovely-bosomed daughter of Nereus," and brought up for Peleus and Thetis "their incomparable child" Achilles, "nurturing his spirit with all fitting things."

How do we explain that the Greeks hated Kentaurs and yet revered one of them as their teacher? Remember, the Greeks identified the Kentaurs with the line of Seth, a strange "branch" of humanity they had difficulty understanding. They held the Kentaurs responsible for beating Kaineus (the line of Kain) into the ground during the Flood. They knew that only the line of Seth; that is, the Kentaurs, survived the Deluge. Initially then, they *had* to be taught by a Kentaur even as they were beginning to gradually reestablish the way of Kain after the Flood. Greek artists pictured Chiron as an intermediate figure wearing Noah's cloak, and he is the one who passed it on to the Greek religious system.

Let's look at some actual vase-paintings of Chiron. In Figure 107, Chiron/

Figure 107: On this vase from ca. 500 BC, Peleus abducts Noah's daughter, Thetis. The transitional Kentaur, Ham/Chiron, wearing Noah's cloak, places a lion on the back of the Zeus-worshipper Peleus as a sign that earthly power is shifting to his religious system. To the right, a sister of Thetis flees.

Ham witnesses the abduction of Thetis, one of the daughters of Nereus/Noah, by the Zeus-worshipper, Peleus. The great religious transformation is not complete, and as we shall see in Chapter 9, it will not be so until Peleus has forced Thetis to marry him before an altar to Zeus with all the Greek gods attending. Yet the transformation is in process, and during the transition, Chiron/Ham wears the star-studded cloak of Noah.

Chiron looks very civilized for a Kentaur and that makes sense, for he was one of the Kentaurs (the line of Seth) on the ark who brought human knowledge and civilization from one side of the Flood to the other. While most Kentaurs are depicted as having the body of a horse and just the upper torso of a man, Chiron is shown fully as a man in front, and the hind legs of a horse projecting behind. He holds the Kentaurs' signature "branch" over his left shoulder, and what appear to be two dead hares, hang from it.

Chiron is often depicted with dead game hanging from his branch. Why? Genesis 1:29 indicates that, before the Flood, humans and "all land life" and "every flyer of the heavens" ate "fruit" and "green herbage," but not meat.

Right after the Flood, Yahweh changed that saying in Genesis 9:3, "And every moving animal which is living is coming to be for food for you. As the

Figure 108: Peleus brings his son Achilles to the friendly Kentaur Chiron.

green herbage I give to you all." Thus the dead game hanging from his branch show Chiron/Ham to be one of the first after the Flood to eat meat.

On the vase on the preceding page, Ham/Chiron places a lion on the back of the Zeus-worshipper, Peleus. A symbol of earthly power, the lion means that Zeus-religion is in the process of becoming dominant in the earth. Sometimes artists put a serpent on the back of Peleus, signifying that it is the serpent's system which is becoming dominant (See Fig. 117, page 122).

The vase-scene above (Fig. 108) takes place several years after the abduction of Thetis. Peleus delivers their son, Achilles, to the friendly Kentaur, Chiron, for instruction. Chiron has passed on knowledge from the pre-Flood world to Peleus, and now he will pass it on to his son, the famous warrior of Homer's *Iliad*.

The cloak, or mantle, of Chiron is a most distinguishing feature, for almost never do we see a Kentaur clothed. Except in special circumstances, Chiron is always depicted with a cloak. This is the cloak of Nereus/Noah. Ham, after all, was the one who, according to Genesis, presumed to take Noah's authority. In Greek eyes, Ham had the right idea, and ought to have been the legitimate owner of the cloak. Chiron, the Ham of Genesis, is an intermediate figure, a transitional figure. As the Greek religious system develops itself, Noah's cloak belongs to Ham—whose idea it was in the first place to take it. Once Zeus-religion is fully established and secure, Noah's cloak passes to Athena whose authority, under the auspices of Zeus, rules the Greek age.

Figure 109: This vase-artist depicts Athena as having the cloak.

On the vases we've been examining, (Figs. 107 and 108) and on Figure 110, the question of the true and ultimate heir of Noah's authority hasn't yet been settled; temporarily the cloak of Noah's authority belongs to Chiron/Ham. Let's look at Figure 109, above, and see how a different artist depicted that ancient situation. On the far right of this vase fragment from ca. 550 BC, we see Peleus approaching with his son, Achilles, to give him over for care and instruction to Chiron. Chiron is fully a man in the front, and he holds a branch. To further identify himself, he holds out his hand which is the Greek meaning of his name. But where is his cloak? This is one of those special circumstances, mentioned above, where he doesn't have it.

Hermes, the Cush of Babylon, and son of Chiron/Ham, and chief prophet of Zeus-religion, follows close on his heels. That is significant but the big difference here is that Athena is in the scene, at the far left. This artist pictures her as now having the cloak. When you think about it, if she's there, she must have it. Greek religion celebrates the birth of Athena—the rebirth of the serpent's Eve after the Flood. Athena's birth full-grown from Zeus signifies her taking authority in the new Greek age, and so the cloak must belong to her because it was hers the moment she came into being.

Figure 110: The friendly Kentaur Chiron/Ham holds the child Achilles in his hand.

Figure 111: Hermes flees with Herakles from the authority of Chiron/Ham.

Chiron (Ham), Hermes (Cush), and Herakles (Nimrod)

On the above vase (Fig. 111), a Greek artist depicts the transition from the rule of Nereus/Noah to that of Hermes and Herakles brilliantly. Nereus is not shown, but his youngest son, Ham, is. The Greeks depicted him as Chiron, the friendly Kentaur who teaches Greek humanity after the Flood. His human front legs make him a benign Kentaur concerned with the fate of his offspring. On the other side of the vase, Ham's son, Cush (Hermes), and Ham's grandson, Nimrod (Herakles), are running away from him.

Over his left shoulder, Chiron/Ham carries a branch, a regular attribute, identifying him as part of that "strange branch" of humanity—the line of Seth. Chiron/Ham desired to have his father's cloak, a symbol of rule and authority. He wears the cloak of Nereus/Noah in the painting, but it's still a Kentaur's cloak. Chiron/Ham felt entitled to Noah's cloak, but he wanted his father's authority for himself as a member of the line of Seth, and not to establish a contrary belief system. But that's exactly what Hermes/Cush wants to do. He flees with his son, Herakles/Nimrod, from the authority of Ham—from the authority of the line of Seth—and he's headed straight for Babylon to begin building the tower there. It is his intention to reestablish the way of Kain, and unite and exalt humanity in the process. In Greek terms, Hermes flees with his son, Herakles, from the authority of the family of Nereus, to establish Zeus-religion and a man-centered culture.

Hermes and Herakles are both named on the vase. Chiron/Ham wears a long beard, a sign of age and wisdom. His pose and open-palmed gesture with his right hand suggest consternation and sadness at Hermes' departure.

Figure 112: Hermes welcomes Herakles in the victorious chariot of Nike.

In the vase-scene (Fig. 111), why doesn't Hermes wear the cloak? Because he hasn't taken authority yet. The development of Zeus-religion is still in its infancy. Herakles is still a child. And it's Herakles' strength as an adult that will wrestle away the power and authority of Nereus/Noah as symbolized in the cloak.

But what end does Hermes have in view? Where does he imagine that his running from the line of Seth will lead? We find the answer on the above vase from the Classical period. Hermes, to the left, the deified Cush from Babylon, rejoices as Nike drives the victorious chariot of Herakles. Herakles, the Nimrod of Genesis, has played the indispensable role in the victory of the gods over the Giants, which is the Greek way of portraying the great victory of Zeus-religion over the Yahweh-believing sons of Noah. Nike's presence in these so-called "mythological" scenes always has to do with the victory of the transfigured serpent's system over the line of Seth.

Hermes looks like the happy coach of the Zeus-religion team, signaling ecstatically that his players have just scored the winning touchdown. That is the very spirit of this vase-scene. Gesture and gaze play important parts in Greek paintings. Nike and Herakles are looking directly at Hermes, taking their cue from him, for he is the chief prophet of Zeus-religion. This victory is the end Hermes had in view when he ran away from Chiron with his child, Herakles.

Hermes Dionysos   Demeter   Ares   Iris   Hera   Zeus

Figure 113: The center of the east frieze of the Parthenon, showing the gods at the conclusion of the cloak ceremony.

Fig. 114: The folding of the cloak after its presentation to the gods.

Now that we understand the religious significance of the cloak, let's get back to its depiction on the east frieze of the Parthenon. Every year, the Athenians celebrated the birth of their goddess. And every fourth year, they presented her with an intricately woven cloak. It was not meant for her huge gold and ivory image (Athena Parthenos) but for a smaller, more ancient wooden statue of the goddess that, according to legend, fell from heaven in the distant past. But before it could cloak the ancient image, the gods had to examine the scenes embroidered on it and express their approval.

In Figure 113, we see the conclusion of the ceremony depicted in marble. The presentation is over, the cloak is being folded, and the happy gods are chatting amiably. As Jenifer Neils has pointed out, by choosing the moment after the presentation of the cloak, the sculptors demonstrate that the ritual is a success, and the well-being of Athenian society, assured.

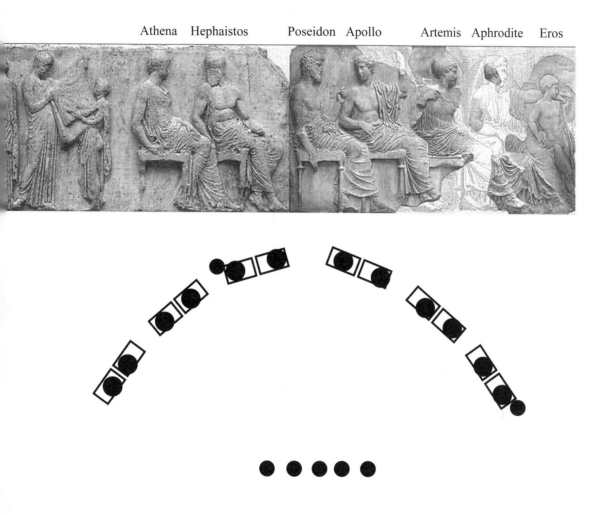

Athena   Hephaistos   Poseidon Apollo   Artemis Aphrodite   Eros

Figure 115: The semi-circular arrangement of the gods in the cloak presentation ceremony.

A priest and his young assistant (akin to a Catholic altar boy) hold the cloak. With her back to them, a priestess of Athena gives instructions to the girls who have each brought a stool to the ceremony, and are now prepared to carry them away on their heads. These original legs of the stools are now broken off. There has been much debate as to the identity of those who sat on these stools. I don't think anyone sat on them. I believe that the priest and the priestess each *stood* on the stools as they unfurled the cloak and presented it to the gods. The cloak was a square piece of wool about eight feet by eight feet. By standing on the stools, while being assisted by the other three persons, they kept the sacred cloak off the ground and presented the best possible view of it to the gods.

Jenifer Neils has also pointed out that although the gods are pictured in a line on the east frieze, their seats were actually arranged for them to view the ceremony in a semicircle, as in Figure 115.

Panathenaia and Passover

Ceremony and ritual are essentially remembrance. Let's look at another ritual celebration with which we can compare the Panathenaia, one that is still practiced 3500 years after the commemorated event. God delivered Israel out of slavery in Egypt through the "Sea of Weeds" (Exodus 10:19) and, after a sojourn in the wilderness, took them into the promised land. In the ancient Scrolls, God, speaking through Moses, set up the annual remembrance of this deliverance:

Remember that you had become a servant in the country of Egypt, and Yahweh your Elohim ransomed you. Therefore I am instructing you to obey this word today . . . You are to observe the month of Aviv and prepare a Passover to Yahweh your Elohim, for in the month of Aviv Yahweh your Elohim brought you forth from Egypt by night. So you will sacrifice the Passover to Yahweh your Elohim from the flock and the herd in the place where Yahweh your Elohim shall choose to tabernacle His name (Deuteronomy 15:15, 16:1-3).

The Passover celebration is a yearly reminder to each Jewish generation of who they are, the hardships they faced in their distant past, and most important, Who saved them. Jews define themselves, not in regard to what they had done, but in regard to *what God had done* when they where imperiled by those who rejected Him. One very important underlying message of Passover is this: "Behold, to Yahweh your Elohim belong the heavens and the heavens of the heavens, the earth and all that is in it" (Deuteronomy 10:14). Passover celebrates the Creator as Deliverer.

The Panathenaia, the celebration of Athena's birthday culminating in the presentation of the cloak, is just the opposite. The Creator God is pushed aside along with his prophet Nereus/Noah. Mankind can save itself. The heavens belong to humanity's deified ancestors, the superhumans worshipped as gods; and the earth belongs to the reconstituted seed of Kain. Erichthonios, the "Earth-born One" was the legendary founder of the Panathenaia—the Festival for All Athenians. Why? He represents the reborn seed of Hephaistos, the very deification of Kain. The stark contrast between Passover and Panathenaia helps us to see more clearly the true significance of both celebrations.

We've seen that an allusion to Nereus/Noah has shown up on the west pediment, the south and east metopes, and on the frieze. We'll see that the remaining sculptural themes (the north and west metopes and the east pediment) also allude to Nereus/Noah in very significant ways. The Akropolis is a place where Noah's spiritual authority and the remembrance of Noah's God have been buried beneath the rising tide of mankind's self-absorbed aspirations. That, essentially, is what the cloak ceremony and the entire Panathenaia celebrated.

Figure 116: The cloak ceremony on the east frieze framed by the central columns.

"As if to capture this image for all time the designer has bracketed it with the two central columns of the eastern peristyle; it is the only self-contained scene in the entire frieze that is framed so carefully for the viewer approaching the temple. In this way, the ritual of the *peplos* is made static and eternalized."

Jenifer Neils, *The Parthenon Frieze*

The spirit of the Greek religious system is the spirit of Babylon: "Build will we for ourselves a city and a tower with its head in the heavens, and make for ourselves a name . . ." (Genesis 11:4). During the Panathenaia itself and on the frieze that memorialized it, the Greeks defined themselves as the ones who had taken the mantel of Noah and passed it on to a humanity eagerly re-embracing the way of Kain after the Flood. Noah's stolen cloak, embroidered with scenes of the gods defeating his Yahweh-believing sons, is the ultimate offering to the superhumans assembled on the heights of the city. This is humanity celebrating itself. This is the religion of humanism and the rite of those who "offer divine service to the creature rather than the Creator . . ." (Romans 1:25).

Chapter 9

Peleus Abducts Thetis, the Daughter of Nereus/Noah

To the Greeks, their history as a powerful race and culture of consequence for humanity, began with Homer's epic, the *Iliad*, the story of the wrath of the hero Achilles in the Trojan War.

Achilles' father, Peleus, a man dedicated to Zeus-religion, stalked the Nereïd Thetis, abducted her, and eventually made her his wife. Seizing wives from the family of Nereus/Noah avenged the taking of the wives from the line of Kain by the line of Seth before the Flood. The wedding of Peleus and Thetis was so important to their religion and history, all the Greek gods attended.

The thirty-two metopes on the north side of the Parthenon depicted the Trojan War, a saga that began with the abduction of Noah's daughter, an abduction fraught with great religious significance for mankind.

The North Metopes

Fig. 117: On one side of this red-figure bobbin, Peleus abducts Thetis, the daughter of Nereus/
Noah. On the other side, Herakles forces Nereus out of the way, negating his authority.

We've seen that Herakles played the key role in defeating the Yahweh-believing sons of Noah, and that artists often depicted him as seizing the power of Nereus/Noah. On opposite sides of the above red-figure bobbin (Fig. 117), the artist connects the abduction of Thetis by Peleus with Herakles' successful efforts to nullify the authority of Nereus/Noah.

On one side of the bobbin, Peleus carries off Thetis, the daughter of Nereus/Noah. Note the serpent on the back of Peleus. Thereby the artist—again, with very simple imagery—tells us that the serpent is *behind* what Peleus is doing. How can Peleus get away with something so brazen? The other side of the bobbin gives us the answer. There, Herakles is pictured as neutralizing the authority of Noah/Nereus so that Peleus can take whatever daughter he likes.

Herakles is not harming Nereus/Noah: he is pushing him out of the way. Mankind revered the "Wet One" for bringing mankind through the Flood. Herakles knocks the fish out of Nereus' hand. Remember, the fish in his hand is a sign of who he is and what he did. Knocking Nereus loose from one of his key identifying symbols suggests that respect for the spiritual authority of Nereus is diminishing while respect for the physical authority of Herakles/Nimrod is becoming paramount. By knocking the fish out of his hand Herakles says, "Your power through association with the Flood is done, and I'm taking over." Note that Nereus still carries the scepter. The artist tells us with his vase-painting that Herakles rebelled against the authority of Nereus; or to use their Judeo-Christian names, Nimrod (whose name means "Rebel") rebelled against the authority of Noah.

Fig. 118: The north side of the Parthenon which once featured thirty-two metopes with sculpted scenes pertaining to the Trojan War.

The long north side of the Parthenon featured thirty-two sculpted metopes with scenes pertaining to the Trojan War. They are too badly battered for us to tell exactly what scenes were where. We can be certain that many of the metopes depicted the most popular vase-scenes concerning the war that have survived. These include the death of Priam, king of Troy; the escape from Troy of Aeneas, the legendary founder of Rome, and his father, Anchises (Fig. 119); Achilles dragging Hector around the walls of Troy; Achilles and Ajax playing a board game; Menelaos seizing Helen (Fig. 120); the rape of Kassandra by the lesser Ajax (Fig. 119); and what really started the war, the abduction of Nereus' daughter, Thetis, by the Zeus-worshipper, Peleus. All the Greeks knew that Peleus and Thetis were the parents of the hero, Achilles, whose exploits are described in Homer's *Iliad*.

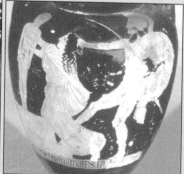

Fig. 119: On the left, Aeneas and his father escape from Troy. On the right, Ajax drags Kassandra away from Athena's idol-image in order to rape her. A metope depicting each of these events most likely appeared on the Parthenon.

Fig. 120: With the Greek victory at Troy, Menelaos seizes his wife, Helen.

Fig. 121: Peleus abducts Thetis, the daughter of Nereus/Noah.

A painting on the interior of a bowl, from about 500 BC, above, with a portion enlarged, opposite, now engages our attention.

With a sheathed sword hanging at his waist, Peleus crouches, capturing Thetis in mid-stride from behind, locking his hands in front of her waist. The surprise and jolt of the seizure causes her to drop a small lion from her right hand. One serpent coils around the left wrist of Thetis; another coils around both wrists of Peleus. Because of paintings like this, a false legend developed that Thetis could change herself into a lion or a serpent. But the obvious truth is that the artist put those animal-figures in this scene to explain the great change in the spiritual orientation of Thetis, and the subsequent great change in the spiritual orientation of Greek humanity.

The lion is a symbol of power on earth. The immediate family of Nereus loses its power—drops its association with it—as the serpent's system takes hold.

As Kathleen Krattenmaker has pointed out in her description of this vase for

Figure 122: Enlargement of Figure 122, opposite, showing two serpents embracing the couple.

the Perseus Project, Thetis "holds another garment in her left hand." Does it represent her father's cloak? This is an Attic red-figure vase from about 500 BC. This means it was painted in the heyday of the Panathenaic Festival by an artist who lived in Athens or the surrounding countryside. The artists from that region during that time period surely understood the significance of the cloak of Nereus/Noah. They understood the meaning of the presentation of the cloak to the gods for their approval during the defining rite of the Panathanaic Festival, and they grasped why it now belonged to Athena. Why wouldn't they depict Thetis as having the cloak, as being the one responsible for taking it from her father and bringing it over into Zeus-religion?

Vase-artists sometimes depicted Thetis as wearing a crown or a tiara (as in Fig. 123 on the following page), suggesting that she is the heiress to her father's authority. Peleus is thus taking her and Noah's authority with him into Zeus-religion. The hand of Thetis which holds the cloak is controlled by her wrist, and a serpent wraps itself around that wrist. The serpent has captured Peleus, Thetis, and Noah's cloak.

Figure 123: Side A: Peleus abducts Thetis from an altar in the midst of her sisters.

Figure 124: Side B: The sisters of Thetis run to their father with the news of her abduction.

Taking Noah's Daughter from One Spiritual Viewpoint to Another——
—From the Altar of Noah's God to the Altar of Zeus-religion

On the page opposite, we see two sides of a red-figure wine jar. The characters are Nereus/Noah, his daughters (Nereïds), and a Zeus-worshipper named Peleus who is in the act of abducting the Nereïd, Thetis, from a position next to an altar. Thetis wears a tiara, indicating her importance in relation to the rule of Nereus/Noah. The abduction causes great distress among the other daughters of Nereus/Noah. All of them appear to be in an agitated state of motion. Two of them run open-armed to their father who holds a scepter, and whose bottom half is a fish.

Peleus is seizing Thetis, abducting her, taking her away to the realm of Zeus-religion. The artist has intentionally placed the scene next to an altar which evokes the idea of worship. According to Genesis, Noah, immediately after departing from the ark, built an altar to Yahweh Elohim. All of the women on the vase are daughters of Nereus/Noah. Not only is Peleus interfering with their worship, he is seizing Thetis and taking her away from it. Taking her from the altar of Noah/ Nereus symbolizes taking her away from the worship of the God of Noah, taking her away from her traditional worship, and making her a part of his own new way of looking at things. We, of course, recognize it as a very old way of looking at things going back to a woman, a fruit tree, and a serpent in an ancient paradise.

Peleus wanted to wed Thetis for himself, and he also wanted to wed her to Zeus-religion. In Figure 125, right, we see Peleus and Thetis in their wedding chariot. Some scenes from the François Vase will give us more details on the importance of their wedding in Greek myth/art.

Figure 125: Peleus and Thetis.

One of the partially damaged bands of the François vase from 560 BC (Fig. 126) features the gods in procession to the wedding of Peleus and Thetis. In Figure 127, opposite top, Thetis sits inside a temple awaiting her husband, Peleus, who stands outside. The parade of gods follows. In front of the palace, Peleus stands before an altar, welcoming the divine guests at his wedding. A kantharos stands on the altar.

As we see in Figure 128, opposite bottom, Iris and the friendly Kentaur, Chiron, lead the

Figure 126: The François Vase. The third band from the top depicted the gods in procession to the wedding of Peleus and Thetis, parents of the hero, Achilles.

procession of gods. Chiron taught Peleus, and then became the teacher of Peleus' and Thetis' son, Achilles. Chiron has a human fore-body, and wears a cloak with a decorated border. He clasps Peleus by the hand, and carries a branch over his shoulder, from which hang two rabbits and another animal. Iris, a messenger of Zeus, carries a *kerykeion*, or herald's staff.

What is the artist trying to tell us? The fact that Thetis is seated within a Greek temple means that this union is taking place within the Greek religious framework. We saw in Figure 123 that Peleus abducted Thetis from an altar erected in the environs of her father, Nereus/Noah. Now Thetis will be married before a Greek altar. The kantharos (meaning "dung-beetle" in Greek) on the altar is a symbol of transformation, as the transformation from an altar to Noah's God and an altar to Zeus is a momentous one, indeed.

We saw in Chapter 5 that the Greeks associated Iris, the rainbow, with the aftermath of the Flood. Her presence helps establish the time period. The Greek religious system is about the reestablishment of the way of Kain after the Flood. One of the serpent heads on the end of the herald's staff of Iris looks to the past dominance of that religious viewpoint; the other serpent head looks to the future dominance of that viewpoint in the Greek age. Once the sign of a covenant between Yahweh and mankind (Genesis 9:12-17), the rainbow now becomes a sign of amity between Greek humanity and the gods of Zeus-religion.

Chiron is also a transitional figure. He represents Noah's youngest son, Ham, who, according to Genesis 9:20-27, had wanted to take his father's cloak, a symbol of his rule and authority. Chiron helps legitimize the development of the Greek religious system. The ancient world did not turn away from Noah's God in a few weeks or months or even years. The transition was gradual, over several generations.

Figure 127: Thetis seated in the temple and Peleus standing outside by the altar.

Fig. 128: Peleus, right, greeting Iris and Chiron at the head of the wedding procession.

Figure 129: Nereus and Doris observe the wedding procession of Thetis and Peleus.

Figure 130: Nereus witnesses the abduction of his daughter, Thetis.

Nereus is Forced to Witness the Marriage of His Daughter

Nereus/Noah is a benchmark. Artists placed him in scenes as the known figure, the constant against which they could portray the great spiritual/ religious change taking place after the Flood. Although I have discussed this in two of the previous chapters, it is well-worth reemphasizing here. Greek artists often put Nereus/Noah in vase-scenes to witness the demise of his religious system. So far we've seen instances where they have forced him to witness the birth of Athena, the gods defeating the Giants (his Yahweh-believing sons), Herakles killing a Kentaur (his relatives in the line of Seth), and his power being seized by Herakles and given to Poseidon. He is always depicted as powerless to act. In Figure 130, the vase-artist forces Nereus/Noah to witness the abduction of his most princess-like daughter, Thetis, by the Zeus-worshipper, Peleus. On the François Vase (Fig. 129), he and his wife, Doris, are not part of the procession celebrating the marriage of Thetis and Peleus: the artist places them in a position where they are forced to watch it pass them by.

Figure 131: On the François Vase, Thetis falls in behind Hermes and Athena.

Thetis Becomes an Integral Part of Greek Religion

Thetis appears again on the François Vase, this time on a different partially damaged band, Figure 131, above. She has fallen in behind Hermes and Athena. She looks directly to Hermes, the chief prophet of Zeus-religion, and her leading gesture parallels his. Noah's daughter is being incorporated into Zeus-religion as a loyal follower of the gods.

The vase-scene below (Fig. 132) takes place years later. Thetis' son, Achilles, has grown to be a great warrior. To obtain her son's armor, Thetis goes to Hephaistos, armorer of the gods. As the eldest son of Zeus and Hera, he is the deification of Kain, and she relies on his technical skill to protect her son. As a young girl, she had resisted her abduction by Peleus. Now as a grown woman and mother, Thetis has become fully integrated into Zeus-religion. Nike's presence on the other side of the vase tells us that this is cause for a victory celebration.

Figure 132: Nike approves as Thetis has Hephaistos make armor for her son, Achilles.

The Consequences of the Abduction of Thetis
from the Standpoint of Scripture

To explain the origin of the Trojan War, Greek artists take us back to the abduction of Thetis. That event set other events in motion which led to the abduction of Helen by the Trojan, Paris. This story is also another way of explaining how the Greeks turned away from the God of Nereus/Noah. A summary of that story, as Greek artists and poets told it, follows.

Peleus abducted Thetis from an altar of her father, Nereus/Noah, and brought her for marriage to an altar of his god, Zeus. All the gods attended the wedding, but they did not invite Eris, goddess of discord and strife. She came anyway, and when they refused her admittance, she threw among the guests a golden apple inscribed, "For the fairest."

The discord and strife began at once because Hera, Athena, and Aphrodite all claimed the apple. Zeus told Hermes to settle it, and he picked the Trojan prince, Paris, the most handsome man in the world, to be the judge of "the fairest." Each goddess offered Paris a bribe; and the one he couldn't resist was Aphrodite's: the love of Helen, the most beautiful woman in the world.

In Figure 133, we see the Judgment of Paris depicted on a red-figure vase. On the far left, Paris sits on a knoll with his goats. The bearded Hermes leads Athena, Hera, and Aphrodite forward while explaining to Paris his task. On a partially damaged part of the same vase (Fig. 135), Paris leads away Helen, his sensual reward. One problem was that Helen was already the wife of the Greek king, Menelaos. According to some versions of the story, Paris took the better part of Menelaos' palace treasure as well as his wife.

The leaders of the largest Greek city-states assembled a great navy and sailed for Troy to recover the supposedly kidnapped queen. The ten-year Trojan War had begun. Some say the Judgment of Paris caused the war, but we've got to go back before that to the wedding of Peleus and Thetis when strife and discord entered the scene, and then back to the true source—the abduction of Thetis from before Nereus/Noah's altar to Yahweh.

Let's moralize for a couple of paragraphs. Everything was fine around Noah's altar to Yahweh; he and his daughters were thankful and content. When Peleus took Thetis from there to an altar of Zeus for marriage, strife and discord (Eris) entered the scene at once. Next came vanity followed by jealousy, bribery, lust, treachery, theft, adultery, hatred, and war. Doesn't that describe the ills of the age in which we live? Hasn't it been that way ever since humanity left the altar to Yahweh built by Noah? The apostle Paul referred to this age as "man's day" and "the present wicked eon" (I Corinthians 4:3 and Galations 1:4).

Figure 133: Hermes leads Athena, Hera, and Aphrodite to Paris for him to judge "the fairest."

Figure 134: Hermes approaching Paris.

Figure 135: Paris leads away Helen.

Greek artists were not one-sided propagandists for their religion. They told the truth about their history and their religious standpoint. Their vases explained how humanity went from the rule of a wise and just paternal figure who looked to the Creator for guidance and understanding, to the rule of men who looked to themselves and deifications of their ancestors for these things.

We've seen that the difference between the way of Seth and the way of Kain involved the question of subjection. The line of Seth in the person of Noah was subject to God; the line of Kain was not. The ancient Greek poet Hesiod wrote in his *Theogony* that "the silver-shod goddess Thetis was *subject* to Peleus and brought forth lion-hearted Achilles, the destroyer of men." Thetis' subjection to Peleus, the Zeus-worshipper, was insubjection to the Creator God of Noah. In such ways did the offspring of Noah embrace the way of Kain.

Chapter 10
The Amazons—Noah's Daughters Turned Warriors

The reason that Greek heroes had to fight and kill Amazons has eluded scholars for centuries. The answer is very simple: they were the outraged sisters of the abducted Thetis, and daughters of Nereus/Noah. As Noah was the Flood-surviving patriarch of the line of Seth, these Amazons were also known as children of Ares, that "other" troublesome son of Zeus and Hera, whom we know to be Seth, the youngest son of Adam and Eve, through whom the line of Christ is traced and from whom Noah was descended.

Unless you see the connection between the Amazons, Nereus/Noah, and the line of Seth, it seems very puzzling that Athena, a warrior-woman herself, would lead the spiritual fight against the warrior-women Amazons. But when we see that Athena represents the rebirth of the serpent's Eve after the Flood, and that she is the nurturing stepmother of Erichthonios of the reborn line of Kain in Athens, the pieces of the puzzle form a logical mosaic.

The West Metopes

Figure 136: The west façade of the Parthenon. The fourteen west metopes below the pediment depicted Greeks fighting and killing Amazons.

The fourteen west metopes of the Parthenon, now badly battered, depicted the Greeks defeating the Amazons. We've seen that the other sculptural themes we've examined so far on Athena's temple portrayed real historical events. Did the Greeks really fight and kill armed women? These metopes, the witness of their poets, and many vase-painters say they did. Greek heroes had to prove themselves by killing Amazons. On Figure 137, left, Achilles kills the Amazon Queen Penthesilea. On Figure 138 opposite top, the Athenian hero, Theseus, kills an Amazon. On Figure 139, Herakles kills an Amazon. But why? Who were these women?

Figure 137: Achilles kills an Amazon.

To find out, we need to take another look at the abduction of Thetis by the Zeus-worshipper, Peleus, focusing this time on the emphatic reaction of her sisters. What these daughters of Nereus do will show that they became the Amazons.

136

Figure 138: The Athenian hero, Theseus, kills an Amazon.

Figure 139: Herakles kills an Amazon.

Fig. 140: Side A: Peleus abducts Thetis surrounded by her sisters.

Figure 141: Side B: Four distraught sisters of Thetis and a fifth, far right, begs
Nereus/Noah to do something about their sister's abduction by Peleus.

Thetis' Sisters React to Her Abduction with Resolve and Action

As the vase-scenes above and opposite demonstrate, the abduction of Thetis by the Zeus-worshipper, Peleus, sent the other daughters of Nereus into fits. On the far right of Figure 141, one of the daughters is clasping her father's head, beseeching him for help, begging him to do something. But on this vase and all the others depicting this event, Nereus/Noah does nothing. In Figures 142 and 143, Noah's daughters react to the abduction by running to each other in a state of extreme agitation. Imagine yourself in such a situation. How would you feel and what would you do if your sister were abducted by a stranger from a religious cult, and your father refused to do anything about it?

Peleus has put the spiritual world of Noah's daughters in great turmoil. The

Figure 142: Two sisters of Thetis express their surprise and shock at her abduction.

Figure 143: Four more sisters of Thetis turn to each other in reaction to the abduction.

women make eye contact. Their frenzied body language speaks: "What are we going to do about this? We've got to do something." On both vases, their hands are very expressive. The artist is telling us that they are "up in arms" over the abduction of their sister.

These vase-paintings and many other similar ones beg the question, what are the daughters of Nereus/Noah going to do about the abduction of their sister, Thetis? You'd think that it was important enough for an ancient vase-artist to show us what they did. It was. In about 490 BC, a vase-artist whom scholars identify as Kleophrades, painted just the vase we're looking for.

The Vase-Painting of Kleophrades

Kleophrades painted two adjacent bands on the neck of a large red-figure storage vase from ca. 490 BC (Fig. 144, below). In the overall composition, the artist as much as insists that the Amazons are the daughters of Nereus/Noah. In the damaged center of the lower band, Peleus abducts Thetis (Fig. 146, opposite). In the enlargement of that area below (Fig. 145), we see the head and two legs of Peleus, the bottom part of the dress of Thetis, and the lower half of a serpent. The friendly Kentaur, Chiron, stands by. On opposite sides of this central scene, the daughters of Nereus/Noah become distraught. On the far right, one of them runs to Nereus gesturing for him to do something. We know that he does nothing. The top band of Figure 146 shows what the Nereïds do about the abduction of their sister into Zeus-religion.

On the far right of the top band, above the Nereïd pleading with her father, a trumpeter issues a call to arms (Fig. 147). The armed female warriors rushing toward her are the end result of that call. The initial response to the call to arms begins further back along the band (Fig. 148). There, five Amazons test their weapons and begin to arm themselves, holding greaves (leg armor for below the knees), shields, spears, and helmets; one tests an arrow with her finger, another prepares to put on a helmet, another puts on her greaves. On that section of the vase, note that Amazons A and B look virtually identical to Nereïds C and D on the band below. That's because that's who they are. The Amazons are the out-raged daughters of Nereus/Noah bent on avenging their sister's abduction into Zeus-religion by Peleus.

Figure 144: The storage jar painted by Kleophrades.

Figure 145: Enlargement of the lower band seen on Figure 146. Peleus abducts Thetis.

Figure 146: On the lower band, Noah's daughters react to the abduction of Thetis. On the top band, these same women arm themselves and fall in line for combat.

Figure 147: Just above a depiction of one of Noah's daughters pleading in vain for him to take action, a trumpeter issues a call to arms to which the daughters respond.

Figure 148: Amazons A and B are Noah's daughters, C and D, arming themselves to fight.

Figure 149: On the upper panel, Herakles kills Amazons who unsuccessfully
try to block his way to the fruit of the serpent's tree, pictured on the lower panel.

We've seen that on one side of the vase, the daughters of Nereus become
Amazons as they arm to fight the emerging Zeus-religion. On the top band on the
other side of the vase (Fig. 149, above), Herakles, the champion and hero of
Zeus-religion, kills these Amazons. Note that the next Amazon to advance
against Herakles has a Kentaur for a shield device, identifying her and her sisters
as part of the line of Seth.

On the partially damaged band just below this scene, Herakles approaches
the serpent's tree in the Garden of the Hesperides. On the right, Atlas elevates the
heavens, pushing them away, and with them the God of the heavens. Nobody is
going to stop Herakles from getting a big bite of one of the serpent's apples. The
Giants, the Yahweh-believing sons of Noah, couldn't stop him, and neither can
the Amazons, Noah's Yahweh-believing daughters.

Read like comic book panels, what does the vase say? First, Zeus-
worshipping Peleus abducts Thetis, a daughter of Nereus/Noah. Second, Noah's
other daughters demand that he take action, which he refuses to do. Third,
Noah's other daughters take action themselves, responding to a call to arms and
becoming Amazons. Fourth, Herakles meets the challenge head-on and kills
these Amazons. Fifth, Herakles cannot be stopped from achieving his objective
of getting humanity back to the serpent's fruit tree in paradise.

Figure 150: E. B. Harrison's drawing of the shield of Athena Parthenos.
Greeks rout the Amazons who storm the Akropolis.

According to legend, the Athenians fought a great battle with the Amazons in Athens. The Amazons attacked the Akropolis from a hill northwest of it that became known as the Areopagus—the Hill of Ares. According to the 1st-century AD Roman writer, Pliny the Elder, the outer part of the shield of Athena's Parthenon idol-image depicted the Greeks defeating the Amazons. E. B. Harrison's recreation of that shield appears above. The Greeks are defending their Akropolis as Amazons attack from the nearby Hill of Ares, the Seth of Genesis. Pliny also wrote that the artists had painted the gods defeating the Giants on the inside of the shield. A shield is an instrument of defense, and the artists' decoration of this shield tells us who it was that Athena and the Greek religious system considered their most significant enemies: Giants and Amazons—Yahweh-believing sons of Noah and Yahweh-believing daughters of Noah turned warriors.

When the apostle Paul visited Athens, he stood on the Areopagus and commented on a pedestal inscribed, "To an Unknown God" (Acts 17:23). This was the Creator Whom Greek religion knew nothing of, but to Whom the line of Seth

143

Figure 151: On this west metope from the temple of Zeus at Olympia, Herakles
kills the Amazon queen Hippolyte, and takes her belt, a symbol of
authority which belonged to her father Ares, the Seth of Genesis.

was devoted. It is worth noting that this little monument did not appear on the
Akropolis, the privileged precinct of the line of Kain, but rather on the hill of the
god Ares whose offspring, both men and women, Herakles sought to kill. Some
Greeks retained a consciousness of the True God. They didn't know His name,
but they knew enough to connect him to Ares.

While our vase-painter, Kleophrades, directly connects the Amazons to Ner-
eus/Noah, many sources directly connect the Amazons to Seth which means the
same thing, for Noah was part of the line of Seth.

Above, we see one of the six metopes from the west side of the temple of
Zeus at Olympia depicting the ninth labor of Herakles. The Greek hero kills the
Amazon queen, Hippolyte, in order to get her war belt, a gift from her father,
Ares. The belt was a sign of the source of her authority, and a token of her supe-
riority over all the other Amazons. Taking the belt of Hippolyte, daughter of
Ares, is an act similar in meaning to the taking of Noah's cloak. Greek artists
chronicled what was essentially an historical religious takeover. It is only logical
that they would express this "takeover" through the "taking" of various symbolic
items. Herakles takes Hippolyte's belt. Athena takes Noah's cloak. Poseidon
takes the trident of Nereus/Noah. Zeus takes the scepter of Nereus/Noah. Peleus
takes the daughter of Nereus/Noah. Each of these "takes" is part of the larger religious "takeover" of the way of Kain from the way of Seth.

The idea that the Amazons cut off their right breast so that it might not inter-
fere with the use of the bow, and that the name thus means "breastless," is a fa-
ble. Greek artists never pictured Amazons without a breast, which they surely

would have if that's what their name meant. Trust the artists: they tell the truth. *Maza* means barley cake. Kain was a "server of the ground" (Genesis 4:2) out of which the barley grows. An "a" in front of a Greek word often is the equivalent of our "non" or "un." The Amazons were known as nomadic and not servers of the ground; that is, not those who raise barley and make cakes. A-mazon would thus identify them as *not* part of the line of Kain, a fact these Yahweh-believing daughters of Nereus/Noah would have been very eager to proclaim.

* * *

In Part II of this book, among many other things, we've found that the murder of Abel by Kain may well have been depicted on the south metopes of the Parthenon; and certainly that the taking of the Kain-women before the Flood by the Kentaurs (Seth-men) was depicted there. We've seen that, having replaced Nereus/Noah with Poseidon, the Greeks depicted the Flood in the center of the west pediment. We've also seen that on the east metopes, the gods routed the Yahweh-believing sons of Noah, and that the same triumph was embroidered on Athena's stolen cloak on the frieze. Examining the theme of the north metopes, we've learned that the true origins of the Trojan War go back to the abduction of Thetis, a daughter of Nereus/Noah; and by studying that abduction and trusting the ancient vase-artists, we've learned of the origin of the warrior women sculpted in defeat on the west metopes.

Where does this new understanding of the Parthenon Code which, by the grace of God we have deciphered, lead us? How do we summarize the import of themes so rich, revealing, and deep? The Greeks have done it for us. The very purpose of the sculpture on the sacred east pediment was to summarize their religious outlook and history in the most simple and direct way possible. In Part III, as we reconstruct the east pediment of the Parthenon with the help of computer artist Holmes Bryant, we shall see that the ancient Greek sculptors achieved their purpose, and then some.

PART III

The East Pediment of the Parthenon— The Greeks' Ultimate Artistic and Religious Statement

Let us imagine ourselves in ancient Athens looking up at the east pediment of the Parthenon as dawn breaks in mid-summer. As shadows of the night back-track, the brightly painted sculptures absorb the red of the rising sun behind us. We begin to make out the scene inside the triangle. As the sunshine spreads to flaxen yellow, we begin to see that the sculptural figures tell a story. We see the triumphant boast of the ancient Athenians' religion and culture, their affirmation of themselves to themselves, and their artistic communication to posterity.

We know many of the details of the story these Greeks tell about themselves from vase-paintings and the other sculptural themes we've examined on Athena's temple. Here on the east pediment, they do us the favor of brilliantly summing up their tale, telling us, in no uncertain terms, who they are, where they came from, and what they believed.

Figure 152: The east pediment.

Figure 153: The center of the east pediment enlarged.

PART III Section I

The Evidence for Reconstructing the East Pediment

Scholars have done a superlative job collecting the evidence. The Genesis connection enables us to make sense of that evidence, and understand what the ancient Greeks were trying to tell us about themselves. The computer reconstructions of Holmes Bryant, based almost entirely on the physical evidence, enable us to see a picture very close to the original one our Greek ancestors created in marble.

Chapter 11

The Pieces of the Puzzle

Figure 154: The Parthenon from the East.

Above, we see the east façade of the Parthenon as it looks today, disencumbered of all the statues. Almost the entire pediment is missing. Surviving sculptures from the left and right sides of the pediment in the British Museum and elsewhere preserve crucial images relating directly to the central scene. We know—from a single sentence written by the ancient travel writer Pausanias—that the central scene represented the birth of Athena.

Figure 155: The east pediment from an engraving by William Pars, 1765.

A Brief History of the Parthenon and Its East Façade

Work began on the Parthenon in 447 BC under the political direction of Perikles, the artistic direction of Phidias, and the architectural direction of Iktinos and Kallikrates. The Greeks dedicated the temple nine years later in 438 BC when Phidias completed the interior gold and ivory statue of Athena Parthenos. Work continued until 432 BC when the sculptors finished their work on all the adorning figures.

Athena's temple remained in continuous use for about a thousand years until Christian officials, in the late fifth or early sixth century, converted it into a church, and removed the central figures of the east pediment. Many of the remaining sculptures undoubtedly suffered deliberate defacement at the hands of zealous believers.

In 1687, the Turks, besieged by the Venetians, used the Parthenon as a gunpowder magazine. On September 26th, the Parthenon took a direct hit from a Venetian shell, and the powder stored there exploded. The blast destroyed most of the interior walls of the temple (apart from the west end), and whole groups of columns on the north and south sides along with much sculpture. Damage to the east pediment was relatively minor. We know this because we have drawings attributed to an artist named Jacques Carrey who visited Athens with the French ambassador to the Turkish Court in 1674. His drawings show that the entire center of the east pediment was missing before the explosion of 1687.

In 1800, when the Akropolis of Athens was a Turkish fortress, the British Crown appointed Thomas Bruce, the seventh earl of Elgin, as its ambassador in Constantinople. From 1801 to 1810, Lord Elgin, largely through the bribery of Turkish officials, removed much sculpture from the Parthenon including almost all of what remained on the east pediment. He shipped it back to England and in 1816 sold his collection to the British Museum where it is on display today.

Since that time and continuing today, scholars have been trying to reconstruct the lost center of the pediment, and to accurately portray and identify the remaining figures. On the pages that follow we will examine the pieces of the puzzle that we have to work with.

The Pieces of the Puzzle—What We Have to Work With

The pieces of our puzzle, the clues available to help us solve the case of the missing east pediment and its meaning are basically these:

- The terse 2nd century AD description of the pediment by the travel writer Pausanias—by far the most important clue (see below).

- The Parthenon sculptures in the British Museum (the so-called Elgin Marbles).

- Sculptural fragments in the Akropolis Museum.

- The 1674 drawings of Jacques Carrey.

- Relevant painting, sculpture, and literature pre-dating the Parthenon, and therefore likely to have influenced the depictions on it.

- Relevant painting, sculpture, and literature post-dating the Parthenon and therefore likely to have been influenced by it.

- Technical evidence gleaned from a detailed architectural examination of what is left of the pediment itself.

The Witness of Pausanias

It seems incredible that although the Parthenon served as a center of worship in Athens for a thousand years, only one writer's description of the Parthenon sculptures survives—that of the 2nd-century AD travel writer Pausanias. He wrote only this about the east pediment:

All the figures in the gable over the entrance to the temple called the Parthenon relate to the birth of Athena.

This single sentence tells us the theme of the pediment and asserts that every piece of sculpture on it relates to that theme. Scholars have been unsuccessful in identifying most of the figures and relating them to Athena's birth because they fail to connect Athena with Eve and the story of Eden in the Book of Genesis.

The Left Side of the East Pediment

A   B C   D   E   F   G

Figure 156: The left side of the east pediment in the British Museum, London.

Above are the sculptures from the left side of the east pediment in the British Museum, London; from the left: a charioteer and two horses (A, B, and C), a naked, muscular male (D), two heavily draped females seated on rectangular chests (E and F), and a third standing female (G) turning abruptly away from the center.

Below are the same figures as drawn by Jacques Carrey in 1674. We can see by the position of G's knee relative to the knee of seated F that Carrey drew G too large. We'll see that G's smaller stature plays a key part in enabling us to identify these surviving sculptures as three very important sisters.

A   B C   D   E   F   G

Figure 157: The left side of the east pediment as drawn by Jacques Carrey in 1674.

Details From the Left Side of the East Pediment

Figure 158: A, B, and C in the British Museum.

Figure 159: D in the British Museum.

Figure 160: E, F, and G in the British Museum.

A, B, and C are universally recognized as the remnants of Helios (the sun) and his quadriga (four-horse chariot).

D has been variously identified as Theseus, a hero who united Attika; Dionysos, the god of revelry and wine; and Herakles. We will see that only one of these scholarly guesses actually fits the theme of the pediment.

The usual identification of E and F as Demeter, goddess of the earth's fertility, and her daughter, Persephone, is not correct because their presence here does not relate to the birth of Athena. The identification of G as Hebe, goddess of youth, or Artemis, goddess of the hunt, is not correct either. Figure G in context lacks the stature of a goddess. And no one until now has been able to explain why E and F seem so at ease while the smaller G turns anxiously.

The Right Side of the East Pediment

Figure 161: K, L, and M in the British Museum.

Above: in the British Museum, K, L, and M. K, far left, is most often identi-fied as Hestia, the goddess of the hearth. L is usually identified as the goddess Dione, with her daughter Aphrodite, M, reclining in her lap. No one has been able to explain their obvious indifference to Athena's birth in the center of the pediment. We'll see that these three are not Olympian goddesses at all, but rather, to the Greeks, familiar figures who form a collective iconograph representing the ancient paradise, or Eden.

Below: the same figures as drawn by Jacques Carrey in 1674. Note that K and M still had heads then.

Figure 162: K, L, and M drawn by Jacques Carrey in 1674.

Sculptures from the Right Side of the East Pediment

Figure 163: N in the Akropolis Museum, Athens

Figure 164: O in the British Museum, London.

Scholars identify N, above, now in the Akropolis Museum, as the torso of the charioteer Selene (the moon), or Nyx (Night or Darkness). We'll see that only one of these beings fits perfectly with the cosmology of the ancient poet Hesiod and the theme of the east pediment, the birth of Athena.

O, above, now in the British Museum, is the outer horse of N's four-horse chariot.

Some believe H, right, now in the Akropolis Museum, is the torso of Poseidon, god of the sea, but the muscular structure identifies H as Atlas, a Titan whose presence relates directly to the birth of Athena and an ancient paradise.

Figure 165: H in the Akropolis Museum, Athens

Chapter 12

The Central Figures—Zeus, Athena, Hera, and Hephaistos

Figure 166: The central figures in the pediment.

The Greeks depicted the birth of Athena in marble only on the Parthenon, and we know about that only from the words of the second-century AD travel writer Pausanias: "All the figures in the gable over the entrance to the temple called the Parthenon relate to the birth of Athena." Of the birth scene itself in the center, we possess only the most fragmentary remains. Fortunately, we do have Athena's birth described in literature and painted on vases. Those sources make up the basis of our reconstruction.

We know from myth that Athena was born full-grown from the head of her father, Zeus, after he devoured Metis, the goddess of cunning. We also know from the ancient poets and many vase-scenes that Hephaistos, the god of the forge, was said to have cracked open the head of Zeus with his axe to release Athena. Thus Zeus, Athena, and Hephaistos must have been part of the central scene on the east pediment.

Hera, the wife of Zeus and queen of the gods, undoubtedly had a place there as well. To omit her from what we will come to see was an all-embracing theme, would have been unthinkable to reverent Greeks. Plus, there is ample physical evidence for Hera's presence in the central scene.

Figure 167: The birth of Athena.

The Birth of Athena Depicted on Vases

The scene on the Attic black-figure cup from ca. 560 BC (Fig. 167, above) depicts the birth of Athena. Zeus sits on a throne, facing right. Both of his hands are raised in a gesture of presentation. His right hand clutches the lightning bolt, a symbol of the "moment of lighting up" in paradise, and his left hand is raised towards Hephaistos. From his head sprouts the head and upper torso of a slightly under life-size Athena carrying her shield. Hephaistos, carrying his axe behind his back, walks to the right, but twists his upper body back to look at Athena after playing his part in her birth. He gestures as if to say, "There, it is done!"

In the Attic red-figure vase-depiction of the birth of Athena from ca. 450 BC (Fig. 168, opposite), Hephaistos, moves to our right carrying his axe, looking intently at Athena's emergence the moment after he is said to have struck the head of Zeus. Athena (under life-size) emerges with her spear ready for immediate battle. The two women framing the scene are probably the *Eileithyiae*, goddesses of childbirth and children of Hera. Hera herself may be the figure at the far left.

Figure 168: Goddesses of childbirth frame the central scene of
Zeus, Athena, and Hephaistos.

But Zeus himself gave birth from his own head to bright-eyed Tritogeneia [Athena], the awful, the strife-stirring, the host-leader, the unwearying one who delights in tumults and wars and battles.

Hesiod, *Theogony*

Athena sprang quickly from the immortal head and **stood before Zeus** who holds the aegis, shaking a sharp spear: great Olympus began to reel horribly at the might of the bright-eyed goddess . . .

Homeric Hymn to Athena

Zeus had intercourse with Metis, who turned many shapes in order to avoid his embraces. When she was with child, Zeus, taking time by the forelock, swallowed her, because Earth said that, after giving birth to the maiden who was then in her womb, Metis would bear a son who should be the lord of heaven. From fear of that, Zeus swallowed her. And when the time came for the birth to take place . . . Hephaistos smote the head of Zeus with an axe, and Athena, fully armed, leaped up from the top of his head . . .

Apollodorus

While it may have seemed appropriate on many "Birth of Athena" vases to have Hera's daughters present but not Hera herself, this would not do for the central scene of the east pediment of the Parthenon. The wife of Zeus and queen of the gods must have been represented prominently there. The technical evidence on the following page bears this out.

Hera Fragments

The drawing by K. Iliakis, right, incorporates non-joining fragments believed to belong to the figure of Hera on the east pediment (Fig. 171, below right). Scholars refer to the combined fragments as "Peplos Figure Wegner" after the type of dress she is wearing and the man who first brought the pieces together. Olga Palagia writes of the figure, "Her striking simplicity, marking a vivid contrast to the baroque exuberance of the corner figures, is best explained by her colossal scale which entails a position close to the pediment axis." No other goddess, save Hera herself, belongs so close to Zeus and Athena in the center.

Figure 169: Athena, Zeus, and Hera.

Figure 170: Fragment of Hera's head.

The majority of Parthenon scholars identify this largest of three fragments of the head of a goddess, above, with the "Peplos Figure Wegner," and thus with Hera. Its dimensions are compatible. According to Olga Palagia, the largest fragment has been in the Akropolis Museum since at least 1890; a second non-joining fragment was recovered in 1984; and a third fragment joining the second came to light in 1990. The figure was turned to its proper right showing the spectator its left profile. The headband is pierced with two rows of holes running across in all fragments for the attachment of metal ornaments making a crown. The back of the head was covered by a veil indicating a matron. This is the head of Hera, queen of Olympus.

Figure 171: Non-joining fragments of Hera's body.

A Standing Zeus in the Center of the Pediment

Since Zeus is seated on vases depicting the birth of Athena, many scholars believe that he was sculpted that way in the center of the east pediment. But because of the weight of the marble, great technical difficulties plague such a possibility. Olga Palagia writes in her *The Pediments of the Parthenon*:

If the pediment represents the aftermath of the birth, there is a possibility that its designer might have departed from what we [scholars] consider the norm. A standing Zeus would eliminate some of the practical problems entailed by a colossal seated figure. [Kristian] Jeppesen sensibly points out that figures near the center of the pediments tend to be standing to reduce their depth. Since Athena is now by his side, Zeus has no reason to sit. He may be envisaged instead rising in response to Olympos' quake.

Figure 172: Zeus from the center of the east pediment of his temple at Olympia, ca. 450 BC.

The vase-painters showed the moment of Athena's birth, and wanted to emphasize that she sprang from the head of Zeus. This would have been an extremely difficult artistic challenge had Zeus been depicted as standing. Where would there have been space for Athena? On the other hand, sculpting a seated Zeus at the apex of a marble pediment with Athena in the process of emerging would have been very awkward, if not impossible. The sculptors most probably followed the *Homeric Hymn to Athena* and depicted her—not in the process of her birth—but after she had emerged and "stood before Zeus."

Furthermore, no Classical pediment is known to have carried a seated figure on its axis. In the center of the east pediment of Zeus' own temple at Olympia, completed ten to twenty years before the Parthenon, he is shown standing (Fig. 172, right). Why would he be depicted differently on Athena's temple? The shape of the triangle itself demands that Zeus stand erect there.

Figure 173: The center of the east pediment looking from the ground up.

In summary, the central scene of the east pediment, the birth of Athena, most likely followed the *Homeric Hymn to Athena*, depicting the moment the fully-formed Athena "stood before Zeus." Common sense would have us put Athena to the proper right of Zeus, Hera to his proper left, and Hephaistos to Hera's left, stepping back. This puts Hera in the shadow of Zeus in relation to Helios, the sun rising in the left corner of the pediment. Hera belongs in the shadow of Zeus in this depiction of the birth of Athena.

Now that we know the central figures on the east pediment were Zeus, Athena, Hephaistos, and Hera, let's move on and find out whom they truly represent.

PART III Section II

The True Identity of the Central Figures

The central figures on the east pediment of the Parthenon take us back to the ancient paradise with Adam and Eve and the serpent. Zeus is the ancient serpent transfigured into an image of Adam; Hera is the original Eve, and the sister/wife of Adam; Hephaistos is Kain, their eldest son; and Athena represents the reborn serpent's Eve after the Flood.

Chapter 13

Zeus—The Serpent Transfigured into an Image of Adam.

Zeus is the true focal point on the east pediment. The scene at the center is almost always referred to as "the birth of Athena," but it is more accurately described as "Zeus birthing Athena." Zeus is the one who brings Athena into being, and he is the one who ordains that all of what we see on the pediment might be so. His lightning bolt in his right hand suggests his power, but more obviously, the moment of lighting up, that instant, that flash of time when Eve received the knowledge of good and evil, and human history as we know it began.

In that ancient garden, the serpent figuratively fathered Eve, subtly coaxing her out of Yahweh's family and welcoming her into his own. Both Zeus and the serpent are father to Athena. It should not surprise us, then, that the Greeks worshipped Zeus as the transfigured serpent.

Figure 174: The relief to the left and the one on the next page were found at Athens' harbor, and date from the 4th century BC. Inscribed above this coiled beast is "to Zeus *Meilichios*," meaning "to Zeus the Easily Entreated One." The beard signifies "the ancient serpent."

John C. Wilson wrote that anthropologist Jane Ellen Harrison "understood, as no one did before her, that in spite of their great intellectual achievements the Greeks belonged in the main to the world of primitive religion." The superstitious Greek, she thought, entered the presence of his gods as though he were approaching the hole of a snake, for the snake had been to his ancestors, and was still to him and many of his contemporaries, literally and actually a god. A lifetime of study led her to believe that Greek religion, for all its superficial serenity, had within it and beneath it elements of a deeper and darker significance. She concluded that Zeus, the Olympian father god, had tended to erase from men's minds the worship of himself when he bore the title Zeus *Meilichios*, "Zeus the Easily Entreated One," and took the form of the serpent who demanded from his devotees the sacrifice of a pig.*

Ms. Harrison examined several ancient stone reliefs of a coiled serpent twice human size inscribed to Zeus. In her *Prolegomena to the Study of Greek Religion*, she wrote:

> **We are brought face-to-face with the astounding fact that Zeus, father of gods and men, is figured by his worshipers as a snake . . . The human-shaped Zeus has slipped himself quietly into the place of the old snake-god. Art sets plainly forth what has been dimly shadowed in ritual and mythology. It is not that Zeus the**

---

*While Ms. Harrison's contributions are invaluable, as an avowed atheist, she was never able to make the Genesis connection.

Olympian has an "underworld aspect;" it is the cruder fact that he of the upper air, of the thunder and lightning, extrudes an ancient serpent-demon of the lower world, Meilichios.

As we have seen, from the earliest times the Greeks took a view of the serpent opposite the one we generally hold today. To them, the serpent freed mankind from bondage to an oppressive God, and was therefore a savior and illuminator of our race. The Greeks worshipped Zeus as both savior and illuminator.

What Zeus itself means is very revealing in this regard. Edward Tripp and others say simply that the name is derived from an Indo-European root meaning to shine or gleam brightly. According to Carl Kerenyi, Zeus, the supreme god of the Greeks and their history, has a transparent name which more directly

Figure 175: A woman and two men approach Zeus as the serpent with gestures of adoration.

betrays his place in Eden. In his book *Zeus and Hera*, Mr. Kerenyi writes that "the actual content of the word *Zeus* is the *moment* of lighting up." He adds:

By the content of his name, "lighting up," Zeus was connected for the Greeks not with the beginning of the world but with the time of which they themselves had historical consciousness, a "new" time contrasted with an "old" time which was not yet ruled by Zeus.

The "old" time is that time when Yahweh ruled, before Eve ate the fruit; the "new" time comes after Eve picks the fruit and the serpent begins his rule. Eve's moment of disobedience from the Judeo-Christian point of view, was to the Greeks the instant she welcomed enlightenment from the serpent—the moment of lighting up, the moment civilization and culture became possible. And with that possibility came the Greek expectation that the serpent's system would raise humanity higher in the scale of creation.

The Greek Scriptures express this more concisely. Revelation 12:9 identifies the "ancient serpent" by the titles Adversary and Satan, and the apostle Paul in II Corinthians 11:14 asserts that "Satan himself [i.e. the ancient serpent] is being transfigured into a messenger of light."

The transfiguration of the serpent into Zeus as a "messenger of light" may be the central architectural message of the Parthenon. The Greeks' first view of the temple as they entered through the gateway to the Akropolis was the west façade. Athena and Poseidon appeared facing each other in the center of that pediment. A depiction of that on a 4th-century BC water pot now in the Hermitage Museum in St. Petersburg, Russia (See Fig. 46, page 56) shows a serpent coiled around a tree between Athena and Poseidon—which would have put the serpent in the very center of that pediment. When we follow the long axis along the roof of the temple from the west pediment to the east pediment, we find Zeus standing in the very center of it. In the space of seventy meters, the serpent has taken the form of a human and become the father of gods and men. The Greeks called their great god Zeus *Phanaios* which means "One Who Appears as Light and Brings Light." The serpent is transfigured into a messenger of light.

Zeus, the god of thunder and lightning, ruled the sky. To the Greeks, his was the sphere of atmospheric phenomena—the air. Scripture matches Greek myth here as well. We read in Ephesians 2:2 that the Adversary (Zeus the transfigured serpent) is "the chief of the jurisdiction of the air."

Greek myth portrays Zeus as the supreme power over all the earth. In Homer, Zeus towers over every other god and goddess and every human order with absolute pre-eminence. Zeus is the one who makes kings and kingdoms. What power Homer gives to Zeus, Scripture gives to Satan. After fasting in the wilderness for forty days and forty nights, Christ encounters the Adversary, sent there to try Him. Matthew 4:8-9 reads:

Again the Adversary takes Him along into a very high mountain, and is showing Him all the kingdoms of the world and their glory. And he said to Him, "All these to you will I be giving, if ever, falling down, you should be worshipping me."

Jesus does not at all dispute the Adversary's express claim that he is ruler of all the kingdoms of the world. The "very high mountain" from which the Adversary makes his offer reminds us of the mythical home of Zeus: Mount Olympus. This mountain characterized the rule of Zeus-religion from the beginning, all the more so in Classical and Hellenistic times when it had become the seat of Father Zeus' entire family of gods and goddesses.

We've seen that Revelation 2:13 also identifies the ancient serpent who is known as the Adversary and Satan with Zeus. In that verse, the voice of God speaks to His Jewish followers in the Ionian city of Pergamum saying, "I am aware where you are dwelling—where the throne of Satan is." Pergamum, near the coast of modern-day Western Turkey, about 50 miles south of ancient Troy, was one of the most beautiful of ancient Greek cities. There, atop a mountain, just above a great amphitheater built into the side of it, 20 miles from the Aegean

Figure 176: A drawing of a relief of the bearded serpent from the sanctuary at Athens harbor. The inscription reads, "Heracleides to the god." Jane Ellen Harrison writes of it, "When and where the snake is simply 'the god,' the fusion with Zeus is made easy."

Sea, stood the magnificent 40-foot-high Altar of Zeus. The throne of Satan—the throne of the ancient transfigured serpent—is the Altar of Zeus.

On the vase below, Zeus sends forth his two primary heralds, Hermes and Iris. To identify themselves as his messengers, each carries a *kerykeion*, or herald's staff (*caduceus* in Latin). The kerykeion features a serpent with two heads facing each other symbolizing the serpent's rule over the past and the future. The kerykeion identifies the authority of Zeus with the authority of the serpent.

The case for the identity of Zeus as the serpent is yet further strengthened when we consider that the idol images of Athena, Apollo, Hermes, Hephaistos, Hera, Artemis, and other Greek gods often appeared attended by serpents, but Zeus never. Why? The presence of snakes around the other gods indicated that they were part of the serpent's system of enlightenment and sacrifice. But Zeus is not a subordinate part of the serpent's system—he *is* the serpent.

Figure 177: Zeus sends forth Hermes and Iris with their serpent-headed kerykeions.

Zeus, the Transfigured Serpent, is a Picture of
Adam at the Moment of Lighting Up

The Greeks worshipped their ancestors. With the exception of some natural elements and forces, such as the North Wind and the sea, the gods are deifications, or immortalizations, of historical humans. Sokrates frankly acknowledged his physical descent from the gods as deified humans in this bit of dialogue from Plato's *Euthydemus*:

> **"No matter, said Dionysodorus, for you admit you have Apollo, Zeus, and Athene."**
> **"Certainly," [Sokrates] said.**
> **"And they are your gods," he said.**
> **"Yes," [Sokrates] said, "my lords and ancestors."**

In the Book of Acts, the apostle Paul, citing Greek literary sources, asserts categorically that the race of the gods and the race of men are one and the same. In Chapter 17 he stands on the Areopagus (the Hill of Ares, across from the Akropolis), and speaks to the inquisitive group gathered there:

> **"Men! Athenians! On all sides am I beholding how unusually religious you are. For, passing through and contemplating the objects of your veneration, I found a pedestal also, on which had been inscribed, 'To an Unknown God.' To Whom then you are ignorantly devout, This One am I announcing to you."**

When Paul says these Greeks are unusually "religious" he means fearful, for the Greek word is *deisidaimon*, literally dread-demon. Zeus-religion was so systematized by Paul's time that it completely obscured the knowledge of Yahweh. Paul attempts to reveal this Unknown God to them, and at the same time expose the futility of idol worship:

> **". . . [N]ot far from each one of us is He [the Unknown God] inherent, for in Him we are living and moving and are, as some poets of yours also have declared, 'For of that race also are we.' The race, then, is inherently of God; we ought not to be inferring that the Divine is like gold, or silver, or stone sculpture of art and human sentiment."**

The exact words "For of that race also are we" occur as part of an invocation to Zeus in a little book called *The Skies* by Aratus (315 – 245 BC) of Cilicia (Paul's native province). Aratus thus asserts that his race and the race of Zeus are one and the same. The Stoic Cleanthes (331 – 232 BC) also uses the phrase in his *Hymn to Zeus*. The Greek word used by Paul and the poets translated race is *genos*. It refers specifically to the race of mankind, making Zeus, in context, part of that race. The race of Zeus and the gods is the race of deified, ancestral men and women.

We've seen that in the Greek religion the serpent took the form of a very powerful-looking father-figure armed with lightning bolts. Both the serpent and the human image had the name Zeus, meaning "the moment of lighting up," or more explicitly according to Carl Kerenyi, "the actual decisive, dynamic moment of becoming light." This meaning of Zeus' name has led us directly back to the Garden of Eden, and to the time when Eve and Adam accepted the serpent's wisdom as their own. It should not surprise us that the enlightener in Greek religion should find suitable human representation for himself right there in the garden.

Unlike Eve, Adam did not need to be convinced of the efficacy of eating the fruit: ". . . and [Eve] is giving, moreover, to her husband with her, and they are eating" (Genesis 3:6). He may very well have desired to possess the knowledge of good and evil for himself for some time before he actually partook. Adam was the enlightener's very first male convert and the progenitor of the entire human race as well. It made sense for the enlightener to represent himself to humanity by means of the image of Adam—a messenger of his (the serpent's) light.

Homer says that Zeus is "the father of men and gods." Every human, living or dead, including those dead who are deified in Greek religion, are descended from Adam, the first man. Zeus, then, is not only a transfiguration of the serpent, but a picture of our first human father, Adam, as well.

Figure 178: The same event depicted from the Judeo-Christian standpoint, and that of Greek religion. In the fresco by Masaccio, shame characterizes the scene. In the sculpture by Tegner, triumph reigns. Athena is born out of Zeus just as Eve came out of Adam, and she has come out exulting in the serpent's enlightenment!

Chapter 14
Athena—The Reborn Serpent's Eve

One of Athena's nicknames was *Tritogenia* or "Thrice-born." She was born for the first time full-grown out of Adam. Then at the apple tree, she was born a second time, as the serpent's Eve, when the serpent birthed her into his system of enlightenment. The Flood wiped out the line of Kain and the serpent's system to which it was dedicated. And so Athena's third birth came after the Flood, as the rebirth of the serpent's Eve.

In their depictions of her, vase-artists and sculptors almost always identified Athena with the ancient serpent, sometimes in more ways than one.

Figure 179: Athena born full-grown and fully-armed from the head of Zeus.

The scene, above, on a large drinking cup from ca. 560 BC depicts the birth of Athena. Hephaistos, his axe slung over his left shoulder, watches Athena emerge from the head of Zeus full-grown and fully-armed.

Athena's coming into being out of Zeus is a marvelously concise picture of the key event—the world-shaking event—in Eden. Zeus is a picture of Adam as "the father of gods and men." Eve came out of Adam. Athena, the Greek Eve, came out of Zeus, a deified picture of Adam. Athena's coming into being out of the head of Zeus also signifies that she is the brain-child of the transfigured serpent. The age in which we live, the age initiated by the Greeks, is a new postdiluvian age, a new beginning, a new system which exalts Eve's wisdom in eating the fruit of the tree in the garden, a wisdom with the power to establish the foundation of a human culture lasting thousands of years. Athena, the new Eve, is fully-armed to fight for Zeus-religion and for the city that bears her name.

Eve's seed, the Book of Genesis said, would bruise the head of the serpent. Noah, a righteous (Yahweh-believing) seed of Eve, figuratively did just that by surviving the Deluge which destroyed the entire line of Kain. After the Flood, with the line of Kain reestablished, Athena, the serpent's Eve, made certain the curse of Genesis could not operate in the Greek age, for she would remain Athena Parthenos, Athena the maiden, Athena the virgin without offspring. There is no seed of this woman to crush the serpent's head in the Greek age. Yahweh's curse is thus broken, and the serpent's promise to Eve—"Ye shall not surely

Figure 180: Hera is the primal Eve; Athena represents the reborn serpent's Eve after the Flood.

die"—is made manifest, for, as we have seen, Athena is A-thana(tos), the death-less one.

The above images help put Athena's birth in its historical perspective. Hera, the sister/wife of Zeus and the original goddess of childbirth and marriage, came first. She represents the primal Eve. By birth alone, Hera holds the scepter of rule. She didn't have to do anything to earn it. Being the motherless mother of all humanity was enough to make her queen of Olympus. Then came the Flood which wiped out the line of Kain.

For several generations, Noah and the line of Seth ruled. The line of Kain had to do battle to reestablish itself, and the reborn serpent's Eve had to emerge ready for that battle. And so Athena is pictured as coming out full-grown and fully-armed, carrying not a scepter, but a spear. Her birth full-grown out of Zeus is a picture of Eve's original full-grown birth out of Adam.

We have seen that Eve was the "mother of all living" and the first woman to marry, and that Hera, worshipped as the goddess of childbirth and marriage, was a deification of Eve in these aspects. According to Greek myth, the golden apples originally belonged to Hera. They had been a wedding present to her from Gaia (Earth) or directly from Zeus who had considered them his most precious posses-sion. So how did Athena get the apples and what did that signify? To answer that, we need to go into more detail about the relation of Herakles to Hera, Athena, and the golden apples of the Hesperides.

Most schoolchildren have heard of the mighty Herakles and his twelve labors. Films and television series about him using his Roman name, Hercules, have attracted great popularity. What is almost always missed in the recounting of his adventures is that within them, we find the story of the transfer of power from Hera to Athena. From the first of his labors to the last, Hera opposed Herakles while Athena assisted him. Ancient Greek artists used the course of Herakles' labors, which included the conquest of Noah's Yahweh-believing sons and daughters, to brilliantly express Athena's rise to preeminence in the post-Flood age. We've seen that Herakles means "the glory of Hera." The great hero's labors testify to Hera's *fading glory* in favor of Athena.

The climax comes in the twelfth labor where Herakles is charged by his mentor, King Eurystheus, with bringing him the golden apples of the Hesperides. The Garden of the Hesperides turned out to be just beyond the place where Atlas stood pushing up the heavens, and the location of the garden was a secret known only to him. Herakles talked Atlas into procuring the golden apples for him. This Atlas did while Herakles temporarily took his place as the elevator of the heavens, with Athena's help. When Atlas returned with the apples, Herakles headed back eastward with them. In his *The Meridian Handbook of Classical Mythology*, Edward Tripp concludes the story:

> **Herakles took the apples to Eurystheus at Tiryns without further interruptions. Eurystheus quickly returned them to Herakles, who as quickly turned them over to Athena, presumably by dedicating them at her shrine. Athena gave them back to their original guardians, the Hesperides, for it was not proper that the sacred fruit should remain in anyone else's keeping.**

The sacred fruit were back where they belonged—in the garden. But the golden apples had changed hands. Originally the apples were a present from Zeus to Hera, from the serpent to Eve. They still belonged to Eve, but not the primal Eve deified as a goddess of marriage and childbirth, but the sophisticated Eve of the new, postdiluvian age deified as Athena. Hera remains the wife of Zeus and is still accorded honor as the queen of heaven, but in the new Greek age, Athena has become the operative wisdom and power of Zeus.

Figure 181: On this vase from ca. 475 BC, Herakles gains control of the two snakes sent by Hera to kill him in his crib. His twin brother, Iphikles, reaches out toward their frightened mother, Alkmene. Athena, with her serpent-trimmed aegis, stands by, calmly extending her left arm over the crib, signifying her protection of Herakles.

Figure 182: Athena, wearing a serpent crown on a pre-Parthenon pedimental sculpture.

Plato wrote that Athena had "the mind of Zeus," and we know Zeus to be the transfigured serpent. Above, we see the head of Athena from the pediment of one of her temples more ancient than the Parthenon. Her crown, a symbol of rule, is a crown of serpents. On that same statue, below, Athena's aegis, as almost always, is serpent-trimmed. In the center of that aegis glared the Gorgon Medusa—the head of serpents. There is no doubt that it is the serpent who ordains Athena's sovereignty and rules her thinking. On the pediment, Athena is in the process of killing a Giant—a Yahweh-believing son of Noah. This is the woman who has the mind of the serpent and conquers in the name of the serpent.

Figure 183: The serpent-crowned Athena kills a Giant.

Let me suggest that the notorious "mother of the prostitutes" mentioned in the Book of Revelation is Athena. Here are verses 17:3-5, which describe a vision of the apostle John:

And I perceived a woman sitting on a scarlet wild beast replete with the names of blasphemy, and having seven heads and ten horns. And the woman was clothed with purple and scarlet, and gilded with gold and precious stones and pearls, having a golden cup in her hand, brimming with abominations and the uncleannesses of the prostitution of her and the earth. And on her forehead is written a name:

Secret
Babylon the Great
the mother of the prostitutes
and the abominations
of the earth.

The prostitution of the woman is not literal, but figurative. She is *spiritually* unfaithful and wanton. And the "mother of the prostitutes;" that is, the mother of all the spiritually unfaithful, is Eve at the moment she disbelieved God and instead believed the serpent.

The woman is sitting on "a scarlet wild beast." The scarlet color associates the wild beast with riches and rule. The Greek word translated "wild beast" is *therion*. In Acts 28:4, a serpent came out of some kindling and fastened onto Paul's hand. It is identified in that passage as a "wild beast" (therion). So the woman sits upon the serpent, which is the basis of her power. The woman sounds like Athena, and the final verse of Chapter 17 seems to confirm it:

"And the woman whom you perceived is the great city which has a kingdom over the kings of the earth."

The woman, Athena, is the city, Athens; and the kingdom over the kings of the earth is a cultural kingdom.

Now it really gets interesting. This written name (the woman's identity), including the fact that it is secret, appears on the woman's forehead. The Greek word for forehead is *metopon*, nearly identical to the word metope that we use to describe the nearly-square sculptures on Classical Greek temples. The Parthenon has a total of ninety-two metopes, with fourteen under the east pediment, which is the front, or forehead, of the building. Athena's idol-image faced this direction. These fourteen metopes depicted the gods defeating the Giants, which as we know, is a picture of Zeus-religion overcoming the righteous (Yahweh-believing) sons of Noah.

In the sight of the Creator, this is one of the main abominations, if not *the* chief abomination, of all "the abominations of the earth." Jesus said to the unbelieving Pharisees in Luke 16:15: "You are those who are justifying yourselves in the sight of men, yet God knows your hearts, for what is high among men is an abomination in the sight of God." The Greeks had elevated their idol-image of the serpent's Eve and her temple to the highest place in their city and memorialized the defeat of the Yahweh-believing sons of Noah in marble on the forehead of her temple. They elevated the serpent and the serpent's system above the Creator of all things in heaven and earth.

The right hand of her Parthenon idol-image holds Nike, which represents both the serpent's victory in the Garden of Eden and the victory over the sons of Noah. Yahweh had condemned the serpent to crawl on its belly, yet all who entered the Parthenon to worship the great statue were forced to look up to both Athena and the serpent. That certainly fits the theme of Revelation 17:3-5. But what of the golden cup said to be in the hand of "the mother of the prostitutes"?

Athena is pictured in several vases, as on the plate below from ca. 480 BC, pouring from her cup into Herakles' wine-drinking cup. This is a great celebration. Herakles is the Athena-led enforcer of Zeus-religion. He wounds Ares, the Seth of Genesis, and kills his sons and daughters. He forces Nereus (Noah) to tell him the location of the serpent's apple tree. He leads the gods in their defeat of the Yahweh-believing sons of Noah. He slays the triple-bodied Geryon who represents the power of Noah's three sons. Athena rewards Herakles for all this and more by pouring him wine from the golden cup which is figuratively "brimming with abominations and the uncleannesses of the [spiritual] prostitution of her and the earth." Athena pours the wine into Herakles' kantharos, a symbol of transformation. The transformation is complete: Zeus-religion has conquered the Yahweh-believing children of Noah.

Figure 184: Athena rewards Herakles.

"Babylon the Great" refers to the place of origin of the serpent- and man-centered religion that the Greeks embraced. Hermes, the Cush of Babylon, is the chief prophet of Zeus-religion. We'll learn more about him, and his place on the east pediment of the Parthenon in Chapter 20.

Chapter 15
Hera—The Primal Eve

Athena is a deification of Eve, but so also is Hera. Hera represents the serpent's Eve before the Flood, and Athena represents the *rebirth* of the serpent's Eve after the Flood.

Zeus and his wife (first known as Dione and then Hera) are deifications of Adam and his wife Eve. Greek myth matches the narrative of Genesis insofar as Eve's creation is concerned. Adam is in paradise, but he is lonely; Yahweh has not yet made "a helper as his complement." And so He set about that work:

And falling is a stupor on the human, caused by Yahweh Elohim, and he is sleeping. And taking is He one of his angular organs and is closing the flesh under it. And Yahweh Elohim is building the angular organ, which He takes from the human, into a woman, and bringing her is He to the human. And saying is the human, "This was once bone of my bones and flesh of my flesh. This shall be called woman, for from her man is this taken."

Figure 185: One of the two temples of Dione, the sister/ wife of Zeus at Dodona, the oldest known site of his worship. Genesis asserts that Eve came out of Adam. Dione is the feminine form of Dios (Zeus), suggesting that they, too, were once a unity.

Therefore a man shall forsake his father and his mother and cling to his wife, and they two become one flesh (Genesis 2:21-24).

The Greek counterpart of this event shows up at the ancient oracle in Dodona in the mountains of Epirus in the north of Greece where, as far as scholars can tell, the Greek worship of Zeus began. According to the cultic myth, a pigeon flying from Egyptian Thebes had lighted on an oak tree at Dodona, and with human voice directed the founding of an oracle of Zeus. By the rustling of the oak's leaves, priests and priestesses divined the will of the god and his wife, Dione. It is her name which reminds us of the creation of Eve, for Dione is the feminine form of Dios, or Zeus. The meaning of the names, identical but for the sex, points to "the moment of lighting up" in Eden, and points to the scriptural idea that the first woman was taken out of the first man to be his complement.

Throughout the rest of Greece, the deification of Eve took the name Hera. She was an ancient pre-Hellenic goddess whose Greek name means "Lady." As Eve immortalized, Hera would, indeed, have to be the preeminent lady. According to Homer, she and Zeus were children of Kronos and Rhea. Rhea is the earth. It is not difficult to see that Adam's "mother" (and therefore Eve's as well) is the earth:

And forming is Yahweh Elohim the human of soil from the ground, and He is blowing into his nostrils the breath of the living, and becoming is the human a living soul (Genesis 2:7).

But who was Kronos? Robert Graves says Kronos means "Crow," and there doesn't seem to be any connection to Eden. We should, then, consider this: the Greek letters kappa (k) and chi (x) sound the same at the beginning of a word;

Figure 186: A young Adam and Eve
by Albrecht Dürer.

Figure 187: A mature Hera and Zeus from
the Temple of Hera at Selinus, ca. 465 BC.

therefore, the Greek word Χρονοσ (Chronos) would sound the same as Kronos. And Chronos, which probably was the original name of the father of Hera and Zeus, means time. It's where we get our word chronology, for example. Yahweh is used hundreds of times in the Hebrew to represent the Supreme God of the Scriptures. It means the Self-Existent One. Yahweh derives from the Hebrew *hâyâh* which has within itself the concepts of past, present, and future—was, is, and will be. Kronos as a misspelling of Chronos could very well be Greek religion's equivalent of Yahweh, the Lord of Time. Zeus is the eldest son of Chronos and Hera is his eldest daughter. As such they are brother and sister.

Adam and Eve are the first couple according to Genesis. Zeus and Hera are the first couple according to Greek myth. Zeus' and Hera's qualities are very, very human. They get angry and resentful. They drink, eat, and party. They become jealous, even furious at times. They make love, and Zeus, in particular, lusts and is unfaithful. In the Greek world, Zeus and Hera are historically and archetypally united as if they were a human pair. The reason for this is obvious: they were originally an actual human pair. They are the original human couple, Adam and Eve, immortalized as the father and mother of all humanity. Understanding this elemental truth of Greek religion, we can say with Paul, Aratus, and Cleanthes, "For of that race also are we." Zeus and Hera are Greek images of our ancestors Adam and Eve.

Figure 188: A wooden loving couple from the island of Samos, ca. 620 BC, height 18 cm. An eagle between their heads, a symbol of the king of the gods, suggests that this is Zeus and Hera—a picture of Adam and Eve, the first couple.

The sacred marriage (*heiros gamos*) of Zeus and Hera according to Greek myth points to their deification as Adam and Eve. The Greeks understood this marriage of their two greatest ancestors to be a prototype of human marriage. The Athenians dedicated the month *Gamelion* (meaning "marriage month") to Hera and sacrificed to her and Zeus *Heraios* (Zeus the husband of Hera). The reenactment of Hera's sacred marriage to Zeus was the most characteristic rite of the goddess in the Greek world. Athenians celebrated it every year on the twenty-sixth of Gamelion.

The problem was that, as a brother and sister union, it violated the strict Greek incest taboo. While on rare occasions children with the same father but different mothers could wed, no Greek bride was allowed to marry a brother who had the same mother as herself. And yet Hera was allowed to transgress this prohibition. Why? Not only does she marry her brother, Zeus, but she becomes the goddess of marriage! Such a marriage is anything but an imitation of human custom—just the reverse—an outright violation of it. The sacred marriage of Zeus and Hera is the one great and shocking exception to the incest taboo.

The marriage of this brother and sister pair doesn't make any sense unless we see it as the reporting of an older mythologem, a story grounded in the reality of the past, a tradition telling the truth about the first couple. The fact that, according to Greek myth, Hera received golden apples as a wedding present from either Earth or Zeus, demands that we look to Eden for the explanation. That is where we find the source of the sacred marriage rite. As the first humans, Adam and Eve were brother and sister. And yet they became husband and wife. The annual celebration and reenactment of the marriage of Zeus and Hera could only have been performed in honor of the original marriage of Adam and his sister Eve.

The Greeks also performed the ritual reenactment of the sacred marriage of Zeus and Hera to ensure fertility. Of course! What more logical pair to propitiate

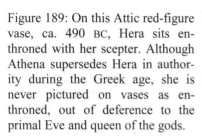

Figure 189: On this Attic red-figure vase, ca. 490 BC, Hera sits enthroned with her scepter. Although Athena supersedes Hera in authority during the Greek age, she is never pictured on vases as enthroned, out of deference to the primal Eve and queen of the gods.

for healthy offspring than the progenitors of the entire race of mankind! Who could ever have more descendants than they?

We can't expect the Greeks to tell the story of Eden in the same way that Genesis does. Their standpoint is different and their sources do not make up a theoretically consistent body of literature. If the Eden story is true, however, we should expect to find bits and pieces of it throughout Greek myth. And we do.

One myth of the "birth" of Zeus says that because of the determination of Chronos to destroy the pregnant Rhea's offspring, she had to flee to Crete in order to save her child Zeus from his wrath. There is a connection between the birth of Zeus (Adam welcoming the serpent's wisdom and his system) and a need to hide from Yahweh. The time and the place are off, but the idea of hiding—associated with shame from the Judeo-Christian viewpoint—is there nonetheless.

Zeus and Hera bickered constantly. Persistent stories of quarrels between the divine pair in myth may reflect the faint memory of the actual state of the marriage of Adam and Eve. They had serious problems with their children (their first-born murdered their second-born) and each undoubtedly could have found good reason to blame the other for the tree incident and the woes that followed.

Myth points directly to Zeus as an image of Adam, and to Hera as an image of the primal Eve. When you stop and think about it, who else could they be?

Figure 190: Hera chafes at the entrance of Herakles into Olympus.

Depicted on the large red-figure mixing bowl from the Classical period, above, and sectional enlargement on the following page, we see Herakles entering Olympus. It is a vase-painting that makes it very easy to explain how Hera and Athena are both deifications of Eve, and to understand the difference between them. Again, let's trust the artist to tell us what Greek religion was about.

On the vase-painting, Herakles, shown naked with his club after having completed his twelve labors, has become immortal and entered Olympus as his reward. Next to him stands his wife Hebe (Youth). An *erotes* hovers between them indicating their love and happiness. Zeus, the king of the gods, looks to Athena and ignores a disgruntled Hera as they welcome Herakles to Olympus. Nike's presence between Zeus and Athena attests to their victory. Hera, hand on hip, looks away from Zeus and Athena in the center toward Hermes with an angry glare, upset with this celebration of Herakles' immortality. But why? The answer is that throughout Herakles' life and labors, Hera opposed him, while Athena assisted him. Hera represents the old order; Athena represents the new. The completion of Herakles' labors represents the reestablishment of the serpent's system after the Flood, and the transfer of power from Hera to Athena.

Eve was the first mother and first wife, deified as Hera, goddess of childbirth and marriage. Athena, as the deification of Eve in the new Greek age, will not marry and will not have children—breaking the curse found in similar forms in

Figure 191: Hera stares at Hermes with a look of blame; and no wonder, for Hermes is the deified Cush from Babylon, the one who is indeed largely responsible for the new order of Zeus-religion after the Flood, an order which pushes Hera into the background in favor of Athena.

Genesis, Hesiod, and Apollodorus. She is the Eve who welcomes and embodies the transfigured serpent's wisdom and power.

As we know from the story of Oedipus, Hera originally controlled the sphinx, a riddle-uttering winged monster with the head of a woman and the body of a lion. By the 5th-century BC when Phidias constructed the great statue of Athena Parthenos, the sphinx and her enigmatic power belonged to Athena, as we know from its image atop her war helmet. Athena's possession of the sphinx shows that her authority supersedes that of Hera. The wings of the sphinx symbolize power in the heavens; the body of the lion, power on earth; and the woman's head represents the mysterious Eve, mother of all living.

Hera and Athena both represent Eve—Eve worshipped in different ways. Mankind originally worshipped Eve as the great mother-goddess of childbirth and marriage. As Greek religion became systematized after the Flood, worship focused on Eve as Athena—the embodiment of the serpent's power and promises. In Genesis, the fruit of the tree was "good for food," brought "a yearning to the eyes," and was "to be coveted as the tree to make one intelligent." It is for embodying this last quality for which Athena, as goddess of the serpent's wisdom, was specifically and especially revered.

Chapter 16
Hephaistos—The Deified Kain

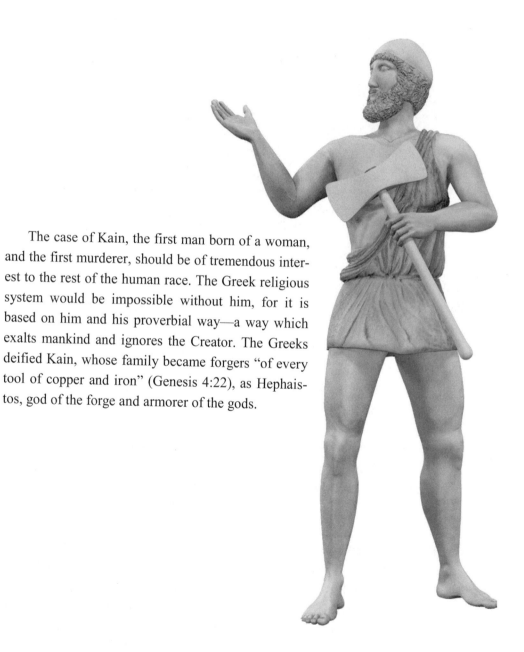

The case of Kain, the first man born of a woman, and the first murderer, should be of tremendous interest to the rest of the human race. The Greek religious system would be impossible without him, for it is based on him and his proverbial way—a way which exalts mankind and ignores the Creator. The Greeks deified Kain, whose family became forgers "of every tool of copper and iron" (Genesis 4:22), as Hephaistos, god of the forge and armorer of the gods.

Figures 192 and 193: The bearded master at the foundry on the Attic black-figure wine jug from ca. 500 BC looks much like the figure of Hephaistos on the Attic red-figure mixing pot from the same period.

We've seen that Greek religion is a sophisticated form of ancestor worship. Zeus is the serpent transfigured into an image of Adam—the head of the race of humanity—and Hera is an image of the primal Eve, the mother of all living. Hephaistos, the eldest son of Zeus and Hera corresponds to Kain, the eldest son of Adam and Eve. According to Genesis, Kain was the first murderer. We must remember, however, that from the point of view of those who embraced the serpent as the enlightener of mankind, Kain was a hero. Through Eve's bold choice, humanity had become liberated at last from the Creator of Eden. Kain's younger brother, Abel, endeavored to reestablish the old order through a blood sacrifice acceptable to his God, while Kain felt pressured to give up a portion of his fruit to a god he did not want running his life. Abel's attempt to reestablish a bond with the God of Genesis was to Kain a step back into bondage. Kain became enraged when he found out that Abel was trying to undo the serpent's work, and so killed him.

By his Roman name, Vulcan, we associate Hephaistos, the deified Kain, immediately with the forge and the foundry. According to Genesis 4:22, the members of Kain's family were the first to become forgers "of every tool of copper and iron." These included the hammer and the axe, the tools most often associated with Hephaistos, the forger of weapons and armor for gods and heroes.

Hephaistos was known as the god who first fashioned axes. He is the god of *techne*, where we, of course, get our word technology. As J. J. Pollitt has pointed out, techne is usually translated as "art" but it means, more precisely, "the orderly application of knowledge for the purpose of producing a specific, predetermined product." It is the techne of Hephaistos that takes humanity from the state of primitive food-gathering and the tending of flocks to the civilized condition. Aeschylus, in his play, *Eumenides*, refers to the Athenians as "the children of Hephaistos." Hephaistos was the deified Kain who had established the first city, and who made the Athenians think of themselves as the most civilized of all human beings.

Figure 194: Kain immortalized as Hephaistos

Greek mythology presents Hephaistos as a cripple from birth, "the renowned lame god," although it is not explained why this is so. This lameness may well be the mark or sign mentioned in Genesis 4:15: "And placing is Yahweh Elohim a sign for Kain, to avoid anyone finding him smiting him."

Since Kain was the eldest son of Eve, we would expect Hephaistos to be the eldest son of the deified primal Eve, Hera. And, indeed, this is so. Zeus, the deified Adam, is his father. One Greek myth suggests that Hera gave birth to Hephaistos parthenogenetically; that is, without the aid of a male god or man. The source of that myth may be found in Genesis, for when Kain was born, Eve spoke in the first person singular, as if Kain were hers alone: "I acquire a man, Yahweh" (Genesis 4:1). Kain, in Hebrew, means "acquired."

After the murder of Abel, Yahweh gave this command to Kain: "a rover and a wanderer shall you become in the earth" (Genesis 4:12). Kain became an outcast, but true to his antipathy toward Yahweh, Kain quickly settled in one place and built the first-ever city which he named after his son, Enoch (Genesis 4:17).

When Kain settled in that city, he ceased being a wanderer and an outcast. This idea comes through in a very important Greek myth as well. Hephaistos was also an outcast for a while. One version says he was thrown out of Olympus by Hera; another version says it was Zeus who threw him out. There came a time, however, when the outcast was welcomed back as part of an emerging order which, instead of exalting the Creator, exalted humanity and the serpent. This is what happened to Kain.

Kain, immortalized as Hephaistos, embraced the serpent's wisdom and through his offspring, systematized belief in it. His figurative cracking open of Zeus' head released Eve's original choice to obey the serpent, and immortalized her as Athena.

Figure 195: The return of Hephaistos to Olympus.

Without Hephaistos, the Deified Kain,
There is no Zeus-Religion

The scene on the Attic red-figure drinking cup from ca. 425 BC (above, and detail on the next two pages) tells us a great deal about how the Greeks viewed Hephaistos. The vase depicts his return to Olympus. It is not clear from Greek myth exactly why he had been thrown out or whether it was Hera or Zeus who did it, but the fact that this myth appeared painted, sculpted, and bronzed throughout the Archaic and Classical periods, tells us that his return to Olympus constituted an essential element of Zeus-religion.

According to the myth, while in exile, Hephaistos sent a golden throne that he had made to his mother, Hera. Once she sat in it, invisible cords bound her to it. On the vase, Hera sits on this golden throne. Playing his double flute, a satyr announces the return of Hephaistos and a female attendant, holding a palmette fan, stands by Hera. A diadem, a symbol of rule, rests on Hera's head, but it is mostly covered with a hood implying that until Hephaistos returns she cannot be free to exercise this rule.

Dionysos, in the center, looks back over his shoulder directly to Hephaistos and beckons him to return with him to Olympus. He displays a kantharos to Hephaistos, suggesting that this wine-drinking cup symbolizes his reward, or what the scene is ultimately about, or both. Hephaistos rides a donkey, carries his hammer and tongs, and follows the lure of the kantharos held up by Dionysos.

What are we to make of this? In all my reading of Greek myths, I have never seen the return of Hephaistos to Olympus explained. That's because it cannot be explained without reference to Kain and Genesis. Keep in mind, as we review some of the early events of Genesis, that a return to Olympus by Hephaistos signifies a return to the authority of the serpent's religious system by Kain.

Now, according to Genesis, after Adam and Eve partook of the forbidden fruit, they became ashamed and then accepted God's provision as a sign of accepting his authority: "And making is Yahweh

Figure 196: Hephaistos returns to Olympus.

Elohim for Adam and for his wife tunics of skin, and is clothing them" (Genesis 3:21). Abel, their youngest son, accepted Yahweh's authority also, but Kain, their eldest, did not. He killed Abel and then defied God's command to wander through the earth as punishment. Kain built a city, settled there, and passed on his defiance to his offspring. From the point of view of Scripture, Kain was "of the wicked one," and "the way of Kain" became a description of behavior opposed to the will and worship of Yahweh Elohim.

Kain's rejection of Yahweh was total. We see this in the names of Kain's immediate offspring. The name of his son, Enoch, means "dedicated," presumably to the ways of his father; the name of his grandson, Irad, means "city suffices;" and the name of his great-grandson, Mehujael, means "wipe out God." When the story of Kain's banishment makes its way into Greek myth, Yahweh no longer even plays a part in it.

Kain's continuous and absolute rejection of Yahweh's ways renewed the serpent's power, and made a virtue of what Eve had done at the serpent's behest. Those who embraced the way of Kain began to idolize Eve's willingness to obey the serpent. From their perspective, Eve's taking of the fruit was the most significant and positive event in the history of humanity. Thus Kain and his line systematized the rejection of Yahweh and set the serpent's wisdom free, ultimately enabling the worship of Kain's mother, Eve, as the queen of the gods.

Figure 197: Hera on her throne.

This is the very message that our vase so succinctly portrays.

To the left, we see Hera seated on the throne given to her by her son Hephaistos. This gift, in itself, shows that Hephaistos (Kain) is in the process of making his mother Hera (Eve) humanity's queen. On the vase, she is poised to rule, but is unable as yet to exercise her authority. Two things had to happen before Hera could take her place as the deified Eve and queen of the gods: first, the God who planted the Garden had to be rejected; and second, what Eve did in the garden—the taking of the fruit making possible the knowledge of good and evil—had to be revered and glorified. Kain and his offspring fulfilled both requirements. And here, on his donkey, comes Hephaistos, the deified Kain, suggesting just that.

In our scene, Hephaistos *is* returning and the hood that symbolizes the covering of Hera's rule *is* receding. We can picture the scene before Hephaistos begins his return—the hood completely covering her crown. And we can picture the scene after the return of Hephaistos is accomplished—Hera's hood shed, her crown glistening, the invisible bonds loosed, and her rule over those who embraced the way of Kain, begun.

The vase shows that it is the promise of the kantharos which entices Hephaistos to return. On one level, it is a symbol of a pleasurable wine-drinking time. But there is a much deeper significance to it. As we have seen, the word kantharos itself means "dung beetle." This religious symbolism comes from Egypt where the dung beetle, or scarab, signifies transformation and immortality. The kantharos here may represent the serpent's promise of immortality: "Not to die shall you be dying . . . in the day you eat of [the tree] unclosed shall be your eyes, and you shall become as gods, knowing good and evil."

When Kain defied Yahweh's command to become a rover and a wanderer in the earth, and established instead a city, he figuratively returned to Olympus—to the realm of Zeus the transfigured serpent—and as his reward, he became immortalized as Hephaistos.

196

We have seen that both Hera and Athena are pictures of the serpent's Eve. Hera is the primal Eve, wife and sister of Zeus, and goddess of childbirth and marriage. Athena is the picture of the more sophisticated Eve, the goddess of the serpent's wisdom, a goddess capable of establishing the rudiments of humanity's central culture in this age, and a goddess capable of ruling the collective mind of that entire culture. It is Hephaistos, the deified Kain, who allows both of these goddesses to take their places of rule, at their respective times. His role in Greek religion is more than important and basic, it is essential. The myth of his return to Olympus and his role in the myth of Athena's birth say so in no uncertain terms: Hera remains bound to her golden throne and cannot rule unless Hephaistos returns to Olympus to release her; and Athena, the reborn serpent's Eve after the Flood, cannot emerge from the mind of Zeus and rule this Greek age unless Hephaistos sets her free with a blow of his axe. In sum, without Hephaistos, without Kain and his way, there is no such thing as Zeus-religion.

Figure 198: The Temple of Hephaistos in Athens on the west side of the agora—the market and meeting place in the center of the city. The Greeks worshipped both Hephaistos and Athena in this temple built from 449 - 444 BC. Ironically, the temple of the "renowned lame god" survives as the least crippled temple in Greece.

Figure 199: A drawing of a bronze relief on a shield band panel from Olympia ca. 550 BC depicting the birth of Athena. The lightning bolt held by Zeus associates "the moment of lighting up"—the actual meaning of the name Zeus—with the birth of Athena. With a blow of his axe, Kain, deified as Hephaistos, initiates the worship of the serpent's Eve as Athena. Eileithyia, a sister of Hephaistos, serves as midwife.

HERMES   ATLAS   THE HESPERIDES   NYX

PART III Section III

The Background of Athena's Birth
The Right Side of the Pediment

The right side of the east pediment tells us where mankind originally came from. Darkness (Nyx), on the far right, departs. The Hesperides, a picture of paradise, come into being. Atlas pushes away the heavens, and with them, the God of the heavens, so that mankind can feast at the serpent's tree. Hermes, the chief prophet of Zeus-religion, connects the ancient paradise and the serpent's tree to the scene in the center, the birth of Athena—the rebirth of the serpent's Eve after the Flood.

Chapter 17
Nyx—The Departing Darkness Out of Which Arose Paradise

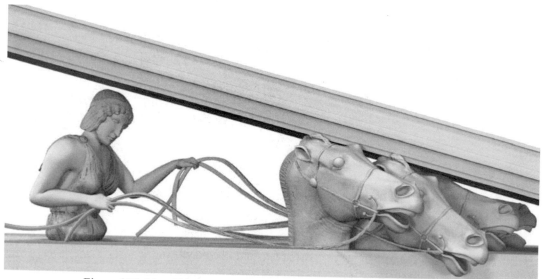

Figure 200: Nyx (Darkness) departs on the far right of the pediment scene.

Zeus' birthing of Athena is the centerpiece of the east pediment; however, that event is not the beginning of the Greeks' figurative account of their origins. The ancient poet Hesiod traces the beginning of the Greek cosmos, or world-system, back to something he calls Chaos. Chaos is not portrayed on the pediment but it is implied for out of Chaos, according to Hesiod, came Nyx, or Darkness, and Nyx is portrayed departing in her four-horse chariot in the right corner of the triangular panorama. Phidias, the chief sculptor, is showing us how, out of Chaos through Darkness (Nyx), order emerged in the Greek view of their world-system.

Nyx . . . bare . . . the Hesperides who guard the rich, golden apples . . . and the ruthless avenging Fates . . . who give men at their birth both evil and good to have . . .

Hesiod, *Theogony*

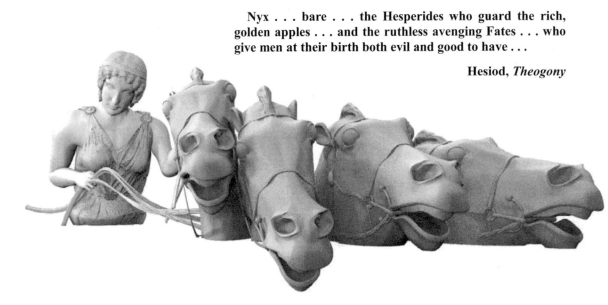

Figure 201: Nyx (Darkness) and her exhausted horses depart the scene.

Hesiod's account of creation does not reach back beyond Chaos to the "Created by God [Elohim] were the heavens and the earth" in Genesis, but begins with Chaos itself, out of which emerged Nyx or Darkness. Out of Nyx emerged the Hesperides, nymphs of the West representing a luxurious and carefree garden, and the Three Fates representing death. According to Hesiod, the Fates "give men at their birth both evil and good to have." Thus, just as in Genesis, the knowledge of good and evil is associated with the beginning of the experience of death for humanity.

On the pediment, Nyx departs. She leaves behind the Hesperides who appear next to her on the pediment and the Three Fates who appear in a corresponding spot on the opposite side of the pediment, setting the stage for the earth-shaking drama in the center—Eve's taking the fruit from the tree of the knowledge of good and evil, her figurative birth from the head of the transfigured serpent.

As we will see from the comparisons on page 204, Greek myth and Genesis tell essentially the same story. These elements are the same: chaos, darkness, a serpent, a fruit tree, the knowledge of good and evil, and death.

The east pediment sculptures are narrative art: they tell a story. Nyx tells us when the crucial event—the taking of the fruit—took place. Nyx is departing, so our scene is set after her departure, at the time the Garden of the Hesperides existed, and more specifically, at the time the Three Fates, representing death, came into being.

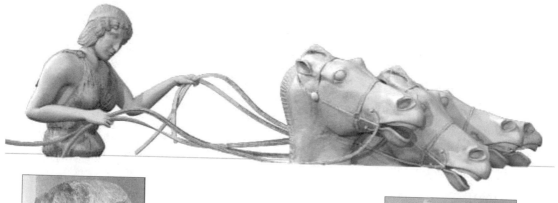

Figure 202, above: Nyx or Darkness.
Figure 203, left: The surviving torso
(N) of the charioteer Nyx.
Figure 204, right: The outer horse (O)
of the four-horse chariot
belonging to Nyx.

Many Parthenon scholars are undecided whether Figure N and her horses in the right corner of the east pediment represent Selene (the Moon), or Nyx (Night or Darkness). From an astronomical point of view, Kristian Jeppesen has explained why it cannot be Selene. He writes in his "Evidence for the Restoration of the East Pediment Reconsidered in the Light of Recent Achievements," a contribution to the *Parthenon Kongress*:

> **Strictly speaking, Selene sinking at the same time as Helios is rising [on the pediment's far left] implies that the moon is in direct opposition to the Sun and therefore full. However, this happens only in the middle of the [lunar] month, while according to ancient sources the birth of Athena took place on the 3rd or on the 28th of the month, that is, either when the new moon had just begun to increase or when the waning moon had nearly disappeared. On both days, the moon was seen at a distance of only some 20 or 30 degrees from the Sun. If, therefore, the birth is supposed to have taken place on one of these days, figure N must logically be assumed to represent Nyx rather than Selene.**

There is an even better reason that this is not Selene, but rather Nyx. According to Hesiod, Chaos was the beginning of the Greek cosmos, or world-system, and Nyx came out of Chaos. Out of Nyx came the Hesperides and the Three Fates, and both of these groupings are found sculpted on the east pediment, and they relate directly to the birth of Athena.

Greek Myth . . . Compared to Genesis

Hesiod, *Theogony*	*Genesis*
	Created by God [Elohim] were the heavens and the earth.
In truth at first Chaos came to be . . .	Yet the earth became a chaos and vacant . . .
From Chaos came forth Erebus (the covered pit) and black Night (Nyx) . . .	And darkness was on the surface of the submerged chaos.
And again the goddess murky Night [Nyx], though she lay with none, bare . . . the Hesperides who guard the rich, golden apples and the trees bearing fruit beyond glorious Ocean.	And planting is Yahweh Elohim [the Lord God] a garden in Eden . . . sprouting is Yahweh Elohim from the ground every tree coveted by the sight and good for food, . . . and the tree of the knowledge of good and evil.
Also [Nyx] bore the Destinies and ruthless avenging Fates, Clotho and Lachesis and Atropos, who give men at their birth both evil and good to have.	. . . "Yet from the tree of the knowledge of good and evil, you are not to be eating from it, for in the day you eat from it, to die shall you be dying."
Apollodorus	
[The apples of the Hesperides] were presented by Earth to Zeus after his marriage with Hera, and were guarded by an immortal dragon.	And taking is [Eve at the serpent's urging] of its fruit and is eating, and she is giving, moreover, to her husband with her, and they are eating.

Greek and Hebrew Post-Creation Stories Match

The parallelism of the Greeks' account of the origin of the cosmos with that of Genesis has been obscured for centuries by mistranslations in the King James Version. One mistranslation obscures the fact that Darkness (Nyx) came out of Chaos—just as the Greeks said. Verses one and two of chapter one of Genesis in the King James Version read:

In the beginning God created the heaven and the earth.
And the earth was without form, and void; and darkness was upon the face of the deep. And the Spirit of God moved upon the face of the waters.

Common sense tells us that there is something very wrong with this translation. Try to picture an earth without form. If you are an artist or have an artist friend, ask him or her to draw you a sketch of an earth without form or an earth that is void. You can't picture it and you can't sketch it because it doesn't make any sense. The Concordant translation of those same verses of Genesis clears up the problem:

Created by Elohim [God] were the heavens and the earth.
Yet the earth became a chaos and vacant, and darkness was on the surface of the submerged chaos. Yet the spirit of the Elohim is vibrating over the surface of the water.

We can picture an earth that *became* a chaos and vacant, and we can even sketch such an earth, and most importantly, that translation agrees with the original Hebrew.*

The Concordant rendering of Isaiah 45:18 also shows that God did not create the earth "without form and void":

For thus says Yahweh, Creator of the heavens,
He is the Elohim, and Former of the earth, and its Maker,
And He, He established it.
He did not create it a chaos.
He formed it to be indwelt.

---

*If the Hebrew verb were *eue*, "was" would be an accurate translation; but it is *eie*, the causative form of be which means become. This causative form (*eie*) appears more than twenty times in chapter one of Genesis alone, and everywhere denotes a change, and not mere existence. (This analysis is the work of A. E. Knoch).

Then ten times in the New Testament, the King James Version mistranslates the Greek word *katabole* as foundation. *Kata* means down, and it comes into English in such words as cataclysm and catastrophe. *Bole* means casting or throwing. Together they mean down-casting. The whole word comes into English as catabolism which means "the breaking down of complex bodies." Katabole is in reality a disruption and is translated that way throughout the accurate and consistent *Concordant Literal New Testament*. The New Testament verses which contain the word katabole, such as Ephesians 1:4 which speaks of believers in Christ as having been chosen in Him "before the *disruption* of the world," refer directly to the disruption which caused the chaos and darkness after the initial creation of the heavens and the earth by God.

Thus, Scripture does not say how much time was involved with Yahweh's original creation of the heavens and the earth. A true reading reveals that in six days, Yahweh is said to have *restored* the disrupted and chaotic earth.

The point is that when we compare the original texts, we find important connections between the Hebrew and Greek accounts of the origin of things. Hesiod says out of Chaos came Nyx, or Darkness. A true rendering of Genesis 1:2 says basically the same thing: the earth became a chaos, and then there was darkness on the surface of that chaos.

Out of the darkness, Yahweh made light, restored the chaotic earth, and created Eden and Adam and Eve; then death became a part of the human experience. Leaving Yahweh out of the picture, Hesiod says essentially the same thing: out of Chaos came Darkness (Nyx); out of Nyx came the Hesperides (a collective iconograph representing paradise) and then the Three Fates who administer death to humanity.

When we break it down to the basics, we see how very close is the order of events in the two accounts. Genesis says that God creates all, then:

Chaos-Darkness-Paradise-Death-Flood

The Greek account leaves out the Creator but the rest is the same:

Chaos-Darkness-Paradise-Death-Flood

The collective cultural memory of the Greeks as to the main events following creation thus matches what is written in the Sacred Scrolls of the Hebrews. It's basically the same story. Now let's take a look at the sculptors' depiction of the ancient paradise on the east pediment of the Parthenon.

Chapter 18

The Hesperides—A Picture of Paradise

Figure 205: K, L, and M restored.

Figure 206: K, L, and M in the British Museum, London.

The three female figures known as K, L, and M are Hesperides, nymphs of the West, whose presence in Greek art is always associated with their garden and a tree with a serpent coiled around it. Their posture suggests a luxurious setting and a state of continuous enchantment and bliss. The Hesperides form a collective iconograph which depicts paradise—what we call the Garden of Eden.

Throughout ancient Greek art, we find an apple tree with three or more golden apples and a serpent wrapped around its trunk. We think of Eden, and rightly so. The spirit-beings associated with this tree and its apples are called Hesperides, a name which means "nymphs of the West." *Hespere* means evening, and that of course signifies the West where the sun sets. This accords with the Genesis account which describes civilization developing to the east of Eden. A trek back to the garden would necessitate traveling west. The Greeks put the Garden of the Hesperides in the Far West.

The existence of the garden and the idea of Herakles obtaining the three apples from its serpent-entwined tree and presenting them to Athena is extremely important in Greek iconography. Depictions of this subject appear on a metope over the entrance to the temple of Zeus at Olympia (See Fig. 241, page 237), inside Zeus's temple on a painting, sculpted next to an image of Athena in Hera's temple at Olympia, carved therein on the cedar wood chest of Kypselos, on a metope on the temple of Hephaistos in Athens (See Fig. 13, page 23), and on numerous red- and black-figure vases from the Archaic and Classical periods. Phidias, the chief artist and sculptor of the Parthenon, featured the Garden of the Hesperides very prominently on the east pediment.

As far as I know, the first person to identify K-L-M as Hesperides was Kristian Jeppesen at the Parthenon Kongress in Basel in 1982. He writes of K-L-M:

Apparently they are not involved in any kind of willful action, but seem to display some slight amazement at being disturbed in the act of performing their morning toilet. This situation agrees perfectly with representations of the Hesperides on vases, where they are always depicted as lovely fairies with little other concern than the preservation of their beauty.

We've seen in Chapter 2 that some of their names mean Golden Order, Star Face, Health, Shining Skin, Dazzling Light, Red Land, Evening Star and Water Fountain. Their names, their body language, and their easy actions establish what kind of a garden this is: a wonderful, carefree place. It is the original paradise. And no, the Greeks did not borrow a copy of Genesis from the Jews to come up with this: it was rather part of the Greek collective cultural memory. They knew that their original ancestors came from a place like this.

On the red-figure water pot from ca. 465 BC, opposite top, Herakles, wearing his familiar lion-skin headdress, makes off with the three golden apples of the Hesperides. They have no power to stop him; their presence simply identifies the scene as paradise. Note that the serpent wears a beard, a symbol of age. The Book of Revelation refers to God's Adversary as "the ancient serpent." On Figure 208, the Hesperides grace a Greek woman's cosmetics container.

Figure 207: Herakles has at last obtained the sacred apples from the serpent's tree.

Figure 208: The Hesperides depicted on a cosmetics container.

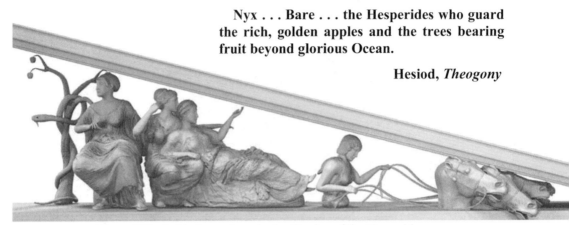

Nyx . . . Bare . . . the Hesperides who guard the rich, golden apples and the trees bearing fruit beyond glorious Ocean.

Hesiod, *Theogony*

Figure 209: As Darkness departs, the Garden of the Hesperides appears.

Above, we see the restoration (from right to left) of Nyx, the Hesperides, and the serpent encoiled tree. The Hesperides occupy cornice blocks 20, 21, and 22. In Greek art, they are always represented with the tree, and it must have appeared on cornice block 19, to their proper right. This particular block was replaced in Roman times and bears no traces of the sculptures it carried. If the attribution of the marble fragments traditionally ascribed to Athena's olive tree in the west pediment holds true, the tree of the Hesperides—the tree of the knowledge of good and evil—is also likely to have been sculpted in marble.*

Figure 210: On one side of this perfume vase, an Hesperid feeds the serpent; on the other side, an Hesperid picks the apples for Herakles.

*Credit to Kristian Jeppesen.

Figure 211: Herakles in the Garden of the Hesperides, ca. 410 BC.

A Greek Artist Uses One of the Parthenon Hesperides as a Model for His Own Vase-Painting of the Subject

In Figure 211 above, we see the serpent, the tree, two Hesperides, Herakles to our right, and Hephaistos to our left. In Hephaistos, the deified Kain, we have the one who systematized belief in the serpent's wisdom before the Flood. In Herakles, the deified Nimrod, we have the man who, through force of arms, overcame Nereus/Noah and the line of Seth after the Flood and, with the aid of Hermes and Athena, re-systematized belief in the serpent's wisdom.

The artist created the vase-painting after the Parthenon sculptures were complete. The lounging Hesperid in the center, resting her left hand comfortably on the serpent, looks very much like the lounging Hesperid, known as M, on the east pediment of the Parthenon (inset). Note the widely-spread breasts and the thin draw-string around the waist. It seems certain that the vase-artist based the central figure in his painting on the sculpted Hesperid from the east pediment of the Parthenon.

211

Figure 212: Four views of the restored Hesperides on the east pediment.

Chapter 19

Atlas Pushes away the Heavens, and with Them, the God of the Heavens

Figure 213: Atlas takes his place in the Garden of the Hesperides.

Above we see Atlas, the Hesperides, and Nyx. As Nyx departs the scene, she leaves behind her offspring, the Hesperides, always depicted in Greek art with the serpent-entwined tree. Next to them, we find Atlas, for according to Hesiod, Zeus himself has placed him there, standing "at the borders of the earth before the clear-voiced Hesperides." The raking cornice represents the skyline or heaven. By lifting here, Atlas enables Zeus, the transfigured serpent, to stand at the apex of the triangle—the center of Greek religion.

When Ludwig Ross dug around the foundations of the Parthenon in 1836, he found, among other fragments of sculptures lying beneath the east front, only one piece which in his opinion might possibly have fallen from the pediment: a male torso preserved from neck and shoulders to the hips (Fig. 215, opposite). Because of the find-spot, the heavy weathering, and indications on the neck that the head was turned a little to the right, the torso is commonly attributed to the right side of the east pediment. The muscular tension [of the sculpture known as Figure H] springs from great physical effort: both arms are raised, the left hip is placed higher, the neck turns to its proper right. The comparatively small scale of the statue necessitates its placement far from the center and therefore at some distance from Zeus.*

Experts from the Institute of Anatomy at the University of Aarhus in Denmark helped Kristian Jeppesen with this technical anatomical analysis of the torso known as Figure H:

The right arm is raised a little more than the left one, as shown by the deltoid muscle. The poise of the head is stooping. The right thigh is almost on a line with the side of the body, while the direction of the left thigh deviates markedly from the axis of the trunk, as indicated by the swelling musculus obliquus externus abdominis on the left side of the torso. That the muscles of the right arm were more tensely activated than those of the left arm is confirmed by the contraction of the trapezoid muscle on the right side of the spine. The sharp dividing line separating the upper and lower musculus rectus abdominis and the deep linia semilunaris on the lower abdomen are obvious signs of physical exertion that cause the lungs to gasp for breath. The contraction of the shoulder blades seems excessive but actually corresponds to an intermediate position.

In Figure 217, opposite, a live model trained in body building poses in an attitude comparable to that of the restored torso.

Figure 214: From right to left: Nyx, the Hesperides, and Atlas.

*From the writings of Olga Palagia and Kristian Jeppesen.

Figure 215: The muscular torso called Figure H discovered beneath the east front of the Parthenon in 1836.

Figure 216: Atlas, three-quarter view.

Figure 217: Body-builder shows the position the strained muscles of the torso (H) would have put him in on the pediment.

Figure 218: Atlas, front view.

Atlas is a Picture of Adam Prior to His Eating the Fruit—and of Mankind in General

Atlas presents us with a picture, from the Greek point of view, of Adam in the Garden of Eden just prior to his eating of the forbidden fruit. Before he could eat of the tree of the knowledge of good and evil, Adam had to put God and the strict spirituality of His law at a distance. In that sense he became the "elevator of the heavens," enabling himself to feel as if heaven were afar off from earth, and to act as if the God of the heavens could not see through the clouds, or did not regard with displeasure one who would flout His instructions.

According to Robert Graves, Atlas means "he who dares," or "he who suffers." Both definitions point to Adam since by eating the forbidden fruit, he was one who dared and as a consequence, became one who suffered. But Atlas is more than simply a picture of Adam: he represents Greek humanity as a whole making room for the gods they believe they are choosing to worship.

Greek religion is the system of Zeus—the transfigured serpent. Athena is the serpent's Eve and goddess of its wisdom. The Supreme God of the heavens has no place in this system. For Greek religion to prosper, mankind must keep pushing away the heavens and the God of the heavens. And the Greeks kept pushing until they lost the knowledge of What they were pushing away and why they were doing it. This is memorialized in this previously cited passage from the Book of Acts:

Now Paul, standing in the center of the Areopagus [the Hill of Ares west of the Akropolis], averred, "Men! Athenians! On all sides am I beholding how unusually religious you are. For, passing through and contemplating the objects of your veneration, I found a pedestal also, on which had been inscribed, 'To an Unknown God.' " (Acts 17:22-23).

It isn't that Greek religion excoriates the Creator, or makes Him into a hated "other," but rather that Zeus, Athena, and the rest of the gods obscure His memory and take His place.

Nyx, the Hesperides, and Atlas share an intimate association in Greek myth. In the Far West of the world, Atlas stands before the "clear-voiced Hesperides" who originated in Nyx. We've seen that the greatest of Greek heroes, Herakles, also had an intimate connection to the Hesperides and Atlas. In Chapter 22, we'll examine that connection in more detail and Herakles' special place on the left side of the east pediment. But first we'll take a look at how the chief sculptor, Phidias, used Hermes to connect this background scene on the right side with the scene of Athena's birth in the center.

216

> **And Atlas through hard constraint upholds the wide heaven with un-wearying head and arms, standing at the borders of the earth before the clear-voiced Hesperides; for this lot wise Zeus assigned to him.**
>
> Hesiod, *Theogony*

Figure 219: A section of a damaged Attic red-figure vase, ca. 490 BC, with part of a scene in the Garden of the Hesperides. We can make out Herakles, most of the serpent, about half the tree, and half of the muscular body of Atlas as he elevates the heavens.

Figure 220: On this bronze relief shield band panel from about 550 BC, Atlas resumes pushing away the heavens after Herakles had taken his place so that Atlas could obtain the apples for him. Herakles will give them to Athena. Before the Flood, Atlas pushed away the heavens so that the way of Kain could develop. After the Flood, Herakles pushed away the heavens so that Zeus-religion could develop.

Chapter 20

Hermes—The Deified Cush Connects Eden with the Rebirth of the Serpent's Eve

Figure 221: Hermes, Atlas, the Hesperides, and Nyx.

As the deified Cush, the high priest of rebellion in Babylon, Hermes links what happened in the ancient paradise (Atlas and the Hesperides) to the central scene of the pediment. For the birth of Athena is in reality the rebirth of the serpent's Eve after the Flood, and Hermes is instrumental in bringing about that rebirth and the accompanying religious rites.

On the east pediment, as in virtually all of his depictions on vases, Hermes carried his kerykeion, or staff with a two-headed serpent. One head looked to the past while the other looked to the future. Hermes also undoubtedly wore his *petasos*, or traveling cap. Hermes traveled around the ancient world spreading Zeus-religion.

Hermes is the son of the friendly Kentaur, Chiron (Ham in Genesis), and the father of Herakles (the Nimrod of Genesis).

Figure 222: By perching the dove on the phallus of Hermes over an altar, the vase-artist insists that the religious orientation of humanity after the Flood is defined by Hermes, the Cush of Babylon, and his powerful seed or son, Herakles, the Nimrod of Genesis.

A Greek Artist Gives Noah's Dove to Hermes/Cush

In Genesis 8:8-12, Noah sends out a dove from the ark three times "to see if the waters are slight over the surface of the ground." The first time, the dove finds no place to land because "water is on the surface of the entire earth." Seven days later, Noah sends it out again. That evening, the dove returns with a "torn-off olive leaf in its beak! And knowing is Noah that the waters are slight above the earth." Seven days later, Noah sends out the dove again and it does not return. As a sign of the new age after the Flood, the dove became a symbol of great significance in the ancient world. Where the dove would land for the third time became very important.

That helps us understand the bizarre vase-depiction in Figure 222. Hermes' phallus stretches across a flaming sacrificial altar as the dove lands on the head of it. This is not intended as an erotic scene at all. The altar lets us know that this has to do with the success of a certain religious orientation. An erect penis is what transfers the seed of mankind from one generation to another. By perching the dove on the phallus of Hermes, the artist is telling us that the spirit of this post-Flood age belongs to the seed of Hermes. Hermes, the deified Cush, and chief prophet of Zeus-religion, was the one who defined this system of worship and sacrifice. And the most important and powerful "seed" of Cush was his son Nimrod, the Herakles of Zeus-religion.

Figure 223: Hermes connects the ancient paradise to the central scene.

The right side of the east pediment explains the background of Athena's birth. Moving from the right corner toward the center: first, there was Darkness (Nyx) and out of it came paradise (the Hesperides, the tree, and serpent); then mankind (Atlas) pushed away the heavens and with them, the God of the heavens, so that humans might partake of the serpent's fruit and become as gods knowing good and evil.

But then came the Great Flood with all of humanity wiped out save the family of righteous (Yahweh-believing) Noah. The Greeks sculpted their interpretation of this event on the west pediment of the Parthenon. In the succeeding generations, Noah's grandson, Cush, deified by the Greeks as Hermes, reconnected a large portion of humanity to the serpent's enlightenment and promises from the time of the Garden of Eden. As such, Cush took a preeminent place in the postdiluvian world, and ultimately in the Greek religious system as Hermes. According to L. H. Martin, he was the "implementer of Zeus' will, or that of the celestial Olympians collectively, among the inhabited world."

Hermes, like many of the gods in the Greek pantheon, was the deification of a dead human being. He is Cush, the son of Ham, and the grandson of Noah. Cush was the man who founded Babylon, and led the effort to unite humanity—without Yahweh—in the building of the infamous tower there. Cush, or Hermes, was the great soothsayer and prophet worshipped in Babylon. Pausanias wrote that he was referred to as Hermes *Agetor*, meaning "Leader of Men."

The Greeks recognized Hermes as the author of their religious rites, and the interpreter of the gods. They understood him to be the grand agent in that movement which produced the division of tongues—they called him the "divider of the speeches of men." According to Plato, Hermes invented language and speech. Hermes in Greek means *translator*. From Hermes, we derive our word hermeneutics which is the science or art of language interpretation. This points us directly to Babylon and the Tower of Babel, where the tongues of mankind were divided, and from then on, an interpreter or translator was required.

In Hermes' Greek genealogy, we find his qualifications to promote the serpent's system. His father was Zeus and his mother was Maia. Being "fathered"

by Zeus meant that he sought after and welcomed the serpent's wisdom and promises. Maia's father was Atlas, the man who pushed away the heavens, and with them, the God of the heavens. Fathered by the transfigured serpent and descended on his mother's side from an archtypal man who pushed away the God of Eden, Hermes had excellent credentials for the job of chief messenger of Zeus.

He was also Hermes *Psychopompus*, literally "the Conductor of Souls" who led humans to the underworld after death. The realm of the dead is the realm of the past, and Hermes was Greek humanity's link with their past. As the god of boundaries, he was naturally able to cross what was for humans the biggest boundary of them all. Zeus had accorded only to Hermes of all the gods, free access to all three worlds—Olympus, Earth, and the Underworld. Thus Hermes, the deified Cush, was the link between the Greek present, humanity's past, and the deified ancestors of the Greek pantheon.

A Herm, like the one pictured on this page, was a rectangular column with a head of the god Hermes at the top and a phallus halfway up. These ubiquitous sculptures stood upon the thresholds of homes and estates, at the gateways of

Figure 224: A Herm.

towns and cities, before temples and gymnasia, at crossroads, along the side of roadways, at the frontiers of territories and upon tombs. The phallus here was not a sexual symbol, but rather an attestation of human seed, of source, of generation, and of origins. The message of the phallus: Zeus-religion, the basis of their civilization, issued forth from Hermes. The most famous Herm was carved by Alkamenes and stood at the entrance to the Akropolis where the sacred precinct began. The ancient travel writer, Pausanias, wrote that a revered wooden Herm stood in a temple on the Akropolis itself. Both of these Herms pointed to the fact that the religious rites performed on the sacred rock of Athens owed their origin to Hermes, the deified Cush of Babylon. At the highest point of their city, the Athenians built a temple, and inside it, a gigantic gold and ivory image elevating Eve to the status of a great and immortal goddess because she had defied the Creator and given to mankind the knowledge of good and

Figure 225: Kekrops, the serpent's man, and legendary first king of Athens, looked to Hermes and Babylon for his religious understanding.

evil. And they adored Hermes on their sacred rock for bringing them Zeus-religion. In Babylon, mankind built a city and a tower; in Greece, mankind built a city and a temple to Athena elevated to the supreme heights. Both cities expressed the same idea: man, not God, is the measure of all things.

The legendary first king of Athens, the half-man/half-serpent (the serpent's man) Kekrops, sacrificed to Hermes (Fig. 225, above). This means that he looked to Hermes as his religious guide. The fact that Kekrops looked to Hermes and Babylon makes perfect sense. That's where the belief structure of Zeus-religion originated. A Greek legend tells that Hermes married a daughter of Kekrops. This may or may not

Figure 226: Hermes explains to Nereus/Noah that the time of his rule is over.

be literally true; it may mean that Hermes figuratively became Kekrops' son-in-law; that is, Kekrops and the Athenians welcomed Hermes and his religious standpoint into their family. Hermes is the "Translator" from the Tower of Babel. Zeus-religion is the spiritual philosophy of Hermes, translated into Greek.

Greek artists had a way of breaking down their message to the basics. On the vase in Figure 226, Hermes explains to Nereus/Noah that everything has changed. He is in charge now and humanity is headed in a different direction.

HELIOS   HERAKLES   THE THREE FATES   NIKE

PART III Section IV

The Power and Promise of Athena's Birth
The Left Side of the Pediment

What did the Greeks believe that Athena, Zeus, Herakles, and the rest of the gods of Zeus-religion had achieved for mankind? We find the answer on the left side of the pediment.

Chapter 21

Helios—The Rising Sun Heralds the Birth of Athena and the New Greek Age

Figure 227: Helios rising out of the ocean and through the pediment floor.

Helios, the personification of the sun, rises through the waters covering the earth to herald a glorious new age after the Flood for Greece and the gods. His light illuminates the immortal hero Herakles, the Nike (Victory) of Athena and Zeus, and the triumphant birth of Athena herself.

As [Helios] rides in his chariot, he shines upon men and deathless gods, and piercingly he gazes with his eyes from his golden helmet. Bright rays beam dazzlingly from him, and his bright locks streaming from the temples of his head gracefully enclose his far-seen face: a rich, fine-spun garment glows upon his body and flutters in the wind: and stallions carry him. Then, when he has stayed his golden-yoked chariot and horses, he rests there upon the highest point of heaven, until he marvelously drives them down again through heaven to Ocean.

From the Homeric *Hymn to Helios*

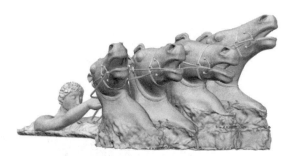

Figure 228: Helios rises out of the Ocean

Figure 229: The remnants of Helios and two of his four horses; and Figure 230: Close-up of the surviving horse-head. British Museum, London.

Homer's *Hymn to Helios*, above, describes the god generally while Homer's *Hymn to Pallas Athen*a, opposite, puts Helios right there at Athena's birth. This information is very helpful since Pausanias has told us that "all the figures . . . relate to the birth of Athena." How so with the personification of the sun? Helios stops "his swift-footed horses a long while" until Athena is able to shed her armor, signifying that the battle is over and her victory is complete. Notice how the surviving horse-head rears back as if stopping—as if depicting that very passage from Homer. Helios shines toward the center of the pediment showing Athena's birth, a birth presaging a new and bright day for the rule of Zeus-religion.

I begin to sing of Pallas Athena, the glorious goddess, bright-eyed, inventive, unbending of heart, pure virgin, saviour of cities, courageous, Tritogeneia. Wise Zeus himself bare her from his awful head, arrayed in warlike arms of flashing gold, and awe seized all the gods as they gazed. But Athena sprang quickly from the immortal head and stood before Zeus who holds the aegis, shaking a sharp spear: great Olympus began to reel horribly at the might of the bright-eyed goddess, and earth round about cried fearfully, and the sea was moved and tossed with dark waves, while foam burst forth suddenly: the bright Son of Hyperion [Helios] stopped his swift-footed horses a long while, until the maiden Pallas Athena had stripped the heavenly armour from her immortal shoulders. And wise Zeus was glad.

From the Homeric *Hymn to Pallas Athene*

Figure 231: Helios steers the solar chariot in this 5th-century BC vase-painting. The young boys leaping before him represent the stars fading in the light of day.

Figure 232: Views of Helios rising out of the water.

Chapter 22
The Immortal Herakles—Nimrod Transplanted to Greek Soil

Figure 233: Herakles basks in the light of Helios.

The Greek sculptors positioned the immortal Herakles so that he might be the first to bathe in the bright light from Helios. Herakles is the Greek counterpart of Nimrod, the great benefactor of humanity in Genesis who, through sheer power and force of arms, reestablished the way of Kain after the Flood. Herakles earned his place on Olympus by overcoming the worshippers of the God of Noah and his three sons, and instituting the serpent's system through the worship of Zeus and Athena. Unlike the Adam of Genesis, Herakles is not ashamed of his nakedness.

Figure 234: Herakles in the British Museum, London.

Figure 235: Herakles restored with his club and kantharos.

Figure 236: Athena presents the reclining, immortal Herakles with a rose.

The Feasting Herakles

The east pediment figure known as D is the immortal Herakles. He reclines in the position of one enjoying a feast on a rock, suggesting pleasure on Mount Olympus. A feline pelt is spread over the rock, undoubtedly his lion skin. The fact that it is under him and not worn by him, indicates his labors are complete. He most likely held his club, his most recognizable attribute, in his right hand. He appears youthful because as a reward for his service to Zeus and Athena, he has received Hebe, the goddess of youth, as his wife.

Scholars agree that D's reclining position suggests a man enjoying a feast, and they often restore a kantharos in one of his hands as a symbol of an enjoyable wine-drinking time. Herakles was certainly one inclined toward soulish pleasures, but as we have seen, the kantharos means much more. The word itself means "dung beetle" referring to the Egyptian scarab, signifying transformation and immortality. On the red-figure storage vase from ca. 520 BC, above, Herakles feasts as Athena presents him with a rose. The reclining position represents the epitome of earthly enjoyment, and thus a similar pose on the Parthenon suggests the beginning of the endless pleasures of immortality.

Figures 237 and 238: Nimrod depicted in Assyria and Greece.

Herakles is the Nimrod of Genesis

The labors of Herakles contain clear reminiscences of an earlier Mesopotamian tradition that connects directly to the great hunter and conqueror, Nimrod, in Genesis. Archaeological evidence from that region shows that the figure of Herakles/Nimrod is found as early as the middle of the 3rd millennium BC. On the Assyrian seal impression from the 9th-century BC, above left, we see the Assyrian king in single combat with a lion. Above right, on an 8th century BC tripod from Athens, it is now Herakles who kills the lion.

Nimrod was the great-grandson of Noah, the grandson of Ham, and the son of Cush. We read in Genesis 10: 8-9:

And Cush generates Nimrod. He starts to become a master in the earth. He becomes a master hunter before Yahweh Elohim. Therefore is it being said, "As Nimrod, the master hunter before Yahweh."

After the Flood, God's powerful operations remained fresh in the minds of humanity. For a considerable period of time, the descendants of Noah were content to live on the same level with their neighbors, and though every man bare rule in his own house, no man pretended any further. That changed with Nimrod who was determined to lord his great strength and cunning over his neighbors.

Nimrod became a great hunter and benefactor of the men and women who were terrified by roaming wild animals after the Flood. This required great courage and adroitness, and thus gave an opportunity for Nimrod to command others, and gradually attach a number of devoted followers to himself. From such a beginning, Nimrod began to rule, and made others submit. He invaded his

234

Figure 239: A Greek vase-artist depicts Herakles (the Mighty One) conquering the Egyptians.

neighbors' rights and properties endeavoring to make all his own by force and violence. These were the same things Herakles did.

Nimrod was the first to organize an army, build walled cities, and establish himself as king. Not content with delivering men from the fear of wild beasts, he set to work also to emancipate them from the fear of the God of Noah. The Book of Genesis says the *beginning* of Nimrod's kingdom was "Babel and Erech and Accad and Calneh, in the land of Shinar." Legend says he ultimately conquered the known world. On the Greek vase, above, from the Archaic period, an artist shows Herakles conquering the Egyptians. Even as eagle-winged and bold as Nimrod's ambitions were, ultimately his accomplishments in life dwarfed them.

The Assyrian tradition and Genesis make Nimrod the first great hunter/ warrior after the Flood. The Greek tradition calls that man Herakles. Herakles' given name was Alcaeüs which means "Mighty One." Herakles and Nimrod are the same historical figure seen through different cultural lenses.

Herakles Overcomes the Rule of Noah's Three Sons

Greek artists depicted the sons of Noah as a three-bodied man called Geryon, a name that relates directly to the patriarch. Except for the addition of one vowel in the center, it's the same as Geron, which means Old Man, a description repeatedly applied to Nereus, the Greek Noah.

Herakles' specific mission in his tenth labor was to obtain the cattle of three-bodied Geryon. These cattle symbolized the wealth of Noah's three sons. Herakles took the cattle, and in the process, killed a herdsman, his dog and the three-bodied Geryon.

Figure 240: On this black-figure vase from ca. 550 BC, Herakles kills the dog, Orthos, his master, Eurytion, and moves forward to overpower the three-bodied Geryon, representing the authority of the three sons of Noah.

The Message at the Entrance to the Temple of Zeus at Olympia

On the temple of Zeus at Olympia, twelve 1.6 meter square metopes, six over the east entrance and six over the west, depicted the twelve labors of Herakles. The metopes shown on the opposite page are numbers three and four on the east side, making them the ones in the center just above the sacred entrance. Thus, they had a very special meaning to the ancient Greeks. The one to the left depicts Herakles killing the triple-bodied Geryon. The one to the right shows Atlas bringing the three golden apples from the tree in the Garden of the Hesperides to Herakles who, aided by Athena, upholds the heavens. Both metopes have to do with the question of spiritual authority in the Greek world.

There were no triple-bodied warriors in ancient days, any more than there are triple-bodied fighters today. And yet Herakles is here shown having killed two of Geryon's bodies, about to kill the third. What could a triple-bodied man signify? Noah had three sons: Shem, Ham, and Japheth. Nimrod's rebellion intensified during the time of their rule, after the death of Noah. By killing the triple-bodied Geryon, Herakles is figuratively overcoming the spiritual authority of Noah's three sons. After their deaths, Nimrod (Herakles) reigned supreme. But where did he get his authority? The adjacent metope answers that question—it shows us whose jurisdiction takes the place of that lost by the sons of Noah.

The metope with Athena, Herakles, and Atlas presents us with a picture of

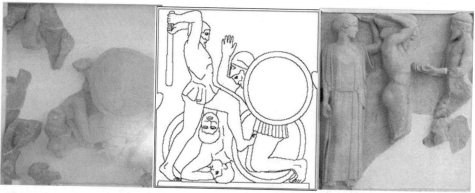

Figure 241: The fragmentary metope of Herakles killing the three-bodied Geryon, a restored drawing of it, and the well-preserved adjacent metope of Athena and Herakles uplifting the heavens as Atlas presents them with the golden apples of the Hesperides. These two metopes over the sacred east entrance to the temple of Zeus at Olympia commemorate Nimrod's rebellion, celebrate an end to the interference of Noah's oppressive God with Greek humanity, and acknowledge the authority of the ancient serpent as supreme.

the serpent's Eve, the serpent's Adam, and Nimrod—the serpent's rebel after the Flood. Eve's part in pushing away God was very easy in the garden. She simply believed the serpent. On the metope, there is neither tension in her arm nor strain on her face as Athena pushes the God of the heavens away. Likewise, with God pushed away, it was no effort at all for Adam to take the fruit. On the metope, Atlas offers the apples to Herakles with ease and confidence.

Herakles' part in pushing away the God of Noah, on the other hand, took superhuman effort. He had to overcome the power of the sons of Noah. He had to fight, train other men as fighters, build walls, establish cities, and destroy wild animals. We see his strain on the metope. He needs a cushion on his shoulder to enable him to effectively put more of his weight into his effort. All this so that he could become the bearer of the golden apples from the serpent's tree, and the serpent's authority could replace that of the God of the three sons of Noah.

With the jurisdiction of Noah's three sons at an end thanks to Nimrod, and the God of Noah pushed away, humanity was again free to enjoy the golden apples from the serpent's tree. Those who felt restricted by the God of Noah could breathe freely and walk at liberty once again as they had done in the days of Kain and his line, and for this, such men could not help but regard Herakles as a great benefactor. Thanks to Herakles (Nimrod), Zeus, the transfigured serpent, ruled the Greek world. That's why these metopes were directly over the sacred east entrance. As the Greeks looked up at these metopes over the doorway and walked under them, they surely understood what it was that enabled Zeus to take his place of rule over the Greek world, and be seated comfortably on the huge throne before them inside his temple.

Figure 242: Athena takes Herakles from his funeral pyre to Olympus in her chariot.

Figure 243: Herakles and Hebe.

The Apotheosis and Marriage of Herakles

On the Attic red-figure vase above (Fig. 242) from ca. 410 BC, Athena, in her chariot, conducts the wreathed Herakles to Olympus. Herakles, naked except for the cloak draped over his left arm, holds his club in his left hand. Below is the flaming funeral pyre where his breast armor lies. Here and on the vase-scene in Figure 243, above, the ancient artists associate Herakles' nakedness with his immortality, perhaps in emulation of his naked sculpted image on the east pediment of the Parthenon.

On the lid of the cosmetics box from ca. 350 BC (Fig. 243) we see the marriage of Herakles and Hebe (Youth) depicted. Herakles is naked but for a piece of draped cloth, and he carries his club in his left hand. With his right hand, Herakles leads Hebe. According to Pindar's *Nemean Ode*, Teiresias, the prophet of Zeus, predicted that Herakles would receive Hebe, the daughter of Hera and goddess of youth, as his bride after his death as a reward for his heroism in the battle of the gods against the Giants. Herakles' heroics turned out to be crucial to the gods' victory over the Giants; thus, after Athena brought Herakles to Olympus in her chariot, he received Hebe in wedlock, becoming immortal in accord with the prophecy.

That is just another way of saying that the Greeks rewarded their greatest hero, Herakles, by making him a god. He is the Nimrod of Genesis who, by force of arms after the Flood, reestablished the way of Kain—the very essence of Zeus-religion. He has more than earned his place on the east pediment.

Chapter 23

The Three Fates—Death Turned Back by the Immortal Athena

Figure 244: E, F, and G in the British Museum, and restored.

The sculptures known as E, F, and G, continue to puzzle scholars. The usual identification of E and F as Demeter, goddess of the earth's fertility, and her daughter Persephone doesn't work because their presence here does not relate to the birth of Athena. The identification of G as Hebe, goddess of youth, or Artemis, goddess of the hunt, runs into the same problem. Also, the standing G, more than a head smaller than seated women E and F, lacks the stature of a goddess. And why would Hebe or Artemis or whoever she is, turn away so abruptly from the central scene, while Demeter and Persephone, or whoever they are, exhibit such relaxed poses?

Figure 245: Helios, Herakles, Clotho, Lachesis, and Atropos

The answer is simple: these are the Three Fates, the *Moirae*. Their name means "parts" or allotted portions. Clotho spins the thread of life, Lachesis measures it, and Atropos cuts it. E is Clotho, F is Lachesis, and G is Atropos. Why is Atropos so much smaller than her sisters? The answer is that Hesiod, in his *The Shield of Herakles*, says she is. He describes a scene on Herakles' shield whereon "the dusky Fates, gnashing their white fangs," hover over a bloody battle. "Clotho and Lachesis were over [the wounded]," he writes, "and Atropos less tall than they, a goddess of no great frame, yet superior to the others and the eldest of them." And so the puzzle of G's lesser stature is solved.

Atropos means unturnable. The idea is that she cannot be stopped from cutting the thread of life when the time has come. But here, on the east pediment of the Parthenon, Atropos is in the very process of turning back. Why? How can that be? Remember what Pausanias wrote—"All the figures . . . relate to the birth of Athena." Athena's birth as the transfigured serpent's immortal Eve has the power to turn back fate. A-tropos, the one who cannot be turned back, must now yield to A-thanatos, the one who cannot die. Clotho and Lachesis, their work done, react in joint amazement at Athena's birth. But Atropos, confronting the birth of the immortal Athena, unable to complete the work of her sisters, turns back abruptly. And so the puzzle of G's turning anxiously back toward the relaxed E and F is solved.

The evidence also shows that the pose of F connects Athena's immortality with that of Herakles. As Kristian Jeppesen has pointed out, indications preserved at the neck of F show that her head was tilted and turned rather sharply to her right. Since she is leaning eagerly forward and seems not to pay any attention to her companion, E, she must be looking to Herakles. F is Lachesis. She is the one who measures the thread of life. What an honor to measure the thread of Athena's powerful and endless life! Thus the arms of Lachesis reach toward Athena in an all-embracing gesture, and she looks over her shoulder to Herakles,

Figure 246: Atropos' dress reacts naturally to her abrupt turning back, masterfully depicting the desired motion in a marble figure. Atropos was the Fate who could not be turned—except by Athana(tos), the deathless one, to whose birth Atropos reacts.

> **Also [Nyx] bore the Destinies and ruthless avenging Fates, Clotho and Lachesis and Atropos, who give men at their birth both evil and good to have . . .**
>
> **Hesiod, *Theogony***

who in turn was rewarded with immortality for his faithful service to Athena and Zeus. Her open arms welcome her sister Atropos also, for the turning back of Atropos relates directly to the birth of the immortal Athena.

Figure 247: Three views of Clotho and Lachesis

Figure 248: Atropos turned back by Nike.

Chapter 24
Nike Amplifies the Victory of Zeus and Athena

Figure 249: Helios, Herakles, the Three Fates, and Nike.

Nike is not the deification of a dead person, but rather the representation of an abstraction. She is Victory. Specifically, she is the Victory of Zeus and Athena. Zeus holds her in his right hand in his temple at Olympia; Athena holds her in her right hand in the Parthenon. Nike is an attribute of Zeus and Athena which means that Victory belongs to Zeus and Athena. Nike is an attribute of no other god or goddess.

Nike symbolizes the Victory of the serpent in the garden. Zeus represents two beings: the transfigured serpent and Adam, and Athena represents Eve. So in a deeper sense, the Nike of Zeus and Athena is the Victory of Adam, Eve, and the serpent over the God Who created the Garden of Eden.

Figure 250: Nike forces Atropos to turn back toward her sisters, Clotho and Lachesis.

Above, Nike, the personification of the Victory of Zeus and Athena, turns back Atropos, the Fate who cuts the thread of life—but not the thread of Athena's immortal life.

In Figure 251, opposite top, we see part of a vase-painting with Nike driving the chariot of Zeus. The overall scene pictures the gods routing the Giants—the Yahweh-believing sons of Noah. Zeus aims his lightning bolt at his enemies. Next to Zeus, Nike with wings outspread, drives his quadriga—a chariot drawn by four horses abreast. Her presence symbolizes the victory of Zeus over all his enemies, and his rule over all earthly kingdoms. Zeus grasps his lightning bolt, a symbol of the moment of lighting up—the dawn of human self-consciousness in Eden. Forgive the pun, but it is very revealing that Zeus is naked. The Judeo-Christian viewpoint has Adam ashamed of himself after eating of the tree. But on this vase we have a picture of an unashamed Adam who has eaten its fruit. From the viewpoint of Zeus-religion, taking the fruit from the tree of the knowledge of good and evil did not bring shame, but Victory. A naked Zeus boasts of the great Victory that is his at the moment of lighting up.

On the Attic red-figure vase from ca. 435 BC, opposite bottom, we see Athena, dressed as Athena Parthenos, holding a spear in her left hand and Nike in her right. Nike, or Victory, belonged jointly to Zeus and Athena.

Figure 251: On this storage jar from ca. 400 BC, Nike (Victory) drives the chariot of Zeus as he routs the Giants—the Yahweh-believing sons of Noah.

Figure 252: A vase-painting of Athena Parthenos with Nike in her right hand.

The black-figure vase, right, from ca. 550 BC, depicts the birth of Athena. Not yet full size, she stands on Zeus' lap while other deities gather around. Zeus holds his lightning bolt in his right hand. Athena is standing on Zeus' lap facing right. Although small in stature, she is fully dressed and is armed with helmet, shield and spear. A small, winged Nike stands beneath the throne, raising the palm of her left arm upward. Her presence tells us that the seat of Zeus at the moment of lighting up has become the throne of Victory for humanity.

Figure 253: Nike at the birth of Athena.

The famous Nike from the Aegean island of Samothrace in the Louvre Museum in Paris (Fig. 255) is an eight-feet-high marble figure, created by a Rhodian sculptor between 220 and 190 BC, portraying the goddess of victory alighting on a ship's prow, with her wings spread and her clinging garments rippling in the wind. The sculptor who created the Nike of Samothrace was most likely inspired by the Nike on the east pediment of the Parthenon.

We've gone over each of the figures on the pediment in some detail. Let's now review the panorama of sculptures from the standpoint of its overall impact.

Figure 254: Holmes Bryant's render of Nike from the east pediment.

Figure 255: Nike of Samothrace, now in the Louvre Museum, Paris.

246

PART IV

A Review of the East Pediment and the Overall Sculptural Theme of the Parthenon

The idol-image of Athena displays Nike in her right hand. Nike also appears on the east pediment above the metopes depicting the gods defeating the Yahweh-believing sons of Nereus/Noah. And Nike appears on the west pediment, above the metopes depicting the Greeks defeating the Yahweh-believing daughters of Nereus/Noah. The theme of the sacred east pediment is the Victory of Athena, the reborn serpent's Eve. The overall theme of the Parthenon and its sculptures is the celebration of the victory of Zeus-religion over the Yahweh-believing children of Noah.

Chapter 25

A Review of the East Pediment Sculptures

Figure 256: Drawing by H. Cook of the Parthenon from the northeast, 1851.

The ancient travel writer, Pausanias, has told us that "All the figures in the gable over the entrance to the temple called the Parthenon relate to the birth of Athena." And we have read Pindar's account, among others, of that most unique birth: "By the skills of Hephaistos with the bronze-forged hatchet, Athena leapt from the top of her father's head and cried aloud with a mighty shout. The Sky and mother Earth shuddered before her." Based on this information, other ancient sources, and the physical evidence, we have been able to reassemble the pieces of the puzzle, and recreate the ancient sculptural panorama.

The sculptures of the east pediment of the Parthenon are narrative art. Two of the most important qualities of Classical art are rationalism and realism, and what the east pediment depicts is both rational (it makes sense) and real (it is history).

The sacred east pediment is a succinct and masterful summary of what the Greeks believed about themselves. The scene, *in toto*, presents us with a story—what the Greeks believed to be a true story. The sculptural presentation straight-forwardly explains how the Greeks accounted for their existence, answering all the important questions: who, what, when, where, why, and how. The east pediment scene speaks for the Greeks. I can imagine the chief sculptor, Phidias, saying to us over the span of centuries, "Welcome to our world. Welcome to what we have painstakingly carved into marble so that you might know what we believe about our world and our place in it."

Athena's Birth
The Central Scene

We have learned that the four figures in the middle of the pediment are Zeus, Hera, Athena, and Hephaistos. These gods present us with the central truth of Greek religion. We will begin our review with the father of gods and men.

Zeus

Zeus is the true focal point on the east pediment. Zeus is the one who brings Athena into being, and he is the one who ordains that all of what we see on the pediment might be so.

Zeus, the serpent transfigured into an image of Adam as the "father of gods and men," is the chief actor in the unfolding drama. His lightning bolt in his right hand suggests his power, but more obviously, the moment of lighting up, that instant, that flash of time when Eve received the knowledge of good and evil, and human history as we know it began. The name Zeus in Greek, *Dios*, means at its deepest level "the moment of lighting up."

Zeus and his wife, Hera, have controlled human destiny up to the point of Athena's birth. But this is a new age, the Greek age, a new beginning for mankind after the Flood. The central figures represent the rebirth of the serpent's system after the Flood. The central event is the rebirth of the serpent's Eve, a picture of the basic precept and boast of Zeus-religion. Zeus will control human destiny through Athena in the Greek age.

Hera

The Greeks knew Hera as the wife of Zeus, and as the goddess of childbirth and marriage. As such, she is a picture of the first woman, the first woman to give birth, and the first woman to marry. She is a picture of the primal Eve. She remains the great queen of heaven, but it is after the Flood now, and Herakles has completed his labors unifying Greek humanity in the service of his father, Zeus. And from the serpent-entwined tree in the paradise of the Hesperides, Herakles has taken the sacred golden apples which once belonged to Hera and given them to his patroness, Athena. In the central scene, Hera is not armed, for it is Athena, as goddess of war and wisdom, who will now do battle for her father Zeus. Hera retains her scepter: as the motherless mother of all humanity, it is her birthright.

ATHENA   ZEUS   HERA   HEPHAISTOS

Athena

Athena's coming into being out of Zeus is a marvelously concise picture of the key event—the world-shaking event—in Eden. Zeus is a picture of Adam as "the father of gods and men." Eve came out of Adam. Athena, the Greek Eve, came out of Zeus, a deified picture of Adam. Athena's coming into being out of the head of Zeus also signifies that she is the brain-child of the transfigured serpent. The age in which we live, the age initiated by the Greeks, is a new postdiluvian age, a new beginning, a new system which exalts Eve's wisdom in eating the fruit of the tree in the garden, a wisdom with the power to establish the foundation of a human culture lasting thousands of years. Athena, the new Eve, is fully-armed to fight for Zeus-religion, and for the city that bears her name.

Hephaistos

Hephaistos, the eldest son of Zeus and Hera, is a deification of Kain, the eldest son of Adam and Eve. His unbelief in the ways of Yahweh releases the serpent's religious system into his mind and heart, and subsequently into the minds and hearts of his offspring. That is why he is the one who is pictured with his axe in the scenes of Athena's birth. He is a hero to all who welcome the serpent's enlightenment. In the Greek age, Hephaistos, the deified Kain, reopens the door to all the serpent had promised to his mother, Hera (the primal Eve).

In about 500 BC, Pindar wrote, "By the skills of Hephaistos with bronze-forged hatchet, Athena leapt from the top of her father's head and cried with a mighty shout." Many artists from the Archaic and Classical periods put Hephaistos and his axe in Athena's birth scenes, but he is never seen hitting the head of Zeus, and Zeus never shows any bad effects. But then Apollodorus, who wrote an uncritical summary of Greek mythology in about 140 BC opined, "*Hephaistos smote the head of Zeus with an axe*, and Athena, fully-armed leaped up from the top of his head." I believe that Apollodorus' unwarranted assumption (italicized), is where the idea that Hephaistos struck Zeus in the head originates. The leaves of time drop stealthily, sometimes obscuring the real meaning of a myth.

I believe Pindar's phrase "By the skills of Hephaistos with bronze-forged hatchet" refers to Kain's killing Abel. That is the original vicious and violent act that set in motion "the way of Kain" and eventually led to the outright glorification of the serpent's enlightenment. Why bring Hephaistos, the deified Kain, into the birth scene if that's not the idea the artists and poets were originally trying to express? The vase-painters are telling us that this new beginning—the rebirth of the serpent's Eve—is based on the old beginning of this religion's spiritual standpoint in a bloody field somewhere east of Eden.

The setting free of the serpent's wisdom after the Flood through the power of Hephaistos' axe is crucial to the development of the Greek religious system. Everything else depends on it. Now let's summarize the meaning of this scene, central to the east pediment and central to Zeus-religion.

Summary of the Central Scene

Zeus' birthing (bringing into being) of Athena as goddess of the new Greek age after the Flood is the central event on the pediment to which all the other sculptures relate. Zeus, the transfigured serpent, stands at the apex of the triangle. This is his system and his religion. He takes the form of Adam whom Scripture identifies as the father of all mankind. Greek myth makes him the father of gods (deified mortals) and men. To Zeus' proper left stands Hera, a picture of the primal Eve. Eve is the mother of all living, and sister and wife of Adam. So Hera, in Greek myth, is the goddess of childbirth, sister and wife of Zeus, and goddess of marriage.

To the proper left of Zeus and Hera stands their eldest son, Hephaistos. This is the deified Kain, the corresponding eldest son of Adam and Eve, standing next to the deifications of his parents. He carries his axe as evidence that this religious viewpoint began with a violent act. We've seen that Kain's murder of Abel may well have been depicted on "the mysterious south central metopes" of the Parthenon (see pages 76-77). As a result of Kain's violent act, Athena is able to emerge from the head (the mind) of Zeus the transfigured serpent, and stand before him to his proper right. The knowledge of good and evil and the serpent's promise of immortality are hers. She imparts the knowledge of good and evil, and the promise of the afterlife to Greek humanity.

Now that we understand who the central figures are, and how Athena's birth relates to Eden, let's review the meaning of the surrounding sculptures which provide the background for, and significance of, the pivotal scene.

The Background of Athena's Birth
The Right Side of the Pediment

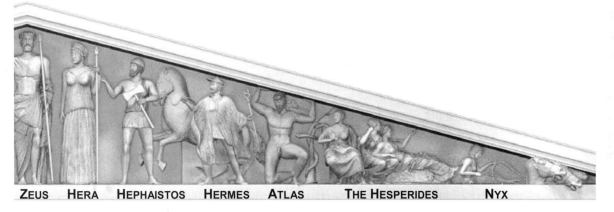

ZEUS   HERA   HEPHAISTOS   HERMES   ATLAS   THE HESPERIDES   NYX

Nyx

The surrounding sculptures should tell us when and where the central scene takes place, and they do. Nyx, representing Night or Darkness, leaves the scene in her chariot to our far right. She gives us the time frame we need. Hesiod tells us that Nyx came out of Chaos. Chaos is as far back as Hesiod is able to trace the origins of the cosmos, and Nyx is the first concept he can truly understand. We see Nyx in the right corner of the pediment but Chaos has disappeared completely, as the Greeks, in this panorama, begin to bring order out of Chaos; that is, they begin to make sense of their place in the universe. Hesiod also tells us that out of Nyx came the Hesperides and the Three Fates, both of which are depicted on the pediment on opposite sides in corresponding positions. Nyx departs, so our scene is set after her departure, at the time the Hesperides existed, and more specifically, at the time the Three Fates, representing death and the giving of the knowledge of good and evil to mankind, came into being.

The Hesperides

The depiction of the Hesperides next to Nyx helps us understand when the central event—the birth of Athena—originally took place, but most importantly, it tells us *where* it took place. The Hesperides are a collective iconograph representing paradise. On the extant vase-paintings, the Hesperides are always pictured with a serpent-entwined apple tree. A paradise, a tree, and a serpent: in terms of Genesis, this is Eden. This is where, Phidias is telling us, the original and central event took place. Figuratively, the serpent's Eve was reborn as Athena throughout the Greek world. The myth that she was born full-grown out of Zeus presents a picture of Eve's full-grown birth out of Adam in the original paradise.

Atlas

The presence of Atlas next to the Hesperides explains how Adam's and Eve's choice became possible. From the Greek viewpoint, the oppressive God Who had temptingly placed the tree of the knowledge of good and evil in the midst of the garden and yet forbade that its fruit be eaten, had to be pushed away from the scene before humanity could make any progress. This idea, Atlas pictures perfectly. He pushes away the heavens and with them, the God of the heavens. The raking cornice represents the lower limit of the heavens. As Atlas pushes upward, he enables the transfigured serpent to stand triumphant at the apex of the triangle. Like Herakles on the opposite side of the pediment, Atlas is naked and unashamed of seeking and exalting the serpent's enlightenment.

Hermes

Like Nike on the opposite side of the central scene, Hermes has a transitional function in our panorama. As the deified Cush, the high priest of rebellion in Babylon, he links what happened in the garden (Atlas and the Hesperides) to the central scene. For the birth of Athena is in reality the *rebirth* of the serpent's Eve after the Flood, and Hermes is instrumental in bringing about that rebirth. Kekrops, depicted as a half-man and half-serpent (the serpent's man), was the king who established Zeus-religion in Athens. The Greeks taught that Kekrops sacrificed to Hermes, meaning that he looked to Hermes, the deified Cush, as his religious mentor. Hermes was the original and chief herald of Zeus-religion (the serpent's system) in the ancient Greek world. As the deified Cush, he is the son of Ham (Chiron) and the father of Nimrod, whom the Greeks worshipped as the great hero, Herakles.

The Power and Promise of Athena's Birth
The Left Side of the Pediment

| HELIOS | HERAKLES | THREE FATES | NIKE | ATHENA | ZEUS |

Nike

Nike, to Athena's proper right, amplifies the great victory of Zeus and Athena. Athena's victorious rebirth forces Atropos, the Fate who cuts the thread of life, the unturnable one, to turn back toward her two sisters. A-tropos, must yield to A-thana(tos), the deathless one. The Greeks believed that the serpent's promise was true; and so to them Eve did not die, but became as the gods, knowing good and evil.

The Three Fates

The presence of the Three Fates on this side of the pediment pinpoints the time of the birth of Athena in the Garden of the Hesperides. Clotho spins the thread of life, Lachesis measures it, and Atropos cuts it, and thus the Three Fates signify death. Death became part of the human condition when Eve picked the fruit in the garden. That is the very moment when Zeus, the transfigured serpent, birthed Athena from his head, the moment Eve became convinced that heeding the serpent was the path to victory, the moment of lighting up, the instant Eve obtained the knowledge of good and evil.

Herakles

On the other side of the Fates, Herakles, the man-become-god, revels in the victory of Zeus and Athena for it is the basis of his Olympian life. The common people looked to him as a helper and giver of strength in their day-to-day difficulties. For them, Herakles bridged the gulf between mortality and immortality. The Greeks understood what it was that gained Herakles a happy, endless life: his unswerving devotion to Athena, and his exemplary obedience to the will of Zeus. Herakles' presence on the east pediment was an example and a lesson for them. Like Atlas on the other side of the pediment, Herakles is naked and unashamed of seeking and exalting the serpent's enlightenment.

Herakles is the Greek version of Nimrod from Genesis, the great benefactor of humanity who reestablished and enforced the way of Kain after the Flood. From the gods' point of view, Herakles earned his place on Olympus by overcoming the worshippers of the God of Nereus/Noah, and instituting Zeus-religion (the serpent's system) through his conquests in the postdiluvian world.

Helios

In the left corner, Helios, the sun, rises to herald the dawn of the great Greek age. His light illuminates the birth of Athena, the Nike (Victory) of Zeus and Athena, and the well-deserved immortality of Herakles. Figuratively, the light from Helios is the serpent's enlightenment in which Zeus-religion glories.

* * *

The artistic balance within the panorama is brilliant. Helios, the light, and Nyx (Night or Darkness), offset each other in the far corners. Atlas and the Hesperides on the right side, balance Herakles and the Three Fates on the left. Before the Flood, Atlas pushed away the heavens and with them, the God of the heavens. After the Flood, Herakles did the same. Both are naked and unashamed. Nike corresponds with Hermes, for the Victory of Zeus-religion is the Victory of Hermes, the Cush of Babylon. On the right side of the central scene, Zeus, Hera, and Hephaistos represent our first parents and Zeus-religion's favorite son, Kain. On the left side of the central scene, Zeus, the transfigured serpent, and Athena, the reborn serpent's Eve of the new Greek age, receive the light of the rising sun, and the way of Kain reasserts itself, and conquers.

On the east pediment of the Parthenon, the Greeks depicted the most momentous events in the history of humanity from their religious viewpoint. This is the story of Eden and the reestablishment of the serpent's system after the Flood. Phidias, the chief sculptor, compressed time and space to relate all the elements of the story at once. I cannot conceive of a way in which those events could have been encapsulated any better, in any medium.

Chapter 26
Noah's Cloak, the Parthenon, and the Christ

The unseen, background presence of Nereus/Noah pervaded the myth/art of the Parthenon. Each of the seven sculptural themes related to him in some meaningful way. His daughter, Amphitrite, and his son-in-law, Poseidon, appeared in the center of the west pediment. As the events leading up to the Trojan War began with the abduction of his daughter, Thetis, by the Zeus-worshipper, Peleus, we can be sure that they were depicted on one of the thirty-two badly battered metopes on the north side. The theme of the east metopes was the gods routing the Giants—Noah's Yahweh-believing sons. The theme of the west metopes was the Greeks' routing the Amazons—his outraged, Yahweh-believing daughters. The south metopes depicted the events leading up to the Flood through which Nereus/Noah had saved humanity. In the center of the east pediment, the rebirth of the serpent's Eve boasted of the return of the way of Kain and the victory of Zeus-religion over Nereus/Noah and his Yahweh-believing children. The immortal Herakles on the left side of that pediment certainly evoked vase-images of his elbowing and pushing Nereus/Noah out of the way and seizing his authority. And finally, the frieze celebrated the Greeks' possession of the cloak of Nereus/Noah. The Greek sculptors did not want us to miss the point that Zeus-religion reigned supreme, not just in general terms, but specifically over Nereus/Noah and his God-centered spiritual viewpoint.

In about 50 AD, Paul arrived in Athens. He knew what the Parthenon was and what it represented. In fact, "his spirit was incited in him at beholding the city being idol-ridden" (Acts 17:16). He most likely had the Parthenon idol-image of Athena in mind when he wrote in Romans 1:22-23 about those who,

> **Alleging themselves to be wise . . . are made stupid, and they change the glory of the incorruptible God into the likes of an image of a corruptible human being [Eve] and flying creatures [the winged griffins on Athena's helmet and Nike in her right hand] and quadrupeds [the griffins and the lion-bodied sphinx on Athena's helmet] and reptiles [the serpent rising up at Athena's side, those trimming her aegis, and the Gorgon Medusa—the head of serpents].**

Zeus-religion boasted of the Greeks' total spiritual alienation from Noah and his God. It was as if the sculptors of the Parthenon had intentionally buried Noah, his God, and their spiritual children beneath their own marble heroes and gods.

In Athens and elsewhere, Paul spoke with anyone who would listen about another Man who had been buried in a different part of the Mediterranean world. On His Father's side, this Man was the only-begotten Son of the God of Noah. On His mother's side, sixty-seven generations removed from Noah, He was the "Seed of the woman" (Genesis 3:15) Who shall crush the serpent's head. Paul testified that this Man, Christ Jesus, had died, and having been resurrected from the dead, now lived. At midday on the road to Damascus, this Man appeared to Paul "as a light from heaven, above the brightness of the sun" (Acts 26:13). Paul had seen the Light through Whom Helios and his far lesser light had been created.

Three of the original twelve apostles had glimpsed the unveiled glory of Christ as well:

And after six days, Jesus is taking aside Peter and James and John and is bringing them up into a very high mountain, privately, alone. And He was transformed in front of them. And His garments became glistening, very white, as snow, such as no fuller on earth is able thus to whiten (Mark 9:2-3).

This is Noah's greatest Son, the legitimate, blameless, and worthy heir of Noah's cloak, the "Mediator of God and mankind" (I Timothy 2:5); and, as "the Image of the Invisible God" (II Corinthians 4:4), the One to Whom mankind rightly looks for instruction in truth.

Let's think back to that young student who asked, "Where does Greek myth come from?" By the grace of God, we have answered her question. We know now that Greek myth is the true story of the origins of the human race, a story told from a rebellious religious orientation that leaves out the Creator of heaven and earth, and shuns His prophets. And we've learned that the Parthenon sculptures were the Greek artists' ultimate expression of the "myths" of Zeus-religion, and of man as the measure of all things. But "O, the depth of the riches and the wisdom and the knowledge of God! How inscrutable are His judgments, and untraceable His ways!" (Romans 11:33). What the Greeks meant to be an unparalleled, intricately chiseled monument to the glory of mankind turns out to be a detailed history of mankind's delusion, and a clear-cut validation of the truth of the Word of God.

* * *

Dedication

Art and Image Credits

Bibliography

Index

DEDICATION:

The Completion of *The Parthenon Code*

Is Dedicated to the Memory of

Bernie Ruck

and

Nate Steele

Their Considerable Contributions are Well-remembered

ART AND IMAGE CREDITS

Part I: Background

Chapter 1: The Ancient Greek Artists' Code

Figure 1. Attribution unknown.
Figure 2. Cutaway drawing (after G. Niemann) of the Parthenon's east façade scanned from page 16 of Cook's *The Elgin Marbles*.
Figure 3. Athena and serpent: Attic red-figure stamnos, ca. 450 BC. St. Petersburg, State Hermitage Museum, B1559. Beazley Archive.

Chapter 2: Ancient Greek Religion—A Summary

Figure 4. *Adam and Eve*, Hans Holbein, 1517. Oil on paper mounted on wood. Kunstmuseum Basel, Basel, Switzerland. Olga's Gallery (Web Site).
Figure 5. Hera and Zeus from the east frieze of the Parthenon courtesy of the British Museum, London.
Figure 6. Zeus, from Berlin F 2531. Photograph by Maria Daniels, courtesy of the Staatliche Museen zu Berlin, Preußischer Kulturbesitz; Antikensammlung. Attic red-figure (Perseus Library).
Figure 7. Hesperides, Attic red-figure hydria, London E224. Photograph courtesy of the Trustees of the British Museum, London (Perseus Library).
Figure 8. Atlas from a Laconian kylix, 6th century BC. Rome, Gregorian Etruscan Museum. Scanned from Plate VI in Carl Kerényi's *Prometheus*.
Figure 9. Hephaistos vase scanned from fig. 272, *Athenian Black Figure Vases*, by Sir John Boardman.
Figure 10. Kaineus on the west frieze of the temple of Hephaistos scanned from fig. 114.7 in *Greek Sculpture: The Classical Period* by Sir John Boardman.
Figure 11. Kaineus, Florence 4209. Scanned from page 15 of *The Centaur's Smile* by J. Michael Padgett, et. al.
Figure 12. Herakles and Nereus shield band panel scanned from figure 87 in T. H. Carpenter's *Art and Myth in Ancient Greece*.
Figure 13. Temple of Hephaistos photograph courtesy of the Department of Archaeology, Boston University, Saul S. Weinberg Collection (Perseus Library). Drawing of Hephaistion metope scanned from page 151 of John Boardman's *Greek Sculpture: The Classical Period*.
Figure 14. *Athena Parthenos*, full-size reproduction in the Nashville Parthenon by Alan LeQuire (Parthenon.org).
Figure 15. Athena with Gorgon on aegis, Attic red-figure, Berlin F 2159. Photograph by Maria Daniels, courtesy of the Staatliche Museen zu Berlin, Preußischer Kulturbesitz: Antikensammlung (Perseus Library).

PART II: Noah and His Children in Greek Vase-art, in Greek History, and on the Parthenon

Figure 15.1. C. R. Cockerell, *The Athens of Pericles: An Imaginary Reconstruction.* Source: H. W. Williams, Select Views in Greece, London 1829; Athens, Gennadios Library. Scanned from page 39 of *The Parthenon and Its Impact on Modern Times* by Panayotis Tournikiotis.

Chapter 3: Nereus—The Greek Noah

Figure 16. Red-figure hydria, Paris, Musée du Louvre, G428. Beazley Archive.

Figure 17. Red-figure skyphos cup from Sorrento, Italy. Berlin, Antikensammlung, 3244. Beazley Archive.

Figure 18. Nereus from Hartford 1961.8: Photograph courtesy of the Wadsworth Atheneum, Hartford, Connecticut. The Ella Gallup Sumner and Mary Catlin Sumner Collection. Attic black-figure hydria.

Figure 19. Etruscan black-figure hydria, Toledo 1982.134. Photograph by Maria Daniels, courtesy of the Toledo Museum of Art (Perseus Library).

Figure 20. Red-figure stamnos, Munich, Antikensammlungen, 8738. Beazley Archive.

Figure 21. Red-figure cup from Camiros, Rhodes. London, British Museum, E73. Beazley Archive.

Figure 22. Attic red-figure kalyx krater, ca. 470 BC. Yale 1985.4.1, Yale University Art Gallery. Photograph by Maria Daniels, (Perseus Library).

Figure 23. Malibu 77. AE.11: Nereus and fleeing Nereids. Collection of the J. Paul Getty Museum, Malibu, California. Attic red-figure volute krater. (Perseus Library).

Figure 24. Würzburg L 540: Side B: Nereus, detail of head and body. Photograph by Maria Daniels, courtesy of he Martin von Wagner Museum, Würzburg. Attic red-figure, dinos and stand.

Figure 25. Black-figure amphora, ca. 525 BC. Geneva, Musée d'Art et d'Histoire, MF154. Beazley Archive.

Figure 26. Ceramic cup, collection of Michael and Judy Steinhardt, scanned from page 341 of *The Centaur's Smile* by J. Michael Padgett, et al.

Chapter 4: Herakles Seizes the Authority of Nereus/Noah

Figure 27. Herakles chasing Nereus and pointing to his club, red-figure stamnos. Vatican City, Museo Gregoriano Etrusco Vaticano. Beazley Archive.

Figure 28. Black-figure cup from Etruria, Vulci. London, British Museum, B428

Figure 29. Band-cup with Poseidon, Herakles, and Nereus from the Carlos collection of ancient Greek art at Emory University, scanned from page 341 of *The Centaur's Smile* by J. Michael Padgett, et. al.

Figure 30. Harvard 1927.150: Triton. Photograph by Maria Daniels, courtesy of Harvard University Art Museums. Attic red-figure neck amphora. (Perseus Library).

Figure 31. Black-figure hydria, from Capua, Italy. Laon, Musée Archeologique Municipal, 37.971, Beazley Archive.

Figure 32. Toledo 1956.69: Herakles and Triton. Photograph by Maria Daniels, courtesy of the Toledo Museum of Art. Attic black-figure hydria. (Perseus Library).

Figure 33 through 35. Attic black-figure zone cup, ca. 520 BC, J. Paul Getty Museum, Malibu (Perseus Library).

Figure 36. Toledo 1956.58: Attic red-figure stamnos. Photograph by Maria Daniels, courtesy of the Toledo Museum of Art.

Chapter 5: The Flood Depicted on the Parthenon

Figure 37. Poseidon, black figure amphora. Mannheim, Reiss-Museum, 58. Beazley Archive.

Figures 38 and 39. Attic red-figure Kalyx Krater, ca. 475 BC, Yale university 1985.4.1. Photo by Maria Daniels, courtesy of the Yale University Art Gallery.

Figure 40. Reconstruction of the west façade of the Parthenon by E. Berger, Skulpturhalle, Basel. Photo: D. Widmer SH 278.

Figure 41. Center of pediment from the Internet.

Figures 42, 43, and 44. Jacques Carrey drawings scanned from figs. 46 and 47 in B. F. Cook's *The Elgin Marbles*.

Figure 45. Photograph of Iris courtesy of the Trustees of the British Museum, London.

Figure 46. Athena/Poseidon hydria scanned from page 454 of John Boardman's (et. al.) *The Art and Architecture of Ancient Greece*.

Figure 47. Poseidon hydria scanned from fig. 11 in Olga Palagia's *The Pediments of the Parthenon*. Pella Museum, Greece.

Chapter 6: Before the Flood, the Kentaurs Take the Line of Kain's Women

Figure 48. Parthenon south metope 30. Photograph by Maria Daniels, courtesy of the Trustees of the British Museum, London.

Figure 49. Parthenon south metope 29. Photograph by Maria Daniels, courtesy of the Trustees of the British Museum, London.

Figure 50. Attic red-figure lekythos, Herakles and Perithous in Hades, Berlin inv. 30035, courtesy of the Staatliche Museen zu Berlin, Preußischer Kulturbesitz: Antiken-sammlung. Photograph by Maria Daniels.

Figure 51. Etruscan black-figure neck amphora, Würzburg L 778, Martin von Wagner Museum, University of Würzburg. Photograph by Maria Daniels. (Perseus Library).

Figure 52. Sculptures scanned from *Olympia: The Sculptures of the Temple of Zeus* by Bernard Ashmole and Nicholas Yalouris.

Figures 53 and 54. Jacques Carrey's drawings scanned from *The Carrey Drawings of the Parthenon Sculptures*, T. Bowie and D. Thimme, eds.

Figure 55. Bassae, near Phigaleia, temple of Apollo, east frieze. Detail of Lapith women beside the image of a goddess. British Museum, London.

Figure 56. Kaineus on the west frieze of the temple of Hephaistos scanned from fig. 114.7 in *Greek Sculpture: The Classical Period* by Sir John Boardman.

Figure 57. Kaineus, Florence 4209. Scanned from page 15 of *The Centaur's Smile* by J. Michael Padgett, et al.

Figure 58. Beazley archive drawing of red-figure stamnos in Musée du Louvre, Paris.

Figure 59. *The Flood*, Michelangelo.

Figure 60. Kaineus: Malibu 86.AE.154: Attic black-figure Siana Cup. Collection of the J. Paul Getty Museum, Malibu, California.

Figure 61. Kaineus vase, ca. 440 BC, Musées Royaux d'Art et d'Histoire, Brussels. Scanned from page 80 of *Greek Mythology* by John Pinsent.

Figure 62. Kalyx krater with Athena, Gaia, and Erichthonios. Richmond, Virginia Museum of Fine Arts, The Arthur and Margaret Glasgow Fund, inv. No. 81.70.

Figure 63. Photograph by S. Mavrommatis scanned from page 72 of *The Parthenon and Its Impact on Modern Times* by Panayotis Tournikiotis.

Figures 64 through 71. Jacques Carrey's drawings scanned from *The Carrey Drawings of the Parthenon Sculptures*, T. Bowie and D. Thimme, eds.

Figure 72. Attic black-figure amphora, ca. 525 BC, J. Paul Getty Museum, Malibu (Perseus Library).

Figure 73. Attic black-figure Tyrrhenian amphora, ca. 550 BC, Munich, Antiken-sammlunge (Perseus Library).

Figure 74. Attic red-figure kantharos, ca. 470 BC, Museum of Fine Arts, Boston. From Caskey & Beazley, plate LXXXV (Perseus Library).

Chapter 7: The Conquest of Noah's Yahweh-Believing Sons

Figure 75. Parthenon Photograph, east façade from the East, courtesy of the Department of Archaeology, Boston University, Saul S. Weinberg Collection. (Perseus Library).

Figure 76. Attribution unknown.

Figure 77. Zeus and Athena, from Berlin F 2531. Photograph by Maria Daniels, courtesy of the Staatliche Museen zu Berlin, Preußischer Kulturbesitz; Antikensammlung. Attic red-figure (Perseus Library).

Figure 78. Athena and Giant, black-figure neck amphora. London, British Museum, 1926.6-28.7.

Figure 79. Dionysos killing Giant Attic red-figure, Berlin F 2321. Berlin, Antikenmuseen. Photograph by Maria Daniels, courtesy of the Staatliche Museen zu Berlin, Preußischer Kulturbesitz: Antikensammlung (Perseus Library).

Figure 80. Athena kills a Giant, image courtesy Hellenic Ministry of Culture, Akropolis Museum Web site.

Figure 81. Athena and Zeus, red-figure hydria. London, British Museum, E165. Beazley archive.

Figure 82. Poseidon, black-figure amphora. Mannheim, Reiss-Museum, 58. Beazley Archive.

Figure 83 through 87. Cleveland 78.59, Cleveland Museum of Art, Attic red-figure lekythos. Athena killing Giant Enkelados. Photograph courtesy Cleveland Museum of Art.

Figure 88. Herakles and Giant, black-figure neck amphora. London, British Museum, 1926.6-28.7.

Figure 89. Herakles, Hermes, and Alkyoneus, Attic red-figure, Munich 2590. Munich Antikensammlunge. Photograph copyright Stattl. Antikensammlungen und Glyptothek, München (Perseus Library).

Figure 90. Reconstructed west front of the altar from Pergamum, Turkey, ca. 166-156 BC. Marble. Staatliche Museen zu Berlin, Preussischer Kulturbesitz, Pergamonmuseum. Scanned from page 213 of *Art History* by Marilyn Stokstad.

Figure 91.Photographs of sculptures scanned from *The Great Altar at Pergamon* by Evamarie Schmidt.

Figure 92. Map created using Perseus 2.0 Compact Disc, Platform Independent Version, *Interactive Sources and Studies on Ancient Greece*. Yale University Press, New Haven and London.

Figure 93. Photograph from an unknown source.

Figure 94 through 98. Photographs of sculptures scanned from *The Great Altar at Pergamon* by Evamarie Schmidt.

Chapter 8: Noah's Cloak on the Parthenon

Figure 99. Cutaway drawing (after G. Niemann) of Parthenon's east façade scanned from page 16 of Cook's *The Elgin Marbles*.

Figure 100. Photograph attribution unknown.

Figures 101 to 103. Frieze sculptures and Jacques Carrey's drawings scanned from *The Carrey Drawings of the Parthenon Sculptures*, T. Bowie and D. Thimme, eds.

Figure 104. Sculpture photograph courtesy of the British Museum, London.

Figure 105. Black-figure hydria from Etruria, Vulci. Paris, Cabinet des Medailles, 255. Beazley Archive.

Figure 106. Birth of Erichthonios: Munich 2413, Munich Antikensammlunge, Attic red-figure stamnos.

Figure 107. Black-figure amphora, Munich Antikensammlungen, Beazley Archive.

Figure 108. Attic red-figure stamnos, ca. 490 BC. Paris, Musée du Louvre. Photograph by Maria Daniels (Perseus Library).

Figure 109. Detail from Athenian black-figure clay vase about 575-525 BC. Palermo. Museo Archeologico Regionale 1856.

Figure 110. Attic red-figure Nikosthenic amphora, ca. 520 BC. Paris, Musée du Louvre. Photograph by Maria Daniels (Perseus Library).

Figure 111. Hermes runs from Chiron, Attic black-figure amphora, Munich 1615A. Photograph fromt Staatl. Antikensammlungen und Glyptothek, München (Perseus library).

Figure 112. Vase of Hermes elated from Beazley archive.

Figures 113 and 114. Photographs courtesy of the British Museum, London.

Figure 115. Diagram by author.

Figure 116. Drawing scanned from page 70 of *The Parthenon Frieze* by Jenifer Neils, then modified.

Chapter 9: Peleus Abducts Thetis, the Daughter of Nereus/Noah

Figure 117. Athens red-figure bobbin, Athens National Museum, Beazley Archive.

Figure 118. Attribution unknown.

Figure 119. Attic red-figure hydria, ca. 480 BC. Naples 2422, Naples Museo Nazionale. Photograph by Maria Daniels, from Furtwangler & Reichhold, pl. 34 (Perseus Library).

Figure 120. Attic red-figure nolan amphora, ca. 440 BC. London E 336, British Museum, London. Photograph courtesy of the Trustees of the British Museum (Perseus Library).

Figures 121 and 122. Red-figure bowl, Berlin F 2279. Photographs by Maria Daniels, courtesy of the Staatliche Museen zu Berlin, Preußischer Kulturbesitz: Antikensammlung (Perseus Library).

Figures 123 and 124. Red-figure cup from Camiros, Rhodes. London, British Museum, E73. Beazley Archive.

Figure 125. Attic black-figure lekythos, ca. 510 BC, Tampa Museum of Art, Tampa 86.44. (Perseus Library).

Figures 126 through 129. Attic black-figure volute krater, ca. 570 BC. Florence, Archaeological Museum. Photograph by Maria Daniels, from Furtwängler & Reichhold, pl. 3 (Perseus Library).

Figure 130. Red-figure pelike, St. Petersburg, State Hermitage Museum, ST1527. Beazley Archive.

Figure 131. Attic black-figure volute krater, ca. 570 BC. Florence, Archaeological Museum. Photograph by Maria Daniels, from Furtwängler & Reichhold, pl. 3 (Perseus library).

Figure 132. Attic red-figure nolan amphora, Boston 13.188. From Caskey & Beazley, plate XLIV. Museum of Fine Arts, Boston.

Figures 133 through 135. Attic red-figure kylix, ca. 490 BC, Berlin, Antikenmuseen, Berlin F 2291. Photographs by Maria Daniels (Perseus Library).

Chapter 10: The Amazons—Noah's Daughters Turned Warriors

Figure 136. Attribution not available.

Figure 137. Achilles killing the Amazon Queen Penthesilea, ca. 530 BC, vase B 210, the British Museum, London.

Figure 138. London 1899.7-21.5, Attic red-figure dinos, Theseus and the Amazons, ca. 460 BC. Photography courtesy of the Trustees of the British Museum, London.

Figure 139. Mississippi 1977.3.57: Herakles and three Amazons. Photograph by Maria Daniels, courtesy of the University Museums, University of Mississippi (Perseus Library).

Figures 140 and 141. Attic red-figure kylix ca. 480 BC, Munich 2648, Munich Antikensammlunge (Perseus Library).

Figure 142 and 143. Attic red-figure dinos ca. 450 BC, Würzburg L 540, Martin von Wagner Museum, University of Würzburg. Photographs by Maria Daniels. (Perseus Library).

Figure 144 through 149. Attic red-figure krater by Kleophrades, Malibu 77.AE.11. J. Paul Getty Museum, Malibu, California (Perseus Library).

Figure 150. Shield scanned from John Boardman's *The Parthenon and Its Sculptures*.

Figure 151. Metope scanned from *Olympia: the Sculptures of the Temple of Zeus* by Bernard Ashmole and Nicholas Yalouris.

PART III Section I: The Evidence for Reconstructing the East Pediment

Figures 152 and 153. Computer renders by Holmes Bryant.

Chapter 11: The Pieces of the Puzzle

Figure 154. Parthenon photograph, east façade from the East, courtesy of the Department of Archaeology, Boston University, Saul S. Weinberg Collection. (Perseus Library).

Figure 155. Pars engraving scanned from page 176 of *The Parthenon and Its Impact on Modern Times* by Panayotis Tournikiotis.

Figure 156. Sculpture photograph courtesy of the British Museum, London.

Figure 157. Carrey drawing scanned from *The Carrey Drawings of the Parthenon Sculptures*, T. Bowie and D. Thimme, eds.

Figures 158 through 161. Sculpture photographs courtesy of the British Museum, London.

Figure 162. Carrey drawing scanned from *The Carrey Drawings of the Parthenon Sculptures*, T. Bowie and D. Thimme, eds.

Figure 163. Figure N (Nyx) is scanned from figure 80.4 in John Boardman's *Greek Sculpture: The Classical Period*.

Figure 164. Sculpture photograph courtesy of the British Museum, London.

Figure 165. Figure H (Atlas) is scanned from *The Parthenon Kongress*, 1982.

Chapter 12: The Central Figures—Zeus, Athena, Hera, and Hephaistos

Figure 166. Computer renders by Holmes Bryant.

Figure 167. Zeus, Athena, Hephaistos black-figure: London B 424. Photograph courtesy of the Trustees of the British Museum, London (Perseus Library).

Figure 168. Birth of Athena, red-figure hydria: Paris, Cabinet des Medailles, 444, Beazley Archive.

Figure 169. Drawing of Athena, Zeus, and Hera by K. Iliakis from *Parthenon Kongress*, 1982.

Figures 170 and 171. Scanned from pages 108 and 107 of *The Parthenon and Its Impact on Modern Times* by Panayotis Tournikiotis.
Figure 172. Olympia East Pediment, Fig. H (Zeus), Olympia Archaeological Museum. Photograph by Maria Daniels, courtesy of the Greek Ministry of Culture (Perseus Library).
Figure 173. Computer renders by Holmes Bryant.

PART III Section II: The True Identities of the Central Figures

Chapter 13: Zeus—The Serpent Transfigured into an Image of Adam

Figure 174. Serpent relief scanned from page 18 of Jane Ellen Harrison's *Prolegomena to the Study of Greek Religion*.
Figure 175. Serpent relief scanned from page 19 of Harrison's *Prolegomena*, above.
Figure 176. Serpent drawing scanned from page 20 of Harrison's *Prolegomena*, above.
Figure 177. Hermes, Zeus, and Iris, Attic red-figure vase. Photograph by Maria Daniels, courtesy of the Musée du Louvre, G 192 (Perseus Library).
Figure 178. Massacio's fresco *Expulsion from the Garden of Eden* in the Brancacci Chapel, Florence, Italy. Image from Web Gallery of Art, created by Emil Kren and Daniel Marx. Rudolph Tegner's *Zeus Giving Birth to Athena* in Rudolph Tegner's Museum, Denmark, image from Carlos Parada's Greek Mythology Link (Web Site). Photo from Maicar Förlag –GML.

Chapter 14: Athena—The Reborn Serpent's Eve

Figure 179. Attic red-figure pelike, ca. 470 BC, London E 410, British Museum London, Photograph courtesy of the Trustees of the British Museum.
Figure 180. Birth of Athena, black-figure vase depiction, Boston 00.330, courtesy Museum of Fine Arts, Boston. H. L. Pierce Fund (Perseus library).
Figure 181. Herakles strangling snakes, Attic red-figure, Louvre G 192. Photograph by Maria Daniels, courtesy of the Musée du Louvre (Perseus Library).
Figure 182 and 183. Athena with serpent crown is scanned from page 218 of John Boardman's *The Parthenon and Its Sculptures*.
Figure 184. Munich 2648: Tondo: Herakles and Athena. Photograph from Staatl. Antikensammlungen und Glyptothek, München. Attic red-figure kylix.

Chapter 15: Hera—The Primal Eve

Figure 185. Temple of Dione. Photograph by Beth McIntosh and Sebastian Heath (Perseus Library).
Figure 186. Albrecht Dürer etching, *Adam and Eve* from Olga's Gallery (Web Site).
Figure 187. Metope from temple of Hera at Selinus. Museo Nazionale, Palermo.
Figure 188. Wooden Zeus and Hera scanned from illus. 57, page 70 of *Greek Art* by John Boardman, fourth edition.
Figure 189. Enthroned Hera, RISD 25.078. Photograph by Maria Daniels, courtesy of the Museum of Art, Rhode Island School of Design, Providence, RI (Perseus Library).
Figures 190 and 191. Herakles entering Olympus, Attic red-figure, Villa Giulia 2382. Rome, Museo Nazionale di Villa Giulia. Photograph by Maria Daniels, from Furtwängler & Reichhold, pl. 20 (Perseus Library).

Chapter 16: Hephaistos—The Deified Kain

Figure 192. Foundry scene, London B 507. Photograph courtesy of the Trustees of the British Museum, London (Perseus Library).

Figure 193. Hephaistos, Attic red-figure. Photograph by Maria Daniels, courtesy of Harvard University Art Museums (Perseus Library).

Figure 194. Hephaistos on winged chariot, cup by the Ambrosios Painter. Scanned from fig. 120, *ARFV The Archaic Period*, by Sir John Boardman. Berlin, Staatliche (East) 2273, from Vulci, ARV 174, 31.

Figures 195 through 197. Return of Hephaistos, Attic red-figure, Toledo 1982.88. Photograph by Maria Daniels, courtesy of the Toledo Museum of Art (Perseus Library).

Figure 198. The Temple of Hephaistos across from the Agora, Athens. Photograph courtesy of the Department of Archaeology, Boston University, Saul S. Weinberg Collection (Perseus Library).

Figure 199. Bronze relief scanned from illustration 98 in T. H. Carpenter's *Art and Myth in Ancient Greece*.

PART III Section III: The Background of Athena's Birth—The Right Side of the Pediment

Chapter 17: Nyx—The Departing Darkness Out of Which Arose Paradise

Figures 200 through 202. Computer renders by Holmes Bryant.

Figure 203. Figure N (Nyx) is scanned from figure 80.4 in John Boardman's *Greek Sculpture: The Classical Period*.

Figure 204. Sculpture photograph courtesy of the British Museum, London.

Chapter 18: The Hesperides—A Picture of Paradise

Figures 205 and 206. Computer renders by Holmes Bryant.

Figure 207. Bearded serpent hydria, Champaign 70.8.4, Krannert Art Museum, University of Illinois. Photograph courtesy of the Krannert Art Museum, University of Illinois (Perseus Library).

Figure 208. Hesperides at fountain, Attic red-figure pyxis, London E 772, British Museum, London. Photograph by Maria Daniels, from Furtwängler & Reichhold, pl. 57, 2 (Perseus Library).

Figure 209. Computer renders by Holmes Bryant.

Figure 210. Vase scanned from illustration 351, *Red Figure Vases of South Italy and Sicily* by A. D. Trendall.

Figure 211. Red-figure vase, ca. 410 BC, Beazley Archive.

Figure 212. Computer renders by Holmes Bryant.

Chapter 19: Atlas Pushes Away the Heavens, and with them, the God of the Heavens

Figure 213 and 214. Computer renders by Holmes Bryant.

Figure 215. Atlas torso scanned from *Parthenon Kongress*.

Figure 216. Computer render by Holmes Bryant.

Figure 217. Model pose scanned from *Parthenon Kongress*.

Figure 218. Computer render by Holmes Bryant.

Figure 219. Attic red-figure krater by Kleophrades, Malibu 77.AE.11. J. Paul Getty Museum, Malibu, California (Perseus Library).

Figure 220. Atlas, Herakles, and Athena: bronze relief, shield band panel, Basel, Antikenmuseum.

Chapter 20: Hermes—The Deified Cush Connects Eden with the Rebirth of the Serpent's Eve

Figure 221. Computer renders by Holmes Bryant.

Figure 222. Hermes with dove scanned from *Athenian Red Figure Vases: The Archaic Period* by Sir John Boardman, Figure 330. Berlin, Statliche Museen 2172, from Etruria, ARV 581, 4.

Figure 223. Computer renders by Holmes Bryant.

Figure 224. Herm scanned from page 29 of Peter Connolly's *The Ancient City*.

Figure 225. Kekrops, Attic red-figure, Berlin F 2537, photograph by Maria Daniels, courtesy of the Staatliche Museen zu Berlin, Preußischer Kulturbesitz: Antikensammlung (Perseus Library). Hermes, Attic black-figure neck amphora ca. 510 BC, photograph by Maria Daniels, courtesy of the Worcester Art Museum, Worcester, MA, Worcester 1966.63, (Perseus Library). The Tower of Babel, by Gustav Doré 1866.

Figure 226. Black-figure neck amphora. Copenhagen, Thoryaldsen Museum, 41. Beazley Archive.

PART III Section IV: The Power and Promise of Athena's Birth— The Left Side of the Pediment

Chapter 21: Helios—The Rising Sun Heralds the Birth of Athena and the New Greek Age

Figures 227 and 228. Computer renders by Holmes Bryant.

Figures 229 and 230. Photographs courtesy of the British Museum, London.

Figure 231. Helios red-figure depiction scanned from page 28 of *Titans and Olympians*, a Time-Life book edited by Tony Allan.

Figure 232. Computer renders by Holmes Bryant.

Chapter 22: The Immortal Herakles—Nimrod Transplanted to Greek Soil

Figure 233. Computer renders by Holmes Bryant.

Figure 234. Photograph courtesy of the British Museum, London.

Figure 235. Computer render by Holmes Bryant.

Figure 236. Herakles feasting with Athena, Munich 2301, Munich Antikensammlunge. Photograph copyright Staatl. Antikensammlungen und Glyptothek, München (Perseus Library).

Figures 237 and 238. Seal and tripod images scanned from T. H. Carpenter's *Art and Myth in Ancient Greece*, figures 174, 175.

Figure 239. Vienna, Kunsthisstorisches Museum, Caeretan hydria, Herakles killing Egyptians. Photograph by Maria Daniels, from Furtwängler & Reichhold, p. 151.

Figure 240. Herakles and Geryon, New York (NY), Metropolitan Museum, 56.171.11. Black-figure amphora, Beazley archive.

Figure 241. Geryon and Atlas metopes, Temple of Zeus. Photographs by Maria Daniels, courtesy of the Greek Ministry of Culture, Olympia. Geryon Metope drawing © C. H. Smith 1990 (Perseus Library).

Figure 242. Apotheosis of Herakles, Attic red-figure pelike, Munich 2360, Munich Antikensammlunge (Perseus Library).
Figure 243. Marriage of Herakles and Hebe, Attic red-figure pyxis, Philadelphia MS5462. University Museum, University of Pennsylania (Perseus Library).

Chapter 23: The Three Fates—Death Turned Back by the Immortal Athena

Figure 244. Photograph courtesy of the British Museum, London. Computer renders by Holmes Bryant.
Figure 245. Computer renders by Holmes Bryant.
Figure 246. Photograph courtesy of the British Museum, London. Computer renders by Holmes Bryant.
Figures 247 and 248. Computer renders by Holmes Bryant.

Chapter 24: Nike Amplifies the Victory of Zeus and Athena

Figure 249 and 250. Computer renders by Holmes Bryant.
Figure 251. Zeus and Nike, Attic red-figure, Louvre S 1677. Photograph by Maria Daniels, courtesy of the Musée du Louvre, Paris (Perseus Library).
Figure 252. Athena Parthenos, Attic red-figure, Berlin V. I. 3199. Photograph by Maria Daniels, courtesy of the Staatliche Museen zu Berlin, Preußischer Kulturbesitz: Antikensammlung (Perseus Library).
Figure 253. Birth of Athena with Nike, Attic black-figure, Philadelphia MS3441. Photograph by Maria Daniels, courtesy of The University Museum, Philadelphia (Perseus Library).
Figure 254. Computer render by Holmes Bryant.
Figure 255. Photo of Nike of Samothrace, courtesy Musée du Louvre, Paris.

PART IV: A Review of the East Pediment and the Overall Sculptural Theme of the Parthenon

Chapter 25: A Review of the East Pediment Sculptures

Figure 256. H. Cook drawing. scanned from page 190 of *The Parthenon and Its Impact on Modern Times* by Panayotis Tournikiotis.

Bibliography

Allan, Tony, ed., 1997. *Titans and Olympians: Greek and Roman Myth*. Time-Life Books BV, Amsterdam.

Ashmole, Bernard and Yalouris, Nicholas, 1967. *Olympia: the Sculptures of the Temple of Zeus*. Phaidon Press, London.

Ashmole, Bernard, 1972. *Architect and Sculpture in Classical Greece* (The Wrightsman Lectures), New York University Press.

Baring, Anne, and Cashford, Jules. 1991. *The Myth of the Goddess, Evolution of an Image*. Viking Arkana, Penguin Books Ltd., London.

Beard, Mary, 2003. *The Parthenon*. Harvard University Press, Cambridge, Massachusetts.

Biers, William R., Second Ed. 1996. *The Archaeology of Greece*. Cornell University Press, Ithaca and London.

Boardman, John; Dörig, José; Fuchs, Werner; and Hirmer, Max, 1967. *The Art and Architecture of Ancient Greece*. Thames and Hudson, London.

Boardman, John, 1985. *Greek Sculpture: the Classical Period, a Handbook*. Thames and Hudson, Ltd., London.

Boardman, John, 1985. *The Parthenon and Its Sculpture*. University of Texas Press, Austin.

Boardman, John, 1985. *Athenian Red Figure Vases The Classical Period: a Handbook*. Thames and Hudson, Ltd., London.

Boardman, John; Griffin, Jasper; and Murray, Oswyn, 1988. *Greece and the Hellenistic World*. Oxford University Press, Oxford, England.

Boardman, John, 1989. *Athenian Red Figure Vases: the Classical Period, a Handbook*. Thames and Hudson, Ltd., London.

Boardman, John, 1996. *Greek Art*. Thames and Hudson, Ltd., London.

Boardman, John, 2000. *Athenian Red Figure Vases The Archaic Period: a Handbook*. Thames and Hudson, Ltd., London.

Bothmer, Dietrich Von, 1957. *Amazons in Greek Art*. Oxford University Press, Oxford.

Bowie, Theodore, and Thimme, Diether, (eds.), 1971. *The Carrey Drawings of the Parthenon Sculptures*. Indiana University Press, Bloomington and London.

Bowra, C. M. and the Editors of Time-Life Books, 1965. *Classical Greece*. Time-Life Books, Alexandria, Virginia.

Burckhardt, Jacob, 1998. *The Greeks and Greek Civilization*. St. Martin's Press, New York.

Burkert, Walter, 1983. *Homo Necans*. University of California Press, Berkeley and Los Angeles.

Camp, John M. 1986. *The Athenian Agora: Excavations in the Heart of Classical Athens*. Thames and Hudson, London.

Campbell, Joseph, 1964. *The Masks of God: Occidental Mythology*. The Viking Press, Inc., New York.

Carpenter, T. H., 1991. *Art and Myth in Ancient Greece*. Thames and Hudson, Ltd., London.

Castriota, David. 1992. *Myth, Ethos, and Actuality—Official Art in Fifth-Century B.C. Athens*. The University of Wisconsin Press.

Charbonneaux, Jean, 1972. *Classical Greek Art*. George Braziller, New York.

Connolly, Peter and Dodge, Hazel 1998. *The Ancient City: Life in Classical Athens and Rome*. Oxford University Press, Oxford and New York.

Cook, B. F., 1997. *The Elgin Marbles*. British Museum Press, London.

Crane, Gregory, ed., 2000, Compact Disc: Perseus 2.0 Platform Independent Version. *Interactive Sources and Studies on Ancient Greece*. Yale University Press, New Haven and London.

Dersin, Denise, ed., *What Life Was Like at the Dawn of Democracy*. Time-Life Books Virginia.

Donohue, A. A. 1988. *Xoana and the Origins of Greek Sculpture*. Scholars Press, Atlanta, Georgia.

Durando, Furio Stewart, 1997. *Ancient Greece: The Dawn of the Western World*. Tabori & Chang, New York.

Durant, Will, 1939. *The Life of Greece*. Simon and Schuster, New York.

Geldard, Richard G. 1989. *The Traveler's Key to Ancient Greece*. Alfred A. Knopf, New York.

Goldhill, Simon and Osborne, Robin, eds. 1994. *Art and Text in Ancient Greek Culture*. Cambridge University Press.

Grant, Michael, 1987. *The Rise of the Greeks*. Charles Scribner's Sons, New York.

Green, Peter, 1978. *The Parthenon*. Newsweek, New York.

Green, Peter, 1995. *Ancient Greece: A Concise History*. Thames and Hudson, Ltd., London.

Grene, David and Lattimore, Richard, eds., 1955. *The Complete Greek Tragedies, Volume III Euripides*, The University of Chicago Press, Chicago.

Hale, W. H., Ed. 1965. *The Horizon Book of Ancient Greece*. American Heritage Publishing Co., Inc., New York.

Harrison, Jane Ellen, 1962. *Epilegomena to the Study of Greek Religion and Themis*. University Books, New Hyde Park, New York.

Harrison, Jane Ellen, 1991. *Prolegomena to the Study of Greek Religion*. Princeton University Press, Princeton, New Jersey.

Hislop, Alexander, 1916. *The Two Babylons*, Loizeaux Brothers, Neptune, New Jersey.

Hornblower, Simon and Spawforth, Anthony, eds., 1998. *The Oxford Companion to Classical Civilization*. Oxford University Press, Oxford / New York.

Johnson, Robert Bowie Jr., 2002. *Athena and Eden: The Hidden Meaning of the Parthenon's East Façade*. Solving Light Books, Annapolis, Maryland.

Johnson, Robert Bowie Jr., 2003. *Athena and Kain: The True Meaning of Greek Myth*. Solving Light Books, Annapolis, Maryland.

Jeppesen, Kristian K., 1982. "Evidence for the Restoration of the East Pediment Reconsidered in the Light of Recent Achievements." *Parthenon Kongress*, Basel.

Kerényi, C., 1951. *The Gods of the Greeks.* Thames and Hudson, New York.

Kerényi, C., 1963. *Prometheus: Archtypal Image of Human Existence*. Pantheon Books, Random House, Inc. New York.

Kerényi, C., 1976. *Dionysos*. Bollinger Series 2, Princeton University Press, Princeton, New Jersey.

Kerényi, C., 1975. *Zeus and Hera*. Princeton University Press, Princeton, New Jersey.

Kokkinou, Sophia, 1989. *Greek Mythology*. Sophia Kokkinou, Athens.

Lagerlöf, Margaretha Rossholm, 2000. *The Sculptures of the Parthenon: Aesthetics and Interpretation*. Yale University Press, New Haven and London.

Lefkowitz, Mary R., 1990. *Women in Greek Myth*. The Johns Hopkins University Press, Baltimore.

Morford, Mark P. O. and Lenardon, Robert J. 1971. *Classical Mythology*. David McKay Company, Inc., New York.

Neils, Jenifer, 2001. *The Parthenon Frieze*. Cambridge University Press, United Kingdom.

Neils, Jenifer., Ed., 1996. *Panathenaia and Parthenon*. The University of Wisconsin Press.

Padgett, Michael J. et. al., 2003. *The Centaur's Smile: The Human Animal in Early Greek Life*. Princeton University Art Museum. Distributed by Yale University Press, New Haven and London.

Palagia, Olga, 1993. *The Pediments of the Parthenon*. E. J. Brill, New York.

Parada, Carlos, 1993. *Genealogical Guide to Greek Mythology*. Paul Astroms Forlag, Jonsered, Sweden.

Parke, H. W. 1977. *Festivals of the Athenians*. Cornell University Press, Ithaca, New York.

Parker, Robert 1996. *Athenian Religion: A History*. Clarendon Press, Oxford, England.

Pinsent, John, 1969. *Greek Mythology*. Peter Bedrick Books, New York.

Pollit, J. J., 1972. *Art and Experience in Classical Greece*. Cambridge University Press, London.

Reeder, Ellen D., Ed. 1995. *Pandora: Women in Classical Greece*. Princeton University Press, Princeton, New Jersey.

Rodenbeck, Christina, ed., 1998. *Triumph of the Hero: Greek and Roman Myth*. Time-Life Books BV, Amsterdam.

Rodocanachi, C. P., 1951. *Athens and the Greek Miracle*. The Beacon Press, Boston.

Schmidt, Evamaria. 1965. *The Great Altar at Pergamon*. Boston Book and Art Shop, Inc., Boston.

Schefold, Karl, 1967. *The Art of Classical Greece*. Greystone Press, New York.

Smith, R. R., 1991. *Hellenistic Sculpture*. Thames and Hudson, Ltd., London.

Spivey, Nigel, 1997. *Understanding Greek Sculpture*. Thames and Hudson, Ltd., London.

Stewart, J. A. 1970 (1905 Reprint). *The Myths of Plato*. Barnes and Noble, Inc.

Stokstad, Marilyn, 1995. *Art History*. Harry N. Abrams, Inc., New York.

Stone, I. F., 1988. *The Trial of Socrates*. Anchor Books, Doubleday, New York.

Toorn, Karel van der and Becking, Bob and Horst, Pieter W. van der, eds. 1999. *Dictionary of Deities and Demons in the Bible*. William B. Eerdmans Publishing Company, Grand Rapids, MI / Cambridge, U. K.

Trendall, A. D., 1989. *Red Figure Vases of South Italy and Sicily*. Thames and Hudson, Ltd., London.

Tripp, Edward 1970. *The Meridian Handbook of Classical Mythology*. New American Library, New York.

Tyrrell, Wm. Blake. 1984. *Amazons: A Study in Athenian Mythmaking*. The Johns Hopkins University Press, Baltimore and London.

Walker, Barbara G. 1983. *The Woman's Encyclopedia of Myths and Secrets*. Harper & Row Publishers, San Francisco.

Ward, Anne G. 1970. *The Quest for Theseus*. Praeger Publishers, Inc. New York.

West, John Anthony 1988. *Serpent in the Sky: The High Wisdom of Ancient Egypt*. Quest Books, Theological Publishing House, Wheaton, Illinois.

Wilde, Lyn Webster, 2000. *On the Trail of the Women Warriors: The Amazons in Myth and History*. Thomas Dunne Books, St. Martin's Press, New York.

From the Concordant Publishing Concern, Santa Clarita, California:

Concordant Literal New Testament with Keyword Concordance, sixth edition, 1976.

Concordant Commentary on the New Testament by A. E. Knoch, 1968.

Concordant Greek Text, fourth edition, 1975.

The Book of Genesis, Concordant Version of the Old Testament, 1957.

The Book of Isaiah, Concordant Version of the Old Testament, 1962.

Unsearchable Riches magazine, issues from 1933 to 2004.

Index

274